BAD
CITY

BAD CITY

PERIL AND POWER
IN THE CITY OF ANGELS

PAUL PRINGLE

CELADON
BOOKS

NEW YORK

Library of Congress Cataloging-in-Publication Data

Names: Pringle, Paul, author.
Title: Bad city : peril and power in the City of Angels / Paul Pringle.
Description: First edition. | New York, NY : Celadon Books, [2022] | Includes
bibliographical references.
Identifiers: LCCN 2021062132 | ISBN 9781250824080 (hardcover) | ISBN
9781250824097 (ebook)
Subjects: LCSH: Puliafito, Carmen A., 1951—Drug use. | University of Southern
California—Corrupt practices—Case studies. | Drug abuse—California—Los
Angeles—Case studies. | Universities and colleges—Corrupt practices—
California—Los Angeles—Case studies. | Corruption—California—Los
Angeles—Case studies. | Investigative reporting—California—Los Angeles—
Case studies.
Classification: LCC HV5833.L67 P75 2022 | DDC 362.2909794/94—dc23/
eng/20220201
LC record available at https://lccn.loc.gov/2021062132

First Edition: 2022

10 9 8 7 6 5 4 3 2 1

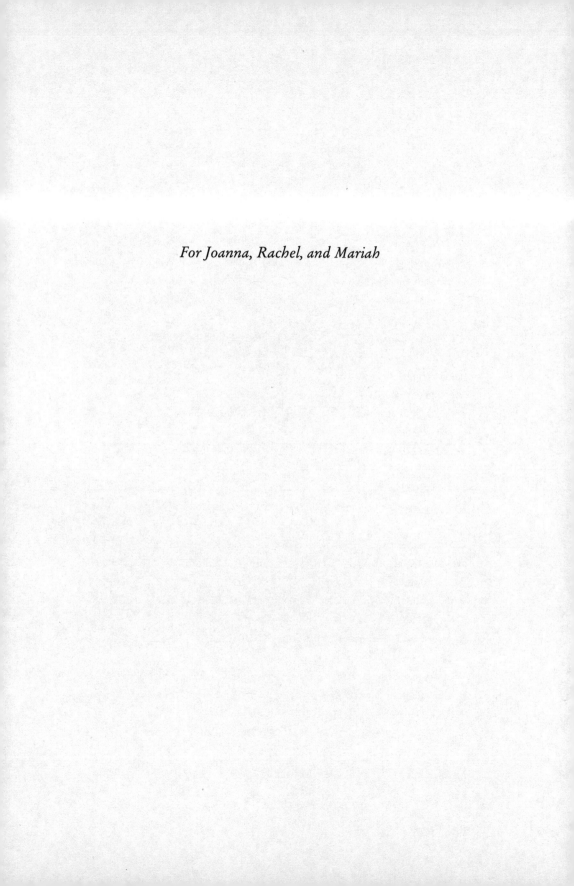

For Joanna, Rachel, and Mariah

CONTENTS

BAD
CITY

PROLOGUE

The tip about the dean of the University of Southern California's medical school hinted at something so salacious, so depraved, so outrageous, that it seemed too good to be true. Or too awful, if you weren't a journalist.

It came to the *Los Angeles Times* through a staff photographer, Ricardo DeAratanha. He got the tip at a house party, purely by chance, and emailed it the next day to a colleague. DeAratanha wrote, "I came across someone last night, who witnessed an apparent coverup involving the Dean of the School of Medicine at USC. It involved lots of drugs and a half dressed unconscious young girl, in the dean's hotel room." He went on to say that the tipster would have more details.

The day after that, another colleague forwarded Ricardo's email to me, writing, "Ricardo has been trying to find someone to drop this tip on. Everybody's been a little skittish about it. I told him you're the one who would know how to handle it."

More often than not, the most tantalizing tips become a fool's errand, a fruitless prospecting for truth from rumors and exaggerations and outright fabrications. Sometimes they are anonymous, sometimes not. The anonymous ones might arrive from an encrypted email account or a hand-scrawled letter with no return address. A large number of these tips, dispiritingly so, are about racist cops and thieving politicians and sexually abusive bosses. Others are meant to exact revenge against business partners in ventures gone south. Unfaithful spouses, especially if they're famous, are a favorite target. So are the lawyers and judges who handled the resulting divorces. It gets even worse when the custody of children is in play.

And yet no matter how colorful they are in the details, no matter how important the story they promise to tell might be, the tips that are particularly over-the-top usually lead nowhere.

But not this one.

This tip was about Dr. Carmen Puliafito, a Harvard-trained eye surgeon, inventor, and big-dollar rainmaker who straddled the highest reaches of the medical world and academia. He was a wizard in the operating room and an innovator in the laboratory. Puliafito estimated that he raised $1 billion for USC. He brought a brainy refinement to the charity circuit of Hollywood and Beverly Hills, mixing as easily with designer-dressed movie stars as he did with the residents in lab coats at the Keck School of Medicine. But as luridly improbable as it seemed at first, the tip about Puliafito not only was on the mark, it merely scratched the surface. And what was revealed beneath that surface was a deep vein of corruption and betrayal that webbed through the Los Angeles establishment and corroded some of the city's most essential institutions, my own newspaper included.

The scandals that followed led to the downfall of powerful men. But it was a close call, a near miss, and many innocent and vulnerable people were hurt along the way. As of this writing, not all of them had gotten the justice they deserved.

1

THE OVERDOSE

A fog scented by canyon pines greeted Devon Khan when he stepped from his front door. It was early in the morning of March 4, 2016, the day of the overdose, and Khan was on his way to work. The low sun lighting the ridges of the San Gabriels promised there would be no rain. The mountains provided a painterly backdrop to the north side of Pasadena, where Khan lived with his wife and their ten-year-old daughter. He was forty-four years old and the reservations supervisor at the Hotel Constance, a boutique inn on the edge of Pasadena's central business district. A veteran of the hotel industry, Khan had bounced from property to property as better opportunities presented themselves. He had worked at the old Ritz-Carlton in Pasadena and its successor, the Langham Huntington. Khan did stints at the Mondrian and Sunset Tower, the West Hollywood haunts of the wealthy and celebrated. Hospitality at this level was a demanding and humbling gig. The default expectation was that every need, wish, whim, and mood of the guests will be catered to, and must be abided with a smile. Even for the guests who were out of line, deference and discretion remained the watchwords. Khan understood that. Polite, soft-spoken, eager to please, and handsome, with a striking resemblance to Los Angeles Laker Rick Fox, he considered himself an excellent fit for the business.

But only to a point. There were limits to what Khan would tolerate to keep his job.

On this Friday morning, he drove the usual way to the Constance, a two-mile jaunt past the palms and tall conifers on Hill Avenue. The avenue ran surveyor-straight from the more affordable neighborhoods on the north end, with their auto body shops and nail salons, south toward the domains of high-walled estates with lawns as broad as meadows. Pasadena was an old-money enclave of L.A. The fortunes that had built it came from the early railroads and banks and land developments, not the movie riches that greened Beverly Hills. Halfway along the drive on Hill Avenue sat the 110-year-old clapboard house where Khan and his late mother had lived for a while, when the structure was a women's shelter. Khan was a middle schooler at the time, and his mother was a crack cocaine addict. One of her principal dealers was her father. Khan's grandfather was a charmer who drove a Cadillac convertible and took a special liking to him, a sentiment Khan could never return.

The family was from Kentucky, by way of Ohio and Michigan, and Khan's mother had moved with him and his older brother to L.A. in hopes of a fresh start. Their fathers were no longer around. Khan's father was a businessman, model, and songwriter. One day in Detroit, as he walked out of a pharmacy, he was shot in the stomach on the orders of a man whose housing fraud scheme he threatened to expose. The bullet nearly killed him, and he later became schizophrenic, which confined him to a mental institution for the rest of his days. Khan's mother had left him long before the shooting. She was loving and engaging and smart, and had studied social work at the University of Louisville. But drugs were her undoing, and L.A. did not change that. Seeing the house on Hill Avenue always reminded Khan of how far he had come in life—from the bouts of homelessness, the weeks spent sleeping on the couches of people he barely knew, the long periods of living with his mother's friends while she did another stretch in jail, and the lonely hospitalizations that came with his battle against sickle cell anemia. Khan had navigated and survived it all, and he would marvel to himself that he was a Pasadena homeowner. Four years ago, he and his German-born wife, Tanja—they had met when she was a flight attendant for Lufthansa—bought the house on Wesley Avenue, a tidy white bungalow boutonniered with a robust growth of bougainvillea. Tanja and their daughter loved Pasadena as much as he did.

Devon Khan was a family man who had put down roots, and he was always mindful of how much he had and how much he had to lose.

A few minutes after 7:00 A.M., he parked across the street from the Hotel Constance. With its butter-smooth arches and cast-stone friezes, the seven-story Constance was a 1926 showpiece of Mediterranean Revival architecture that fronted a corner of Colorado Boulevard, the route of the Rose Parade. Khan was the first of the Constance morning shift to arrive, as he usually was. He liked to get a jump on the overnight reservations, many of which came from the eastern time zones. Khan spent most of the hours in his office off the lobby, making sure the online reservations were processed, fielding questions about rates—the routine tasks. Around 4:00 P.M., he was preparing to head home when he got the MOD—manager on duty—call from the front desk.

Khan was the highest-ranking employee on the premises; the other managers were in a meeting at the hotel corporate offices across the street. He was annoyed that he had to handle the call, in part because he had been denied a promotion to front office manager, the person who normally would deal with whatever headache the call signaled. Khan believed he was more than qualified for the position. He had to wonder if he was passed over because he sometimes questioned the actions of the guests or his superiors. That's who he was. One time, at a different property, a Russian businessman who was a frequent guest blew up at one of Khan's colleagues when she asked him for an ID card required for entry to the hotel's membership-only spa. Khan came to his coworker's defense, telling the Russian that was no way to speak to people. The Russian complained, and Khan got written up. At another hotel, a manager instructed Khan to downgrade a guest's suite reservation to make the premium room available for a legendary actress who arrived without a booking. The guest is a nobody—stick him in a regular room, the manager said. Khan made his displeasure known, which was not appreciated. On one occasion, he had to consider if his being Black was a factor, if a white executive viewed him as, well, *uppity.*

He walked to the front desk to inquire about the MOD call. "What's the issue?"

A clerk told him that the guest in 304 wanted to stay another night and specifically in that room. The guest sounded "jittery." The problem was that 304 had already been reserved by another party who was due to check in at any time. And the room was prized for its balcony. Before Khan could suggest a solution, the desk phone rang. It was the housekeeping supervisor; she needed a manager on the third floor right away.

Okay, Khan thought, *the guest probably wants to make a complaint.*

He quickly checked the computer for 304. The room was registered to a Carmen Puliafito. Khan didn't recognize the name. Puliafito— was Carmen a man or a woman?—wasn't listed as a repeat patron or VIP. Khan took the elevator to the third floor. As he stepped out, the housekeeping supervisor and the hotel security guard were waiting for him in the hallway. Beyond them, outside 304, a bellman waited with a cart piled with luggage and unpacked clothing. Khan was confused. *Why is the guest demanding to extend his stay in the room*

if all of his luggage is on the cart? He must have agreed to move to another room.

Then the housekeeping supervisor told Khan there was an unconscious woman in 304.

"Unconscious?"

She nodded and looked toward the closed door of the room with concern.

"I'll get my eyes on her," Khan said.

It was hotel protocol that Khan could not simply walk into the room. He knocked. An older man with a wan, off-center face opened the door halfway and asked if Khan had the key to his new room. The man appeared to be in his sixties and was dressed in rumpled jeans and a stretched-out polo shirt. He had dimmed, spidery eyes, and his thinning hair went in several different directions. Clearly, he'd had a rough night and a rough day that followed. Khan knew all the tells: drugs and alcohol. The only question was how much had been consumed in 304, particularly by the woman. He couldn't see her from the doorway. Khan decided that the quickest and least confrontational way to check on her was to remain courteous and help the man move her and their belongings to the second room. He told him he would be right back with the key. Looking relieved, the man thanked him and closed the door.

And that's when Khan got the rest of the story from the housekeeping supervisor and security guard. They said that the day before, when the man and woman were out, a housekeeper had found drugs scattered around the room. The security staff was alerted and took photographs of the drugs. What type of drugs they were wasn't apparent. Management did not ask the man and woman to check out. When it came to drinking and drugging, the policy of the Constance and most other hotels was to live and let live, unless the staff witnessed laws being broken or someone getting hurt. Prudishness was bad for the partying side of the business. And no one

had actually seen the occupants of 304 take drugs. The photos were a precautionary measure, in case the guests did get out of hand in a way management couldn't ignore or if there were legal issues down the road.

There was more from the supervisor and security guard—all of it news to Khan, because none of it had to do with reservations. At the man's request, the bellman had already brought a wheelchair to 304 to move the woman. They said she was in the chair at that moment, out cold.

Khan hurried down to the lobby to get the key to a new room—312 was available. When Khan returned, the man let him into 304, resigned that he could no longer keep him out. Khan stepped into the room and drew himself up at what he saw. The woman, blond and very young, looked as if she had been plopped into the wheelchair like a sack of feed. Her head rested heavily on her shoulder, her gossamer hair matted on her brow. She wore only a white hotel robe and pink panties. Her limbs hung straight down, as if they were weighted; one leg dangled off the chair where a footrest was missing. Khan could not be sure she was breathing.

"Ma'am?" he said. "Ma'am? Ma'am?" Nothing.

Khan took in the room, which was 1920s small, updated in a swirly modern decor, and with the balcony that offered a view of the boulevard. Strewn over the carpet were empty beer bottles, a plastic bag of whip-it cartridges—the small canisters of nitrous oxide inhaled for an illicit high—a half-inflated balloon used to enhance that high, and a palm-size container for a butane torch, the type favored for a meth pipe. Burn marks scarred the bed. The room had a sweet-and-sour odor of sweat.

"Ma'am?" Not a sound.

It didn't take a medical degree to conclude she had overdosed. *Drug debris everywhere.*

The man was silent. He was old enough to be the woman's father or even her grandfather.

Khan noticed a small camera tripod sitting on top of the television. *What kind of degenerate is this guy?*

"Are you okay, ma'am?"

There wasn't the slightest flutter along the alabaster face, although Khan could see she was breathing, if only faintly. He decided to move her and the man to 312—and leave 304 in just the state it was in for the police. He asked the man to lift her leg where the footrest used to be so it wouldn't drag on the floor. Khan guided the chair out of the room and into the hallway, the man awkwardly keeping up with the woman's calf in his hand. *If we were down in the parking lot wheeling away a woman like this, people would think we were carting off a murder victim.*

"Can you hear me, ma'am?" Khan said as they rolled through the hallway. Even the one-legged ride didn't stir her.

Before he gave the man the new key, he asked for an ID. The man produced his driver's license: Carmen Puliafito. So the room was registered to him, not the woman. Once they were inside 312, Khan told Puliafito he would call 911. Puliafito looked stricken, as if this was just the beginning of the day's troubles.

"That's not necessary," Puliafito said. "She just had too much to drink." He paused. "Listen, I'm a doctor."

A doctor? Bullshit. A doctor would have called the paramedics himself. This squeezed-out old man was just another john, a fool with enough cash for an afternoon rollick at the Constance. Now he was panicked about getting busted—and a scumbag for trying to deny the girl help. She could be Khan's daughter. She certainly was somebody's daughter.

"I'm caring for her," Puliafito said.

Khan knew he had to choose his words carefully. He said, "I would be derelict in my responsibilities if I didn't seek medical attention for her."

With that, Khan walked out of the room and returned to his office to call 911. A woman dispatcher answered.

"Firefighter paramedics."

"Hi. I'm calling from the Hotel Constance in Pasadena."

Khan gave her the address and said a woman needed help.

"She's up in her room, passed out, unresponsive."

"Is she breathing?"

"Yes."

The dispatcher asked him to transfer the call to the room, and he did so.

Khan had no way of knowing if Puliafito answered—or if anyone answered—when the call was transferred.

"Hello?" Puliafito said.

"Hi, this is the fire department. Did you call for 911?"

"Uh," Puliafito said, "not me, basically." He was rattled. "Um, I had, ah, my girlfriend here had a bunch of drinks, and, uh, she's breathing . . ."

"Is she breathing right now?"

"Yes, she's absolutely breathing." Now Puliafito's voice was edged with annoyance. "Absolutely breathing."

"Is she vomiting at all?"

"No, she's sitting up in bed, she's passed out. I mean, I'm a doctor, actually, so . . ."

"Okay, all right."

"She's sitting up in bed with normal respirations, I mean . . ."

"You have her sitting up?"

"Well, she's sitting up now, yeah." More annoyance.

"Is she awake now?"

"No, she's sort of, very groggy, you know. So . . ."

"Okay, just make sure she doesn't fall over. We're going to be there shortly to check her out, okay?"

"Okay, fine, fine, fine. Thank you." He sounded like he couldn't wait to get off the line.

"Do you know how much she drank?"

"You know, a bunch. I mean, I came in the room, and there were lots of, uh, you know, cans of . . ."

"Okay, but did she take anything else with it or just the alcohol?"

"I think just the alcohol."

"All right, we're going to be there shortly, sir."

And they were. Khan heard the sirens approach as he phoned the offices across the street in search of a manager; a higher-up needed to be there to deal with the authorities. The HR director picked up and said she'd be right over. The sirens got louder and louder and then went silent. A fire engine and a paramedic wagon had pulled up to the curb on the lobby side of the hotel. Two firefighter paramedics walked into the lobby with a gurney in tow, the rumbling noises of the boulevard following them through the door. Right behind them was an older firefighter, a tall man with graying hair. As Khan directed them to the elevator, the older firefighter began asking questions.

"Do you know what kind of drugs are involved?"

"Let's go to the room," Khan said, by way of an answer.

On the third floor, the two paramedics headed to 312 with the gurney while Khan led the older firefighter into 304. The firefighter got an eyeful of the paraphernalia on the floor and the scorched bed. The security guard had opened the guest safe and, sure enough, inside was a small plastic bag of white powder. Khan had seen enough of the powder around his mom to recognize it as crystal meth.

"Don't let anyone in here until the police get here," the firefighter said. "Leave this room exactly how it is." He left to join the paramedics.

The police still had not arrived, so another staffer made a second 911 call to make sure they were on their way. By that time, the hotel general manager had returned from the corporate offices. Khan briefed him as they stood looking at the mess in 304. In the hallway, the paramedics had the woman on the gurney and were loading her into the service elevator. In attempts to rouse her, they called out, "Sarah? Sarah? Can you hear us, Sarah?"

Sarah.

A chill came over Khan. His daughter's name was Sarah. It drove home that he was a witness to a father's nightmare—someone's daughter strapped to a gurney, unconscious, looking as if she may never wake up. Helpless, voiceless, her life in the hands of strangers. Khan again thought of the man's attempts to stop him from calling the paramedics. And he thought of the tripod on the TV. He figured the man—this Puliafito—used it to film on his phone whatever was happening in the room that led to the overdose.

"When the police get here, you should tell them to get the guy's phone," Khan said to the general manager. "I'm sure there's some nasty stuff on there."

There was nothing left for Khan to do. Five minutes later, he was driving home. He didn't wait to see what he assumed would be the cops hooking the man in handcuffs and hauling him away.

Khan spent much of that weekend driving for Uber. The money in the hotel trade wasn't what it should be, and the Khans had a mortgage to pay and Sarah's college education to save for. Tanja contributed with her shifts as a server at a popular Mexican restaurant in Santa Monica. They juggled their work schedules—"like ships passing in the night," Khan would say—to make sure one of them was always home for their daughter.

When he told Tanja about the overdose and his decision to alert the authorities, she immediately became concerned. He knew she would. His wife was a worrier.

"You called the police?" Tanja said to him. She feared the older man might be in a position to hurt her husband. People with money stayed at the Constance. "Who knows who those people are?"

Khan assured her it would be fine.

There was nothing on the local news websites about the overdose or an arrest. Khan wasn't surprised. Routine drug busts didn't necessarily make the news. He wanted to believe the young woman had survived. But how could he be certain? Fatal overdoses also didn't make the news, unless the dead person was famous.

The following Monday, Khan reported to work at his usual time, the morning sun barely over the mountains. He bumped into a colleague who was getting coffee in a service kitchen near the hotel's front entrance; the small space smelled of toasted bagels. The colleague had been on duty after Khan left Friday. Khan asked him if the police arrested the man involved in the overdose. The question was more of a conversation starter than a genuine query, since an arrest had seemed guaranteed.

"No," the coworker said. He shook his head. "Nothing happened."

Khan was taken aback. "What do you mean, nothing?"

"It's like, when the police got here, they already knew who the guy was. They didn't arrest him; they didn't do anything. They said something like, 'Drug abuse isn't a crime, it's a disease.'"

That made no sense. "Didn't they get his phone?"

"They didn't take his phone." He shrugged as if to say it couldn't be explained. "Oh, and the guy really is a doctor."

Khan still didn't buy that. "No way."

"Yeah, and he isn't just *any* doctor—he's the dean of medicine at USC."

"*What?*"

"He's the dean, yeah. At USC."

Khan stared at him. It took only a moment for disbelief to turn to outrage and then to disgust. And Khan knew that he would do something about it. He had to. It was his code.

2

SARAH AND TONY

Two months earlier, on a January night, Dr. Carmen Puliafito was behind the wheel of his Porsche, tooling up Pacific Coast Highway in Malibu. PCH could be a crawl during commute times, but the traffic sailed at this hour. Below the road, moonlight silkened the dark surf break, the crashing waves soundless at this distance. Puliafito turned onto Trancas Canyon, driving north into the steep and striated bluffs of the Santa Monica Mountains. This was one of the most expensive zip codes in the world, even though the residents had to cope with wildfires in the dry months and mudslides when the rains came. Puliafito was headed to Creative Care, one of many addiction treatment centers that had set up shop in Malibu. The location went to their marketing strategy; these were luxury rehabs, the five-star retreat version of halfway houses. They pillowed the prohibition on drugs and drink with ocean views, gourmet chefs, and masseuses. The frills came at a price. Places like Creative Care charged upward of $30,000 a month, and often more. They drew clients like Charlie Sheen, Lindsay Lohan, and Robert Downey Jr., which was another selling point for addicts who lacked fame but not money.

Puliafito had plenty of money. He made more than $1 million a year at USC, and he and his wife owned a Pasadena home valued in the vicinity of $6 million. And during the short time he had known Sarah Warren, who was not his wife, he had spent lavishly on her—hundreds of thousands of dollars. He was paying all her living expenses, starting with the rent on one apartment after another, in Pasadena and then Huntington Beach. Puliafito covered her car payments, her community college fees, even her cable TV bills. He paid for her furniture, clothing, makeup, and dental work. The spending money he gave her set him back as much as $1,000 a week. And there were the trips to New York, Miami, and Boston, even Switzerland. In New York, they stayed at the Plaza—in the same suite that someone said Leonardo DiCaprio favored. Puliafito treated her to a shopping binge at Bergdorf Goodman on Fifth Avenue. It cost him a grand just for a pair of earrings and a necklace.

The expenses meant nothing to Puliafito. Sarah had become the singular focus of his life, his obsession. Sarah called him Tony, after his middle name, Anthony. Sometimes she even called him honey—honey! He told her he loved her.

More important than love was his need to control her. Sarah knew that was the foundation of their relationship. The minute she slipped out of his grip, the minute she really got clean, it would be over—he would mean nothing to her. Puliafito could not let that happen. Which was why he was making the hour-long drive to Malibu, nosing the Porsche up the narrow curves of the canyon. Sarah had checked in to Creative Care that very day. Her parents persuaded her to do it. This was her second stay at the place. She walked out two weeks into her first, some months ago; it had just been too hard to give up the drugs. It wasn't looking good this time around, either, because Puliafito called her on the house phone—cell phones were confiscated at check-in—to say she had left her illicit stash of Xanax in his car. Sarah had no prescription for Xanax, and she could never get one in rehab, but Puliafito kept her supplied. When she took enough Xanax—several times the normal dosage of the benzo, which could be highly addictive in such amounts—it took the edge off her cravings for meth and heroin. She told Puliafito on the phone to bring the drugs up. And the dean of the Keck School of Medicine was doing just that. He was delivering drugs to a young addict in re-hab. He was breaking the law and shattering every ethical standard of his profession—of any profession devoted to human wellness. Puliafito was providing her with drugs because they maintained his hold on her. She was helpless—young and desperate and helpless.

Puliafito pulled off Trancas and into the parking area of the Cre-ative Care compound, whose seven buildings were clustered along the hillsides. Smuggling in the Xanax wouldn't be easy. Staffers at the center knew Puliafito from his visits during Sarah's previous stay. They remembered him well—the brusque and meddling doc-tor who threw his credentials around and barked at them that Sarah needed this or required that. They remembered that the relationship between Sarah and him, supposedly a professional one, did not seem right. And they knew his Porsche.

Even before he encountered Sarah, Puliafito had become bored with the straitlaced life of a dean, a physician, a husband, and a father. It didn't matter that he held one of the loftiest positions in his profession or that he had worked hard to build a sterling reputation—or that he had grown rich. Puliafito was an Italian kid from the suburbs of Buffalo, the son of an electrical engineer father and a homemaker mother. He was exceptionally smart and ambitious and was admitted to Harvard College and then Harvard Medical School. Puliafito graduated magna cum laude in earning his medical degree, and he put in the extra years to become an ophthalmologist. And it wasn't long after he finished his studies that his brilliance as a clinician and surgeon became known in the discipline. Puliafito co-invented optical coherence tomography, a breakthrough technology that employed light waves to take images of the retina to help diag-nose and treat diseases of the eye. Art restorers also used it to image the layers of a painting. Puliafito knew eyeballs the way the impressionists knew color. He wasn't your average contact lens prescriber.

The medical side of academia had taken notice early. Puliafito founded the Laser Research Laboratory at Harvard's Massachusetts Eye and Ear infirmary. Then the teaching hospital of the Tufts University School of Medicine brought Puliafito on board. There, he launched the New England Eye Center. His next stop was the University of Miami, where he led the medical school's eye institute and oversaw its return to the number one position in the all-important rankings by *U.S. News & World Report* magazine, the annual beauty contest of American universities and their professional schools. The rankings were seen as an instrument to accelerate fundraising and help schools recruit from among the aristocracy of professor-researchers who were magnets for seven-figure research grants. A high placement by *U.S. News* made alums proud of their school, and proud alums tended to donate more generously, which provided cash for big-name hires in the money-generating research fields. During Puliafito's term at Miami, research funding for the school tripled.

Puliafito knew more about money than how to spend it. As if his education credentials weren't stellar enough, he added a master's degree from the Wharton School at the University of Pennsylvania.

In August 2007, the provost of the University of Southern California sold Puliafito on heading its medical school. The provost was C. L. Max Nikias, a man with a boxy smile who spoke with the vaguely Spanish-sounding accent of his native Cyprus. Nikias was smitten with Puliafito's achievements at Miami, particularly his success in landing those research grants. That sort of performance was just what USC's Keck School of Medicine needed. Keck was in a long and unending competition with the medical school of the crosstown University of California, Los Angeles, which was more accomplished and more prestigious. The competition was for the best students, the fattest grants, and, in the end, the *name.* Which meant *status,* which came from a better showing in the *U.S. News* rankings. It did not mean much to campus presidents and fundraising directors that news organizations and others had taken the rankings apart and found them to be lacking (and even corruptible) as real measures of a university's excellence. The rankings had become a brand, a seal of approval, a hallmark of which schools to attend and which schools were most worthy of donations to their endowments.

Puliafito accepted Nikias's offer. Miami had been rewarding, but he couldn't resist the prospect of heading the medical school at the largest private university in the West. The day USC hired Puliafito, the university issued a news release. "I am honored to be part of the leadership team at the Keck School and at the University of Southern California," Puliafito said in the release. "The Keck School is poised to become a leader in American medicine."

The release included this statement from Nikias: "We believe this appointment heralds a moment of transformation for the Keck School."

Puliafito and his wife, Janet Pine, a psychiatrist, made the move to L.A. with their three children. Puliafito and Pine were schoolmates at Harvard. The couple became a USC package; the university hired Pine as an associate professor of psychiatry. They bought one of Pasadena's signature homes, a century-old Tudor revival mansion whose eleven thousand square feet presided over more than an acre and a half of rolling lawn and mature trees along a graceful curve of South Los Robles Avenue. It was designed by the acclaimed architectural firm of Hudson and Munsell, whose works included the domed and pillared Natural History Museum of Los Angeles County in Exposition Park, just across the way from USC.

The deanship was high pressure. When Puliafito took the job, *U.S. News* ranked Keck *twenty-five* spots below UCLA's medical school, a daunting gap, maybe an unbridgeable one. But Puliafito plugged away. Keck was a staid and entrenched institution—the school dated to 1885—and he shook it up. He wasn't always gentle about it. Some of the department chairs and faculty members, especially the longer-tenured ones, complained about his abrasiveness, his disdain for collegiality. But no one in the offices of the provost or the president seemed to care. What mattered to them was that Puliafito had lured more than seventy professors to Keck, including researchers who brought those bundles of grant money with them. He even managed to poach a University of California, San Diego, professor and his lab, which was an international leader in the search for an Alzheimer's cure. The lab was conducting drug trials around the world and expected to receive hundreds of millions of dollars in funding as its work blossomed. That was game-changing money, and it was just one lab.

Puliafito had been dean for a little over eight years and, by his count, had secured $1 billion in new funding for the school. He promoted Keck and USC as a featured speaker at national conventions and training seminars. And when he wasn't talking jargon to a ballroom of physicians and researchers, he was representing USC at gala fundraisers, grinning in publicity photos with Hollywood luminaries like Warren Beatty and Jay Leno and chatting with business titans such as Larry Ellison. That was the fun part of the job, yes, but Puliafito also kept up with the less glamorous demands of a professional of his stature. He had coauthored dozens of articles in leading medical journals. He held a seat on the governing board of the California Institute for Regenerative Medicine, which funds billions of dollars in research into stem cell treatments for diseases that had no cure.

And yet none of it was enough for Puliafito. That extended to his pastime, which was stamp collecting. He picked it up in childhood, and the hobby had long relaxed him and helped him to stay centered. Always the overachiever, Puliafito was an award-winning philatelist, and his collections were said to be worth hundreds of thousands of dollars. An upcoming auction offered the "Dr. Carmen A. Puliafito Collection of United States Independent Mails," which consisted of nineteenth-century stamps that private firms issued separately from the government postal service. Fellow philatelists praised the collection, declaring it one of the finest of its kind.

But it was *stamps.* Puliafito needed something more than that. He was tumbling headlong into his midsixties, well into old-man territory. He and his wife were in their fourth decade of marriage. Their children were grown. His job and all the perks that came with it had become less and less important to him. He needed something more engaging. Something thrilling, risky, even dangerous—something *life-affirming.*

Sarah was that something.

Puliafito parked the Porsche and climbed out with the ziplock bag of fifty or so Xanax. He walked in the cool gloom toward the building where Sarah was trying to kick.

3

THE TIP

Devon Khan couldn't let it go.

More to the point, he *wouldn't* let it go. He could drop it if he wanted to—forget about it, keep his mouth shut, walk away. And that would be a relief to his wife. Tanja had every reason to be anxious. Puliafito obviously had the wherewithal to beat an arrest in the face of overwhelming evidence of multiple crimes—*the hotel room was a yard sale of drugs and paraphernalia*—and that meant he should be feared. On Khan's short acquaintance, Carmen A. Puliafito was dissipated and desperate, a fool of an old man, a creep hollowed out by his baser weaknesses. But he was also the big-deal medical school dean whose name and face were all over Google, without a blemish. He was an important person doing important work for an important university. Puliafito was a Harvard man, he was rich, and he was *white*. Khan was none of those things. His degree was n associate of arts from Riverside City College. If Khan spoke out about what he knew about the overdose, Puliafito would have more than one way to crush him.

But it ate at him. Again and again, Khan thought about what should have happened to Puliafito and did not. He could not stop thinking about the young woman, the other Sarah, and how Puli-afito tried to stop him from getting her help. A *doctor.* A so-called healer. It gnawed at Khan as he sat in his office, alone; on the other side of his closed door, the lobby of the Constance was quiet. It had been a full week since the cops let Puliafito go. Khan had considered that there could still be an arrest, perhaps after the police investigated further. But then he thought, no, if the cops didn't have enough to make a bust with what they found in 304, it was because they didn't want enough. They were committed to looking the other way.

What could Khan do about it? Sure, he could call the Pasadena Police Department and ask to speak to a supervisor, maybe even the chief, and demand to know why Puliafito was allowed to skate. But what would that accomplish? Confronting the cops would only piss them off. Would it be smart to get on the bad side of the Pasadena police? The department wasn't known for maintaining a good relationship with the Black residents of the city. There had been questionable police shootings of Black men. And last summer, they arrested an organizer for Black Lives Matter Pasadena and charged her with a felony under California's old lynching law (although the term had been removed from the statute earlier that year). The police claimed she tried to stop them from arresting another woman, which they said was a form of lynching. *Seriously, forget about getting into the face of the cops.*

So then . . . what? Who? Going to the media could be dicey because reporters would want to speak to him and probably use his name. And if Khan was publicly attached to any effort to expose the circumstances of the overdose, he could be fired for violating the cardinal rule of guest privacy. His future in the hotel business could vanish in an instant.

He stared at his computer screen. It was a little after ten thirty in the morning. *Puliafito cannot get away with it. The police cannot get away with it.* If Khan couldn't go to the cops, maybe he could reach out to city hall. And if he couldn't go to the media, maybe he could bluff city hall on that score by claiming the press *was* looking into the overdose. Maybe that would get someone to act.

A lot of maybes.

Khan hunched over his keyboard and called up the city of Pasadena's website. He clicked through the department links until he settled on the page of city attorney Michele Beal Bagneris. The page had a portal that invited residents to submit comments on an email form.

Perfect.

But then Khan hesitated. He didn't trust anonymity on the Web, and he would never use his personal computer for something like this. Contacting the city from his work computer was safer, but he couldn't be sure how much safer; it wouldn't be surprising if an anonymous submission to the city attorney could be traced back to the computer on his desk and to his sign-on credentials. For all Khan knew, if an investigation he triggered led to him, the first to be informed of his involvement would be his bosses and the second would be Puliafito.

And the harm that Khan felt was lying in wait, the threat, was exactly what people like Puliafito counted on to silence people.

Well, fuck them.

Khan began typing. He identified himself on the email form only as *Concerned Citizen.* He wrote:

A story regarding the incident that occurred on March 4, 2016 involving Carmen A Puliafito, Dean of Keck School of Medicine, is forthcoming. I have close ties with Pasadena and would hate to see Pasadena PD portrayed in a bad light due to a possible cover up. Please look into this matter before it is too late.

He took a deep breath, and then he sent it.

There was no indication that the city attorney's office took any action in response to Khan's email. Not that Friday nor in the weeks that followed. It was as if his message had vaporized somewhere between the Constance and city hall.

Khan had figured the email was an outside chance. He was realistic about the fact that the city attorney and her staff worked side by side with the police. The city attorney was more or less the police department's lawyer. Why would she complicate that relationship to go after a heavyweight like Puliafito? Khan hedged his bets. And he didn't wait weeks to do it. On the Monday after he sent the email, he decided to report what he knew about Puliafito to the president of USC—*a man named C. L. Max Nikias.* Khan could not be certain that this Nikias or the people around him were not already part of the cover-up. The only way to be sure was to drop the Puliafito matter right in the man's lap. He found the number to Nikias's office on the USC website. Khan knew that calling it, even from a blocked number, would again pose the risk that he could be discovered. If the cops wanted to find him, couldn't they unmask his blocked number through the carrier? He wasn't sure USC could do that without the police, but he had to assume it could. Either way, calling Nikias probably was no more perilous than contacting the city attorney.

He was at work when he made up his mind to place the call. It had to be done. Khan needed to be able to tell himself that he had tried everything that reasonably could be tried. Calling from the Constance was not a good idea, though—because if Nikias did speak to him, he could be on the phone for a while. Khan intended to provide plenty of details of what happened at the hotel. The longer he was on the call, the greater the chance one of his coworkers would interrupt him or even overhear him. When his lunch break rolled around, Khan tapped the number to Nikias's office into his phone without calling it and left the hotel. The day was windless and bright. He walked around the corner and headed south on Mentor Avenue, past the bistro that occupied a neon-ribboned deco building beyond the Constance garage, past the Normandy apartment house across the street that was as old as the hotel. The apartments beyond Green Street were newer and boxy. As he crossed Green, Khan called the number.

A woman answered. She sounded young. Maybe a grad student assistant? Once Khan ascertained he had the president's office, he asked to speak to Nikias. The girlish voice wanted to know Khan's name and the reason for the call. He replied that he would not give his name, and then he began trotting out the information he had about the dean of the medical school. Khan spoke in the same calm and unhurried manner that he did to the 911 dispatcher ten days earlier. The woman politely broke in to ask if he could send his information to the office in writing.

"No, I'm not interested in doing that," Khan said.

The woman said she was transferring him. The line went silent for a few moments, and then a second woman came on and asked Khan how she might be able to help him. Like the first woman, she did not identify herself by name. Khan repeated his request to speak to Nikias. The woman said the president was not available and suggested she was as far as Khan would get.

The call was taking longer than Khan had thought. He had crossed Cordova and Del Mar, walking by the apartment buildings, and was nearing San Pasqual, where a canopy of oaks kept Mentor in shadow.

Khan laid it all out for the second woman: The dean of the medical school, Carmen Puliafito, was at the scene of an overdose on March 4 at the Hotel Constance in Pasadena. The victim was a young woman. There were drugs in the room. The police were called.

Khan could sense that the woman was taking notes. He kept talking.

The woman said he would have to put his complaint in writing for the school to proceed. *Complaint? Is that how his information was perceived?*

"I've done my part," Khan told her.

He then advised the woman that reporters were looking into the incident. Another bluff. She said nothing.

Khan thanked her and hung up.

"Are you sure nothing will happen to you?" Tanja Khan asked. "What about these people in power?"

She waited for Devon's response, although she knew what it would be: *He would be fine, the family would be fine.* That's what he said about making the 911 call, she thought, and then about the city attorney. But this time, he called the president of USC. If that got the dean in trouble, her husband could pay. Tanja's mind raced. *Whatever people the dean knows, that ugly man, they would take revenge on Devon.* She remembered what happened after he stood up to the Russian businessman, the one with the foul mouth, another one with money. How could she forget? Because of the Russian, her husband eventually lost his job. And this dean and the president of USC were much bigger than the Russian.

"We'll be fine," Devon said now.

He had just arrived home from work, and Tanja was about to leave for her dinner shift at the restaurant. The bungalow was far from a palace, but it was the kind of house in the type of neighborhood they once thought they could never afford. And their daughter was thriving in school—so smart! Their life was good.

"Just be careful," she told her husband.

The days fell away, and there was nothing about an investigation of Puliafito or an overdose at the Hotel Constance. Nothing about the police not doing their job. Nothing in the newspapers or on their websites. Nothing on television. Khan had brought his information to the two institutions responsible for making things right—the government and the university—and they ignored it. Buried it.

The cover-up seemed to be set in stone.

Khan would not have it. He was tormented. When he resolved

that there would be no investigation, he found himself willing to take one more chance. He made a final call, again after blocking his number—and this one was to the *L.A. Times.* No more bluffing about the media. He found the number for a tip line on the *Times* website, which was promoting the newspaper's upcoming Festival of Books at the USC campus, an annual event that was the largest of its kind in the nation. Khan took no notice of that and called the number. A switchboard operator answered. Khan told her that he needed to speak to a reporter about an important story—a local story. The operator patched the call through to a voice mail prompt.

Leaving a voice mail was out of the question. He could be identified by his voice. Khan ended the call.

It had been a month since the overdose. Khan had to accept that he had hit a wall. Maybe Tanja's bleak calculation had been correct all along: You could not go up against these people, not without suffering consequences. In Khan's case, the consequences might simply be the anger and frustration he couldn't shake, that low boil that came from knowing that the bad guys were getting away with it. He had been prepared to come forward if an investigation was launched. If his testimony was needed, he'd have taken the stand. But he refused to do the lone-wolf thing, to go public as the whistleblower. Since the day he made the 911 call, everything that had happened—and had *not* happened—confirmed his instincts that he and his family would be hurt if he took that path.

Khan stopped monitoring the news for any report on Puliafito. Time to move on.

Five days after the overdose, and forty-seven miles from Pasadena, the funeral motorcade of former first lady Nancy Reagan wound its way up Madera Road in Simi Valley. A public viewing of Mrs. Reagan was scheduled for that day at the Ronald Reagan Presidential Library & Museum, where she would be interred alongside her husband. The library was shouldered into a sun-browned hillside above the road, fronting a panorama of the Santa Susana Mountains, whose boulders and crags framed the filming locations of many Westerns. Veteran *L.A. Times* photographer Ricardo DeAratanha covered the motorcade. He pulled onto a side street and parked, downhill from the library, to transmit his photos from a laptop. He draped a tarp over the front of the car to block the sun so he could better see the images on the computer screen. That looked suspicious to someone in the neighborhood, and that person called the Simi Valley police. A motorcycle officer arrived quickly and then a patrol car. DeAratanha was startled when three officers confronted him. He identified himself as a *Times* photographer and showed the cops his media credentials, but that didn't satisfy them. DeAratanha suggested they were bracing him because he was nonwhite—a Brazilian.

Race was a touchy subject in Simi Valley, a predominantly white suburb where a jury acquitted four Los Angeles Police Department officers who were charged in the infamous Rodney King beating. The not-guilty verdicts sparked the 1992 L.A. rebellion. According to DeAratanha's attorney, the Simi Valley cops swarmed his sixty-five-year-old client, forced him to the ground, and handcuffed him. They arrested him on suspicion of resisting and obstructing a law enforcement officer.

DeAratanha was outraged then and even more so when prosecutors later decided to charge him with a misdemeanor based on his arrest. He assumed the case would be dropped. It wasn't as though he had been a threat to anyone. The day after he was charged, DeAratanha drove from his home in Agoura Hills across the San Fernando Valley to Pasadena, where his nephew was hosting a small party. It wasn't long before DeAratanha began venting at the gathering about his legal predicament, the photo assignment that ended with his arrest.

Khan was a guest at the party. DeAratanha's nephew lived two doors down from him and was a close friend of the family. They vacationed together, and their daughters played together. Khan did not know DeAratanha, but he was sitting across the kitchen table from him when he told the story of his arrest. DeAratanha's main point was that he was just doing his job.

"Where do you work?" Khan asked him.

"The *L.A. Times,*" DeAratanha said.

As he recalled later, Khan's "eyes became as big as moons." Here he was in the house of a buddy, someone he could trust, and his buddy's uncle happened to be someone who could help him finally get the word out about Puliafito and the cover-up.

"Man," he said to DeAratanha, "do I have a story for you."

DeAratanha listened closely, and I got Khan's tip two days later. The editors decided I should check it out because of my experience with USC investigations. Seven years earlier, my reporting disclosed that USC head football coach Pete Carroll, a revered figure on campus, violated NCAA rules by secretly retaining a former NFL coach to help run the Trojan kicking and punting squads, known as the special teams. The violation later became part of the NCAA's blistering sanctions of USC—among the harshest the association ever imposed on a school—that centered on unrelated allegations against Trojan running back Reggie Bush, who won the Heisman Trophy, and basketball star O. J. Mayo. And when the tip about the overdose arrived, my colleague Nathan Fenno and I were deep into an investigation of USC's most golden of golden boys, Pat Haden, then the university's athletic director.

Haden was the starting Trojan quarterback in 1973 and 1974 and went on to play the same position for the L.A. Rams—the rare athlete who reached that summit in college and professional sports in his hometown. After his days on the field, he became a fixture on national broadcasts of college and pro football, particularly for Notre Dame games. The clean-cut and studious Haden was more than an accomplished jock. He was a Rhodes Scholar, an attorney, and a wealthy investment adviser. Fenno and I reported that Haden continued to hold lucrative positions on corporate boards while athletic director—moonlighting that was perfectly legal but perhaps a distraction from his USC duties. That wasn't nearly as bad as our finding that he had taken control of a scholarship charity for low-income students and then bled it to pay himself and his relatives more than $2.4 million in fees for what nonprofit watchdogs said should have been volunteer work.

What could be worse than that for the USC leadership? I was about to find out.

I emailed DeAratanha for the name and phone number of the source he knew only as Devon. When I called, Khan immediately said he needed to be off the record. He explained that he would be fired if he were found to have released information about a hotel guest. I granted him anonymity; the potential loss of a job was among the circumstances under which the *Times* allows sources to go unnamed. Khan gave me his account of the overdose and the failure of the police to make an arrest. It was a shocking story—if it held up to scrutiny. Khan was precise in the details, including the times of day that events occurred. But a piece of information Khan did not have was the young woman's last name. He said he knew her first name only because he had overheard it. And he said he did not know if the woman named Sarah recovered from the overdose—if she lived.

"The fact that this guy's in charge of future doctors makes me sick," Khan said.

After twenty minutes or so, I thanked him and said I'd be back in touch. I then did a quick check of the *Times*'s electronic library and found that, eleven days earlier, the paper published a four-paragraph story reporting that Puliafito had "stepped down" as dean. Khan apparently had missed it. The story provided no reason for his resignation, which was strange. But Puliafito's abrupt departure from the deanship, in the middle of the school term, on a Thursday, suggested that Khan was telling the truth.

My sense then was that the overdose story would be scandalous but straightforward—that is, easy to report. I saw it as fundamentally a police story that wouldn't take much time to wrap up and get into the paper. A quick-and-dirty tale about another powerful man behaving in unspeakable ways.

That's what I'd thought. Until I visited the Pasadena Police Department.

4

HITTING A WALL

With its gable stones and red brick and soaring windows, the Los Angeles County coroner's office looked more like a small Parisian opera house than a repository of cadaver slabs and coolers. The 1909 beaux arts building sat on the edge of the town-size USC Health Sciences campus in Boyle Heights, home to the Keck School of Medicine. Health Sciences was about seven miles from the university's main campus in South L.A. The coroner's office was the work of the same architects who designed Carmen Puliafito's mansion in Pasadena. It also was the first place to check on the well-being of the young woman who had been gurneyed out of his hotel room. Did "Sarah" die from the overdose? Given Khan's account, the possibility could not be dismissed; yes, the woman had been breathing, but she was chin-to-shoulder limp. If she didn't make it, the death became a coroner's case, and an autopsy would have been performed. And the questions for Puliafito, the Pasadena police, and USC would be more pointed.

It took me a few days to determine if anyone who matched Sarah's description had died of drug-related causes during a period of several weeks following the overdose. In my query to the coroner's office, I extended the timeline of the possible death in case the woman had lingered before succumbing. The delay in the office's response was not unexpected. The office served a population of more than ten million people, the largest for any coroner in the nation, and it received about eighteen thousand death reports that year and performed thirty-three hundred autopsies. The office was perennially short on both money and the staff the dollars could hire. The dead didn't have much of a political lobby, so funding for more pathologists was not a high priority for the county board of supervisors.

As I waited to hear from the coroner, I began to scrub the *Times*'s public records databases—LexisNexis, Accurint, and TLO—for anything on Puliafito. No criminal filings against him popped up. The only legal case that surfaced was a recent divorce petition filed by his wife, a psychiatrist named Janet Pine. That was intriguing. Divorce records can provide rich material on one or both of the spouses' personality traits, finances, sexual practices, propensity for violence, drug and alcohol abuse, and other vices—the behaviors that might lead to a scene like the one at the Hotel Constance. Some divorce files grew thick as books from the jousting by the parties. But the Pine filing was thin, short on details, and offered nothing about hotels or infidelities or overdoses. A bust.

Then the coroner's office got back to me: In the weeks after the incident at the Constance, there had been a sobering tally of deaths of young Angelenos, including from car crashes, suicides, murders, and, yes, drug overdoses. But none of the dead remotely resembled "Sarah" as Khan described her.

So the next step was to confront the Pasadena police. Going to the police before engaging USC was a tactical decision. USC president Max Nikias and his administrators had a long record of not responding in a helpful way to inquiries from the *Times* that weren't about positive stories—the gushy pieces that promoted the school's relentless campaign to burnish its national reputation. I had to make the calculation of whether contacting USC first would sink my prospects of getting the police to talk. And that equation had to include the ties between USC and Pasadena, at least the ones on the surface. In some respects, the city of 141,000 seemed like a satellite campus of the university. Like the school, Pasadena was an early bastion of L.A.'s elite, having evolved from orchard land into a warm-weather resort town and one of the first affluent communities of the burgeoning Southern California metropolis. A Pasadena thoroughfare, Orange Grove Boulevard, became known as "Millionaires Row" because of the baronial homes that lined it. The Valley Hunt Club in Pasadena was among the pioneers of private social clubs in the L.A. region; it created what later became the Rose Parade in 1890.

A century and more later, Pasadena was home to USC faculty members and administrators and to well-heeled alumni and donors who worked in the law firms, banks, and brokerage firms of downtown L.A. USC graduates served on the Pasadena City Council. The mayor of the city from 1999 to 2015 had taught law at the university. Pasadena's pricey private high schools were feeders to USC. The university's name was on Pasadena's Pacific Asia Museum, and, for decades, the school managed the Gamble House, the city's internationally hailed masterpiece of arts and crafts architecture. Keck Medicine had a treatment center in Pasadena. And the USC president's residence was in neighboring San Marino, a sort of a wealthier appendage of Pasadena. The eight-bedroom, eleven-bathroom American colonial mansion rested on seven regally landscaped acres that had been donated in part by U.S. Army general George S. Patton, whose maternal grandfather was the second mayor of L.A. and whose father was an L.A. district attorney. Nikias used the estate to entertain and schmooze local power brokers and court others from Washington, D.C., to foreign capitals.

Altogether, it seemed reasonable to conclude that if there was one private institution outside its boundaries that Pasadena City Hall took particular notice of and cared about, it was the University of Southern California. So I had to assume that a call or visit to USC about Puliafito would prompt the university to reach out to a friendly and influential contact in the city, if only to get ahead of my reporting. And that could lead to silence all around.

I was still of the mind that getting the basic story of the overdose would not take long. USC might not aid in my reporting, but it couldn't *deny* that the overdose occurred. It *could* deny knowing about Puliafito's presence at the overdose, although that would seem a huge stretch considering Khan's call to Nikias's office. I believed any denial would become irrelevant once I shared what I knew with Nikias and his administrators. They would be forced to address Puliafito's role in the overdose and whether it led to his resignation as dean.

Or would they?

On a Tuesday afternoon, I drove out to Pasadena and parked in a metered lot across from city hall, another local gem of a building, which was constructed during the City Beautiful movement of the 1920s. The fish-scale-tiled dome that rose six stories above Mediterranean archways was magnificent enough to crown a state capitol. The politicians who commissioned city hall promised it would be "suited to a land of flowers and sunshine." Ninety years on, its grace and richness still spoke to a presumed gentility that governed the affairs of the city. But official Pasadena had its share of rough edges. There were the controversial shootings of Black men by the police. And city hall itself became a crime scene in late 2014, when an analyst for its public works department was charged with embezzling more than $6 million from the municipal coffers. The thievery had gone on for years.

I walked the block from the parking lot to the Pasadena Police Department headquarters, whose tall whitewashed arches were a nod to the look of city hall. The lobby for the records office closed off the light of the day. I explained why I was there to a woman who sat behind a long reception window spangled with intercom speakers. She summoned someone from the inner warrens of the building, and, a few minutes later, Lieutenant Tracey Ibarra emerged from behind a secured door. Ibarra was a longtime veteran of the department and its media spokesperson and she did not look happy to see me. Maybe it was because my visit was unannounced—because I had not called or emailed ahead. Or maybe it was because the *Times* waged a long legal battle with Pasadena and the police union to get access to records on the fatal shooting of an unarmed nineteen-year-old Black man. The newspaper won that fight. I told Ibarra what I was looking for, starting with an incident or crime report on the overdose. I made the case that the report should be readily available. The lieutenant gave no ground other than to say she would look into it. I left empty-handed.

It was a three-minute walk from the police headquarters to the administrative office of the Pasadena Fire Department, which leased space in a low-rise commercial building with checkerboard windows. The fire department was a required stop because of the paramedic call, but patient privacy laws made it unlikely that my visit would yield much information. I told the woman who greeted visitors in the office that I wanted to speak to the fire chief or his representative. Neither was in, but the woman gave me the email address of the department's media contact, Lisa Derderian. I walked back to my car and sent her an email from my phone, marking it "urgent":

"Hi. I need information about a paramedic call last month for a story that I'm wrapping up. I'm only looking for the basic material that is released to the public."

To say I was wrapping up the story might have been part wishful thinking, but I was determined to get it filed quickly in case any other news outlet was snooping around. I ended the message to Derderian with my phone number, and she called me within the hour. Derderian gave me some details of the paramedic call, including that it was about an overdose, the location, times of day, and the hospital the woman was taken to—Huntington Hospital. It wasn't much; there were no names of any of the people involved. But the times of day were important because they matched almost to the minute the times Khan had given me. The more I learned about the events of March 4 and their aftermath, the more credible he became.

Later that day, shortly before 6:30 P.M., I received an email from Melissa Trujillo, a police department supervisor. She wrote:

> Mr. Pringle, I received your request for incident 6PA0021560 from Lt. Ibarra. Attached you will find a redacted copy of the incident [report] you requested.

Whoa! I hadn't expected Ibarra to release the report that quickly—if at all. Could the Pasadena PD be committing itself to transparency? Was it tired of being sued? Even before I read the attachment, I asked myself if there was time to get a story posted on the *Times*'s website that night, based on the police report. It would be tight—I would have to reach out to Puliafito and USC before filing—but I had to worry about the possible competition. What if Ibarra was releasing the report to the two Pasadena newspapers? Or to the broadcast stations? All would love a story about a medical school dean mixed up in a drug overdose.

Then I opened the attachment . . . *Never mind*. It wasn't a police report but a Call for Service log, a record of the police response in an assistance capacity to a paramedic call. The document was two pages of call times and puzzling acronyms and abbreviations, with just a snippet of narrative. The name of the reporting party was redacted— blacked out. But the log had several references to either an "overdose," "odose" or "OD, " and a misspelled one to "chrystal meth."

It had no other details that I could hang a story on. Nothing about a potential crime.

Four lines on the log said either "Disposition: RPT," "Dispo: RPT," or "Closed dispo: REPORT." So some type of report must have been filed about the overdose. Was the Call for Service log considered a report? That would be strange—a notation on a report referring to the report itself? I supposed it was possible, in view of the quirky and often inscrutable ways bureaucracies communicated with themselves.

An interview could clear it up. I called Ibarra to request one with police chief Phillip Sanchez. I wanted to ask him why a *crime* report hadn't been taken and filed. Ibarra suggested the incident at the Hotel Constance might have been a medical emergency and not a police matter, so there was no reason to file a crime report. That didn't seem right. What about Puliafito? He didn't overdose, and illegal drugs were found in his hotel room. Didn't that make him a potential crime suspect? Didn't that require a report? Those are questions I had for Sanchez. Except he was unwilling to be interviewed, which I took to mean he saw no upside for himself, the police department, or city hall to breathe any life into my story. If everything was aboveboard, the chief should have been happy to speak to me.

But what I surmised was different from what I could report. All I had to place Puliafito at the scene of the overdose was Khan's off-the-record account. Which wasn't enough for publication.

It was time to take matters to USC.

Ideally, I would have first gathered more information that I could use to arm-twist the Nikias administration into coming clean about Puliafito, such as a witness to confirm what Khan had told me. I would have hounded my USC sources for anything they might be hearing. I would have searched the Web for the names and social media accounts of Pasadena police officers and paramedics, used that information to scour the *Times*'s databases for their addresses, and then knocked on their doors. But that would take time, which I believed I didn't have. I had to act on the presumption that my queries of the police would fly up the chains of command, including those in city hall, and reach USC. And that could get people talking—including to rival media outlets. Apart from the Pasadena newspapers and TV stations, I worried about USC's student paper and news website. Those kids were smart, resourceful, and aggressive about covering their own school. They must be wondering why the dean of the medical school gave up his post on a random Thursday afternoon. I needed to move fast.

I began calling the USC executive offices to inquire about Puliafito's sudden resignation as dean. I did not divulge that I knew about the overdose, but I did stress that I had questions about the circumstances that might have prompted his resignation. I did not hear back from Nikias or his inner circle.

Then, out of the blue, I received an email from Puliafito, whom I had yet to contact. With the subject line "Transition from Deanship," it read:

> I understand from colleagues here at USC that you've been inquiring about my stepping down as Dean of the medical school. I wanted to reach out to you directly and let you know that my decision was entirely my own. The timing of my decision was related to a unique, time limited opportunity in the biotech industry, something which I am looking forward to sharing with others soon. USC was nice enough to grant me a sabbatical to explore this opportunity. Bottom line, I was Dean for almost a decade. It was great, but I was ready and open to jumping on these opportunities when they came along.

Nothing, of course, about a young woman or an overdose at the Hotel Constance.

It occurred to me that Puliafito never would have sent the email if he wasn't confident that Nikias would not contradict it—that USC would protect him.

I hadn't expected USC to grant me much in the way of cooperation. That was based on my earlier reporting on the university, including the investigations of Pete Carroll and Pat Haden as well as a broader one into the Los Angeles Memorial Coliseum, where USC played football. Max Nikias and the people around him had behaved more like bunkered corporate executives than stewards of an academic institution. Silence and secrecy were their preferred methods of engagement with me. They rarely agreed to interviews, and they responded to my written queries largely with parsed answers that were meant to frustrate my reporting. There was no mistaking that they didn't believe they had to deal with me, a lowly reporter, because they represented the real power in L.A.

The Coliseum investigation brought a lesson in how much weight USC carried in the city. The publicly owned stadium, a National Historic Landmark whose peristyled bowl sits across Exposition Boulevard from the campus, is an L.A. crown jewel. It hosted the Olympic Summer Games in 1932 and 1984. Over the years, it also had served as home for the Rams, the Los Angeles Raiders, UCLA football, and briefly the Los Angeles Dodgers and Los Angeles Chargers. The Coliseum was where John F. Kennedy delivered his acceptance speech for the 1960 Democratic presidential nomination, and where Pope John Paul II celebrated a Mass that drew one hundred thousand worshippers. In 2011, I and my colleagues Andrew Blankstein and Rong-Gong Lin II published a series of stories showing that Coliseum managers took millions in bribes and kickbacks from concert promoters and a stadium contractor. We also reported that the managers directed Coliseum business to companies they owned, delivered suitcases of cash to union bosses, and spent tens of thousands in public funds on massages, golf tournaments, luxury cars, and other perks. Ron and I went on to disclose that someone at the Coliseum allowed a porn producer to do a night shoot of *Gangbang Girl #32* on the football field. All together, our stories led to six indictments that resulted in a string of guilty and no-contest pleas. The scandal showed that corruption of an impressive temerity was alive and well in the

City of Angels—that a nonfiction take on L.A. noir was not a thing of the past. And it presented USC, which had not been implicated in any of the wrongdoing, with an opportunity to flex its political muscles.

The school had always been merely a tenant at the Coliseum, the Trojans playing there under lease agreements with the government commission that operated the stadium. But USC had long coveted control of the property, and now that the commissioners were red-faced over our findings, the university went to work on them. They were a mix of elected officials and appointees representing the city and county of L.A. and the state. USC and Nikias had sway with most of them. In the heat of our reporting, the commission president, David Israel, a Hollywood producer, pushed to give USC what it wanted—a ninety-nine-year master lease of the Coliseum, the next best thing to outright ownership. Israel was originally appointed to the body by Governor Arnold Schwarzenegger. As the commission prepared to hand over the Coliseum to USC, Nikias accepted a combined $20 million donation and fundraising pledge from the then former governor to establish the nebulously named USC Schwarzenegger Institute for State and Global Policy. USC also granted the movie-star-turned-politician a professorship. There were whispers of revulsion among the faculty. This was nine years after the *Times,* in the run-up to Schwarzenegger's 2003 election as governor, reported on his history of sexual harassment. But it was five years before the dawn of the #MeToo movement. Women faculty members who were appalled by Nikias's money-minded indulgence of Schwarzenegger could not stop the arrangement. Nikias was two years into his presidency, and my sources at the university were telling me the tenor of his administration had made it plain that open rebukes of him would not be tolerated.

The commission voted 8–1 to give USC its master lease (delays reduced its term to ninety-eight years), in exchange for the university's pledge to make at least $70 million in near-term improvements to the stadium, which had been valued at $650 million after planned renovations. The lease gave USC all receipts from ticket and concession sales, parking fees, and stadium advertising buys, in return for an annual rent outlay that started at $1 million. The university got 95 percent of the millions of dollars in naming rights to the Coliseum. USC agreed to a small split of the stadium profits with the government if the school reported any. Experts on such deals predicted the university would be careful to never show a profit on paper.

To sweeten the terms even more, the commission threw in the Sports Arena, which USC later had razed to make way for a flashy soccer stadium for the professional Los Angeles Football Club, another source of revenue for the school.

The lone holdout in the commission's vote was Bernard Parks, a former L.A. police chief and city councilman. Parks was a Trojan himself, but he believed the lease ripped off the taxpayers and particularly those who lived in USC's South L.A. neighborhood, most of them nonwhite and lower income. He said the deal demonstrated that USC knew how to "turn their alumni out to work on people," meaning the university's trustees and those graduates with big bank accounts and connections.

"It was basically a club of wealthy people," Parks said. "It was all about entitlement and money."

Ron and I reported on the Coliseum giveaway, but there wasn't much of an outcry over the public getting stiffed. The muted response wasn't uncharacteristic for L.A. A small network of political movers and shakers usually managed to accommodate the likes of USC without drawing crowds of vocal skeptics. In that sense, L.A. lived up to its "laid-back" image.

It was a city where people didn't look too hard at things—if they looked at all.

And that made life easier for the Max Nikiases.

• • •

Before I became an investigative reporter, I worked for three decades as a general assignment writer and L.A.-based bureau chief. I covered local, state, national, and occasionally foreign news, writing breaking news stories and longer-term feature pieces on subjects ranging from earthquakes and riots to celebrity murder trials and orchestra pits to presidential campaigns and the war in Northern Ireland. I loved every minute of it. But by the mid-2000s, investigative reporting had become a critical priority as newspapers shrank under financial pressures from the Web. Newspapers still did investigative reporting better and in much greater volume than any other medium, and that had to continue. So I decided it was time to make a transition to investigations, and they gradually became my specialty.

They were challenging in a motivating way. Many investigative stories required us to uncover or even solve crimes with little more than our wits and powers of persuasion. There were many times when that wasn't enough, and we couldn't get sufficient corroborating information to publish our findings, which allowed the bad guys to escape. But when we pulled it off, the intrinsic rewards were enormous, because we had brought justice to people who otherwise would have been denied it. I had seen plenty of injustice go uncorrected in my years of covering breaking news and writing feature stories—defenseless folks being crushed by the people and institutions responsible for serving and safeguarding them. It was gratifying to direct light on their suffering through day-to-day news reporting or longer features. But it was *infinitely* more fulfilling to take down the villains with an investigative project. In this late stage of my career, that's what I was all about as a journalist.

I learned much about the leadership culture at USC from an insider who became my source during the Coliseum reporting. He insisted on complete anonymity, so I nicknamed him "Tommy Trojan," after a bronze statue of a helmeted warrior that stands in the center of campus. The great care he took in communicating with me underscored the fear that gripped USC employees about publicly knocking the school's administrators and especially Nikias. Tommy went to pre-digital lengths—and then some—to avoid leaving any traces of our exchanges. He would not meet face-to-face, believing the risk of someone with USC connections spotting us was too high. He never sent me an email or text message—*never*—not even over encryption apps such as Signal, which he did not trust. He was dubious about burner phones and declined my offer to equip him with one. Tommy did not allow me to call him; he initiated every call and always from a blocked number. When he needed to deliver documents to me, he dropped them off at a Federal Express office where I would pick them up. They were left in an envelope with my name on it—but not his.

I didn't use the nickname in our conversations; he didn't want me to utter any name for him, particularly his own, in case someone overheard it and somehow concluded he was talking to the *L.A. Times.*

Tommy often spoke in a sardonic manner. "Six or seven," he told me about Pat Haden's side work on corporate boards, at a time when Trojan football coach Steve Sarkisian was under scrutiny for alcohol-fueled carousing. "That's a lot of boards. No wonder he couldn't pay attention to Sark's drinking. Poor Pat just didn't have the time."

I didn't hear from Tommy during my first few weeks pursuing the Puliafito tip, but thinking about him made me wonder if Nikias had pull in our own newsroom. Fenno and I were trying to get the Haden charity piece published—Tommy was a source for it—and pushing it through the upper ranks of editors took much more than the usual effort. Davan Maharaj, then a twenty-two-year veteran of the *Times,* had become editor in chief in late 2011 and eventually selected Marc Duvoisin for the number two post, managing editor.

I was not the only one who felt that under Maharaj and Duvoisin, stories that were tough on USC drew extraordinary scrutiny and were assigned little urgency, a pattern that had been hardening. I should have seen trouble coming on the charity story. Because I was busy with other investigations, I'd passed Tommy's tip about Haden's corporate board commitments on to our Sports Department. Sports queried Haden about it as part of a longer Q and A story but did nothing more. I complained in writing to my supervisor, city editor Matt Lait, and copied Duvoisin on the email. As part of my complaint, I asked for permission to freelance a story on Haden's corporate entanglements for another news outlet, since the *Times* seemed uninterested in giving the subject the attention it deserved.

I then met with Duvoisin in his office and asked him point-blank, "Is the *Times* in the tank for USC?"

Duvoisin said nothing. He just looked at me with a flat expression.

Lait encouraged me to do the Haden story for the *Times* rather than freelance it. So I partnered on it with Fenno, who I later learned had his own difficulties getting USC stories published. Neither Maharaj nor Duvoisin had seemed inclined to publish a story Fenno cowrote that revealed Sarkisian's drinking problem. The piece only ran after Sarkisian failed to show up for a practice and Haden placed him on indefinite leave because he was "not healthy." Hours after the story appeared, Sarkisian was fired.

Fenno had much worse luck with a previous story that Nikias would not have liked. It explored a claim by former Trojan football player Armond Armstead that he suffered a heart attack at age twenty-one because a USC team physician had repeatedly injected him with a potent painkiller. The story said the drug, Toradol, was regularly used on USC athletes. Fenno's reporting was based on two thousand pages of sworn statements and other court records in the player's lawsuit against USC and the physician, which the school settled. The story glided through Fenno's immediate editor and the

Sports editor. The draft then went to Duvoisin for approval before publication. Fenno thought that would be routine. It was not. The story died with Duvoisin. And he never told Fenno why. There was no discussion of whether there were flaws in the draft or whether more reporting was needed. Duvoisin seemed to have killed the story through the newsroom equivalent of a pocket veto. Fenno could not believe it. But he was young and new to the *Times* and felt he did not have the standing to confront Duvoisin. Fenno had hoped the Sports editors could change Duvoisin's mind, but they could not.

The *Times* had become a newsroom where the editors in charge did not welcome pushback from the lower orders. Much like USC.

Fenno did not tell me about this story until two years after it was killed. If he had told me earlier, I would have been outraged but not surprised. Maharaj made no secret of his high regard for USC and Nikias. A good while after he settled into the editor's chair, Maharaj invited me into his office to chat—something he often did back then—and our conversation turned to the economic and cultural revival of downtown, which was in full swing. I was astonished to hear him credit the resurgence mostly to Nikias's USC; the university did not have a dominant presence downtown. And then he used his fingers to tick off all the ways he believed the school had surpassed UCLA—its superiority in the sciences, medicine, technology, and, now, economic development. Maharaj, whose accent summoned his Trinidadian background, could not have been more ebullient in his praise if he were Nikias's public relations manager. It disturbed me to the point that, when I returned to my desk, I made a note of his remarks and began researching some of his assertions about USC, many of which I found to be false.

So I knew there were risks in writing anything about USC that wasn't soft. Our investigation of the Haden charity had to grind through a gauntlet of editors, causing weeks of delays. One of our most embarrassing findings was axed in the final edit—the fact that, for seven years, the foundation's tax returns identified a dead man as one of the nonprofit's directors. But even after that experience, I would not have imagined that a story like Fenno's painkiller piece could be spiked outright.

And that would have been good to know as I chased the Puliafito story.

5

SEARCHING FOR SARAH

No one was talking.

Not Puliafito. He still wasn't returning my calls. I replied to his email in which he said he voluntarily relinquished the deanship; I told him I had questions and asked for his phone number. No response. I called the numbers I found for him, and he did not return my messages. He apparently saw no need to say more about the "unique, time limited opportunity" that he claimed inspired him to walk away from the Keck post.

I then sent him this email:

Dr. Puliafito—

I have detailed knowledge of the events of March 4 at the Hotel Constance in Pasadena. I very much would like to give you the opportunity to address the information I've gathered. Either way, though, I will continue to pursue the story.

I ended the message by urging him to contact me as soon as possible. There was no reply.

My interview requests for Nikias met with what had become the customary silence.

I thought I could persuade Thomas Sayles, a USC vice president who oversaw media relations, to get Nikias to open up. I left Sayles a phone message and emailed him to say I needed to speak to him as soon as possible. I was deliberately vague about the subject of my queries, because sometimes that kindles sufficient curiosity or concern to prompt a response. It didn't with Sayles. So I sent him a follow-up email similar to the one I had sent Puliafito, saying I was "aware of the circumstances that preceded" the dean's resignation.

Again, Sayles didn't even acknowledge receiving the email. And he seemingly was *paid* to communicate with the news media.

I'd been stonewalled on many stories in the past, including by institutions that had become expert at ruthlessly stymieing journalists, such as the Pentagon and the Roman Catholic Church. But this cover-up was as adamantine as any that I had faced—maybe more so, given how routine my inquiries were. Here was a major university and the government of a well-to-do city closing off nearly every avenue of information about an incident that involved paramedics and police officers and the dean of a medical school. Considering their legal duel with the *Times,* I could understand why the Pasadena officials might stiff-arm me as a reflex. That didn't make it right, but at least the motivation could be explained. USC was a different matter. This story was not about cheating in the football program or milking a charity. It concerned the overdose of a young woman in the presence of the man who oversees the university's training of future physicians—an incident that occurred in a hotel room on a Friday afternoon when school was in session, with cops and firefighters in the Constance lobby, the emergency lights of the vehicles spinning red on the well-traveled street outside. Did Nikias and his administration really believe they could bury something so egregious and public simply by not talking?

That again got me wondering—and worrying—about Nikias's relationship with the leadership of the *Times.* I was at my computer in the Metro Department of the third-floor newsroom, drafting email requests under the California Public Records Act to send to the Pasadena police and city attorney. The newsroom was an aesthetic affront to the downtown building that housed it—the stout-ribbed, art deco classic on Spring Street by architect Gordon Kaufmann, designer of the Hoover Dam. The room was a long rectangular hive of metal desks and filing cabinets arranged in pods and piled in papery rubble. Much of it had a patchwork, almost makeshift look that came from a succession of function-over-form upgrades and retrofits. The ceiling was low and false and supported by bulbous columns spaced inelegantly along the floor. In the corridors, steel girders angled overhead to improve the building's chances of surviving an earthquake. Glassed-in offices for editors lined the walls. Reporters had begun referring to the occupants of the offices (mostly good-humoredly) as "glassholes" long before the term became popular for the wearers of Google glasses.

My first CPRA request was to the Pasadena city attorney Bagneris, asking for a copy of the anonymous note Khan sent to her office about his knowledge of the overdose and Puliafito's involvement. Khan and I were confident my query could not lead back to him. A copy of the note from Bagneris would be an official government record that I could cite in my story as evidence of the city's inaction on Puliafito. My request for the Pasadena police, addressed to Ibarra, sought copies of "all communications involving Chief Sanchez and/or his management staff relating to an incident at the Dusit D2 Hotel Constance in Pasadena and/or any employees or representatives of the University of Southern California, from March 3, 2016 to the date you fulfill this request. The incident in question, which occurred on March 4, involved a suspected drug overdose and/or suspected drug possession."

I was looking for any email or text message or memo that showed

Sanchez or his staff had reached out to USC about Puliafito's presence at the overdose or vice versa.

I also asked Ibarra to unredact the Call for Service log.

It was a few minutes before 5:00 P.M.—early deadline. The noise and energy in the newsroom were shifting from the reporters' pods to the editing desks. Voices carried in the room, along with alternatively too-cold and too-hot currents of air from the schizoid HVAC system. Kaufmann's monument-evoking structure was the fourth Times Building, all of them in the part of downtown that served not just as the L.A. Civic Center but, for decades, the city's financial district as well—Spring Street was once known as "the Wall Street of the West." The *Times* was founded in 1881, a year after USC. The paper and the university had grown up together and, for better and worse, helped shape L.A.'s character and culture. Some ties between the *Times* and USC bordered on the familial. At the request of the school's athletic director, a young *Times* sports columnist, Owen Bird, came up with "Trojans" as the university's nickname in 1912. (Bird later went to prison for shooting his best friend to death after coming home to find him chatting with his wife.) Richard Nixon represented another USC-*Times* nexus: The road to the White House for Nixon had been largely paved by the *Times* when it was run by Norman Chandler, whose extended family had controlled the paper since shortly after its founding. Nixon surrounded himself with a number of aides who were USC alums and became known as his USC mafia. Among them were Dwight L. Chapin, Donald Segretti, and Herbert Porter, all of whom were convicted in the Watergate scandal. (Nixon himself was a graduate of Whittier College and Duke University Law School.) The *Times* had long been a merciless backer of Republican politicians—to such an extreme that editors forbade their reporters from even covering some Democratic candidates. The paper all but sponsored Nixon's career, promoting him both in its reporting and in the opinion pages.

That only ended in the news columns after Chandler's son, Otis, became publisher in 1960 and set about transforming the *Times* from a partisan sheet with mediocre aspirations into a behemoth of world-class journalism.

But now the legacy of Otis Chandler's two decades as publisher was under assault. I joined the *Times* in 2001, a year after the Chicago-based Tribune Company bought the paper along with the rest of Times Mirror Company, whose stable of publications included *Newsday, The Baltimore Sun,* and the *Hartford Courant.* The $8 billion merger was a victory for what journalists called the "dark side" of the Chandler family—the shareholders who saw Otis's commitment to journalism as a drain on earnings. Under Tribune, slashing the staff became a core business strategy. It cost the *Times* the first two editors in chief Tribune hired—John Carroll and Dean Baquet, both of whom were at the top of their game and beloved by the staff. Carroll resigned in 2005 rather than adhere to Tribune's unending demands to thin the lineup of reporters and editors. Baquet, who succeeded Carroll, subsequently was fired for refusing to do the same. By 2016, the newsroom had shrunk from some 1,200 journalists to barely more than 400. The reporters and editors who survived the carnage were stretched thin. I was juggling three other investigations with my work on USC. Once upon a time, I had the license to dedicate every hour and day to a single long-term story.

As the *Times* lost more and more readers and advertisers to competition from the Web, Tribune tired of the dwindling returns and sold the paper and its sister properties to billionaire real estate wheeler-dealer Sam Zell of Chicago in 2007. In less than twelve months, Zell drove Tribune into bankruptcy—the largest ever for an American media company—where it festered for four years. Zell populated Tribune's corporate offices with cronies from his earlier foray into the radio business, including chief executive officer Randy Michaels and chief innovation officer Lee Abrams. Zell and his team were Philistines—vulgarians. A *New York Times* story on

Michaels's boorish and sexually charged workplace behavior forced him to resign in 2010. That was shortly after Abrams quit under pressure after sending a memo to the staff with a link to a satirical and graphic video titled "Sluts." And the losses in staff, circulation, and revenue at the *Times* accelerated.

The fortunes of Tribune had diminished to such a state by 2016 that Michael Ferro, another rich Chicagoan, was able to become its biggest shareholder with a $44 million investment and install himself as company chair. About four years earlier, Ferro, a tech entrepreneur, led an investment group that bought the *Chicago Sun-Times*. One of his early moves at Tribune was to eliminate the stand-alone position of publisher at the *Times* and the company's other papers and marry the job to the editorships. So Maharaj became the editor *and* publisher of the *Times*, placing him in charge of the news operations and the business functions that paid for them. For a range of ethical reasons, this was not normal in the realm of major newspapers. Maharaj suddenly had a foot on either side of the long-unbreachable wall between the paper's journalists and the people who sold subscriptions and advertising and engaged in other commercial ventures for the *Times*, all of which were supposed to be kept well clear of the newsroom to avoid conflicts of interest (or even the appearance of them). Staffers braced for the worst; Maharaj already was an unpopular editor, viewed by many in the newsroom as someone who, depending on the circumstances, would pursue his personal ambitions at the expense of the paper's journalistic mission. His enthusiastic acceptance of the publisher's job was seen as an example of that. In his new role, Maharaj had become the supreme point person for the paper's business dealings with USC, including the advertising the university regularly purchased and the *Times*'s Festival of Books, which was staged on the university's campus.

I wondered if he might be influenced, consciously or unconsciously, by another bond between the school and the paper: For many years, USC had been a parachute zone for editors and other staffers who left the *Times*. One of Maharaj's predecessors as top editor, Michael Parks, landed at the university after departing the *Times* in the wake of an ethics scandal over the paper's revenue-sharing arrangement with Staples Center, the downtown basketball and hockey arena. In a conversation about the threat of newsroom layoffs, Duvoisin had told me that USC would be a good next stop for both of us. And at the time of the Puliafito reporting, two former *Times* staffers were working for the school's administration. (I would later learn from a USC insider that some in the university administration had considered Maharaj a prospective candidate for a high-ranking position at the school before he became publisher. When I asked Maharaj if he had been in talks for a USC job, he denied it through his lawyer. Nikias, through a spokesperson, denied having "any knowledge" of such talks.)

All of that sat in the back of my mind as I looked for daylight on the Puliafito story. I didn't expect much from my CPRA requests. The act required the city to respond to me within ten days but allowed it to assert an additional fourteen-day delay as it searched for records to be released. So I knew it could be more than three weeks before I received a single document—and that wasn't guaranteed. USC didn't have to worry about records requests under the act. As a private university, the school was free of the requirements of disclosure, despite the hundreds of millions in taxpayer dollars it received through research grants and other government sources. USC was a 501(c)(3) public charity under the Internal Revenue Service code, as most universities were, and that freed it from paying millions in taxes. Because of their tax-exempt privileges, 501(c)(3) organizations were expected by charity watchdogs to operate with an abundance of transparency.

I had never gotten that from USC. And I didn't believe I would get it on this story without more information to squeeze Nikias. I hoped that information would eventually come from my records requests, but that was only a hope.

I had to find Sarah. I had to find her, and I had to persuade her to talk.

Khan's description of her was a running start, although it came with a guardrail. To protect him as a source, I couldn't simply breeze into the Constance and start quizzing employees about an overdose and a young woman named Sarah. Doing so wouldn't automatically finger Khan as my source; as far as his bosses would know, I could've learned the woman's name from any number of other people, including the police officers and paramedics, or someone at the hospital. But all of them had honest deniability, and I couldn't risk directing suspicion at Khan. So I began my search for Sarah with sweeps of databases such as LexisNexis and Accurint and TLO, with the help of the *Times*'s research library. One lucky break was Puliafito's last name—it was not that common. I scrubbed the databases for matches of his name and a Sarah in connection with any addresses, employers, possible relatives and business associates, and criminal and civil court records. No hits. That wasn't too surprising: younger people often didn't leave many traces on these databases. And if Sarah was a prostitute, her presence on them likely would be even smaller, apart from an arrest sheet—and Sarah might not be her real name.

I next turned to the Web for any links, no matter how remote, between Puliafito and her. I added *USC* as a search term in my initial sweeps, in the belief Sarah could be a current or former student of the school. I found a half dozen or so Sarahs, including a Ph.D. and a medical doctor. None came close to Khan's description, even when I added ten years to his estimated age of Sarah or subtracted five. I used a similarly broad age range in examining Web images of Sarahs associated with Puliafito, and I assumed she might not always have been blond.

Nothing.

Social media was a whole other haystack that could be hiding the needle. I searched for any references to the overdose itself, perhaps in a tweet or a Facebook post. Nope. I found a few possible Sarahs

on Facebook and Instagram, but they didn't pan out on closer inspection.

I tried variations on her name: Sara. Sera. Serra. *How about Sierra?* Khan was very precise in his account, but the ears could play tricks. And maybe the paramedics he overheard got the pronunciation wrong.

The more I widened my searches, the flimsier the hits—and the faster they evaporated when I drilled down.

I checked with Tommy and a USC source who had law enforcement contacts; they hadn't heard anything.

I was tempted to confront Puliafito with what I knew about Sarah—to try something of a bluff: If he believed I had learned who she was, he might crack and tell the truth (or some version of it) about the overdose. But it would be a long shot. Puliafito would have been prepared for me—ready to fend off much more than my knowledge of the woman's first name. That wouldn't be enough. Confronting Puliafito with so little information would just give him reason to cover his tracks further. I dropped the idea.

I had to find Sarah.

I was the father of two daughters who, based on Khan's description, were not much older than the woman named Sarah. And from childhood into adulthood, I lived with the wreckage of alcohol and drug abuse in my own family. My father became a heavy drinker after my parents divorced, and he was unemployed for several years. Three of his five children lived with him during that time, me included, and we survived on government welfare benefits, handouts from relatives, and whatever after-school jobs we could find. Addiction crossed generations with the Pringles. My older brother, the best man at my wedding, died of alcoholism after a long decline that included a stretch in state prison for bank robbery. The coroner told me the abuse of prescription drugs might have been a contributing factor in his death—a thicket of pill bottles had been found on his nightstand in the halfway house that was the end of his road.

My younger brother, a bighearted guy when he was sober, also died young from drinking. Before it took his life, the bottle cost him a once-thriving business, a home in the suburbs, and his family's financial security. We remained close through his ups and downs until there were only downs and a normal relationship with him became impossible.

I felt fortunate to have stayed a step ahead of all that with my wife and daughters. But I knew how quickly that kind of good fortune can turn, as it likely did for Sarah and her family.

Who was this Sarah?

Where was she?

6

THE WARRENS

Sarah Warren was spending a December day in an old graveyard. It was nine months after the overdose, and nearly a year after she got tossed from Creative Care. Civil War veterans were buried in the cemetery; their tombstones were scarred at the edges and streaked black from a hundred years of sun and rain. Events over the past months had led Sarah to Magnolia Memorial Park. And on this overcast morning, in the quiet of the place, a moment came when she saw something that made her want to scream.

It was the orange BMW that rolled into the parking lot—the car Carmen drove when he wasn't in the Porsche or his vintage Mercedes.

No!

Sarah took a breath.

Carmen Puliafito alighted from the BMW.

And he was wearing a trench coat and a fedora.

Are you kidding me?

Sarah was on broom duty, sweeping the leaves and dirt from the footpaths of the cemetery, a chore that fulfilled part of her court-ordered community service following her third arrest since she took up with Puliafito. Magnolia Memorial borrowed its name from the street it was on and some of the trees that shaded the sidewalks. It was in Garden Grove, a twenty-five-minute drive from Ocean Recovery in Newport Beach, Sarah's latest stop in what had become her road tour of Southern California rehabs.

She kept an eye on Carmen as he walked from the car. The fact that she was back in rehab meant nothing to him. *Carmen sees rehab as just another means of controlling me,* Sarah thought. He'd pay the rehab bill, or much of it, and then deliver drugs to her, even as she was in treatment. He picked up the tab for the disease *and* the cure. As long as Sarah needed money, as long as she needed to get high, Carmen would be there. *He figures he owns me.* Her stays in rehab only made it easier for him to keep her on a leash, because he knew where she was day and night. He knew she wasn't hanging out with one of the younger men who'd been around her—*much* younger men like Kyle or Don. Carmen didn't like any of them. They were all a threat to him, even if they depended on him for drugs like she did. Just keeping them at bay, away from her, was enough to make Carmen happy to pay for her rehab—*My "vacations," as he regarded them.* If she checked out of rehab without telling him, if she tried to break free of him—tried to *escape*—he would see it as useless. It would be her throwing a tantrum again, nothing more than that, wasting her energy and his time. Because she would always have her needs, and he would always be there to provide for them. Any escape, if that's what it could be called, would be short-lived.

As she stood there with the broom in her hand, Sarah remembered that Carmen had bragged to her that he had the skills and the means to track her down wherever she went, wherever she might try to hide from him.

"I am a detective," he told her.

And now there he was, dressed up like a detective from some ancient movie. Ancient like him. A *fedora*? He looked ridiculous.

She supposed it was his idea of a joke. But did he realize *he* was the joke? Was Carmen in on the joke he had become? Or was he just shit-crazy? His mind fried from all the nights and days of meth and heroin?

Carmen looked in her direction. Did he see her?

Sarah thought about her dad. She had been back home, during one of her breaks from Carmen, and her dad was pleading with her to get back into rehab. "Please, Sarah. Please, Sarah." And then he started to cry.

Her dad.

She had never seen him cry like that. A sadness rose in her, bringing its own tears. Sarah could never again bear to see her dad cry. So she checked into Ocean Recovery. The Ocean staff was tough, no bullshit—brutal enforcers of the rules. *But that's what she wanted, right? . . . Right?*

Carmen drew closer. Maybe he didn't care whether he was a joke or if he had gone crazy. Maybe all he cared about was satisfying *his* needs. And his needs came down to her. Sarah knew that he needed her much more than he needed the drugs. Maybe not her as a person—as Sarah Warren—but her body. Her youth. The resurrection of his own youth. It was the transaction they had entered into.

Waiting for her in that pumpkin carriage of a BMW was her end of the bargain with Carmen—anything she asked for, starting with drugs and money. All she had to do was get in.

She tried not to think about her dad. *Jesus, what a dreary day.* Half the grass around the graves was as dead as the people underneath it. Sarah looked toward the street—people coming and going, living their lives, doing whatever they pleased. Like her friends. And here she was, doing grunt work.

Anything she wanted. Right there in the parking lot.

Anything.

And no more spooky tombstones from history. No more brooms.

• • •

Sarah had never meant to hurt anybody.

Not her parents. She loved them, and she knew they loved her. They loved her even when they were going too far, to her mind, in trying to keep her under their thumb—and even when she defied them. And they loved her even when she hurt them. She hurt them with her boyfriends and her drugs, but it wasn't like it was part of some plan, anything intentional. Sarah had no plan when it came to the bad decisions she made—the decisions that seemed good at the time. She couldn't explain *why* she made those decisions in a way that could justify them, at least not while she was making them. How could she explain her decisions when she was still figuring herself out? Her *whole* self.

She was very young when the worst of this started. Sarah was a kid who grew up too fast because of the choices she made—the boyfriends and the drugs and Carmen—and then she did not grow up fast enough to recognize the damage she was causing. *Why? Why did she let herself lose control? Why did she allow herself to bring misery to the people she loved? Did she suffer from a sort of clinical mania? An impulse disorder? Anxiety? Depression? All of the above? Or was she making excuses for herself?* Those questions came into focus later, after the pain she was inflicting on her parents—and then, to her horror, on her baby brother, Charles—became clear to her.

It started in Spring, Texas, where the Warrens were living the suburban dream, on a street hushed by trees, in a house that embraced them with spacious rooms and light-filled windows. The Warrens were loving and close and, in the way of families, trip-wired for drama. Sarah was a teenager possessed of the type of restless intelligence that was both a strength and a weakness. Earning good grades was a breeze, but she was always bored in the classroom. *Why is the teacher droning on about something so simple? What does any of this have to do with my life?* She loved to sing and had the voice for it, and she had a lively presence that was made for the stage. But after performing in a school production of *Oklahoma!*, she grew bored with singing and acting, too. Boredom could lead to trouble, especially when boys and booze became available.

Sarah got into plenty of trouble.

"Listen, I was a difficult child," she said years later. "I needed more stimuli. I was *wild.*"

The older Sarah got, the more her mother annoyed her, and vice versa, sometimes for good reason, and other times for no reason. Sarah and Mary Ann had a relationship that was not uncommon for mothers and daughters of strong wills: They battled. They found faults in each other that, in moments of clarity, they might well have seen in themselves. Truces were uneasy.

Partying became Sarah's release, aided by marijuana and then alcohol and boys—men, actually, young and not so young. Exploitation and betrayal arrived early in her romantic coming of age. Sarah's first lover during her years at The Woodlands High School had more than sex in mind. One day, he made his move on her just as she wanted, smothered her with his affection, kept her in his arms—and it was a ruse, a distraction so that his buddy could sneak into the Warrens' house and steal their prescription drugs. It wasn't a well-executed caper, and the thieves were soon found out. And then it all got worse: Sarah's parents knew the boyfriend's parents, and Mary Ann made her retrieve the bottles of pills from her lover.

Sarah was humiliated, traumatized. As she put it together long afterward, that experience sent her into a spiral of self-debasement, and the people closest to her paid the price.

"It affected my family's life forever," she said.

She entered her first rehab at age eighteen. It was for her drinking.

Her smarts shone through the fog of hangovers and highs. She kept her grades up and entered the University of Texas at San Antonio, more than two hundred miles from home. It was a new beginning, a clean slate. Sarah thought college *must* be more diverting than high school. And it was. But the other diversions were hard to give up. She was nineteen when she began seeing a drug dealer who was seven years older. Two days after Thanksgiving, she was with him in a car and did not resist his compulsion to have sex. The problem was it was daylight and they were in a parking lot and the parking lot was not empty. Someone called the police, and Sarah and her cocaine-peddling diversion were arrested. The charge was public lewdness. Sarah now had a criminal record, a rap sheet, and one that could be interpreted to mean she was some kind of pervert, when she really had just made a dumb, youthful mistake.

She didn't take it out on the guy. Sarah was drawn to his fuck-all rebelliousness, something she always felt in herself. And so she stayed with him. Her mother wouldn't understand her attraction to him. Her dad certainly wouldn't. Which is why Sarah could never tell them how he made his living. She knew what their reaction would be, and she didn't want to hear it.

And then her dad landed a high-paying job in Southern California, and he announced that the family was moving west. Paul and Mary Ann Warren believed L.A. could be the perfect place for the family to recharge and set out on a better course. It was a place of blue skies, even bluer than Houston's, and of optimism. L.A. was where the future starts.

No—not for me, Sarah said. She had her own life in Texas. She had her bad-boy boyfriend, and she wasn't going anywhere. Her decision was final.

It wasn't final to Mary Ann. Mother and daughter squared off again—the yelling, the anger, the ultimatums, the threats. Sarah gave it her all. But Mary Ann prevailed.

"Me wanting to stay just infuriated my mother," Sarah recalled. "She basically *dragged* me out."

L.A.'s sunny promise proved to be overrated. Sarah had waited a long time to run away from home, but when she did, she did it in L.A., and in a big way. Simply getting out of the house, beyond her

parents' prying eyes, free from her mom's controlling maneuvers—
all of that wasn't enough. She opted for a complete break from everything she was supposed to be, everything expected of her. Sarah
went full *outlaw*. It was an impulse, a reaction. She hadn't thought
it through, but Sarah had barely unpacked her getaway clothes at an
Airbnb in downtown L.A. when she decided that prostitution was
the quickest and easiest way to finance her liberation.

Why not? she told herself. *I like sex, and I'd like to maintain my
lifestyle.*

Within twenty minutes of posting her Backpage.com ad, she had
two tricks. The demand for her body grew by the hour. *L.A. must
have a surplus of desperate men.* Most of Sarah's "clients" were more
pathetic than creepy. But there were creeps, too, and her new line of
work got scary fast. Sarah came to appreciate how pimps could bring
added value to the trade. A woman pimp named Vicky found her
through the Backpage ad and offered Sarah her services. That was fine
by Sarah. Now she had someone screen out the worst of the johns, the
ones sliming around for something rough, acts bordering on violence,
or half-mooching for a discount. But then it didn't take long for her to
figure out that Vicky was ripping her off, especially given the amount
of business Sarah was generating. It was as if a line of men had formed
outside the door of her hotel room and stretched around the building.
Sarah hated the work and no longer associated prostitution with sex,
but instead with injury-grade pain. Looking back at that time, she
said, "Vicky wanted volume, and she got it. I was in so much pain, I
started crying once and it turned the client off."

The client wasn't Carmen. Tears wouldn't be enough to turn him
off. Sarah had a hard time imagining anything that would. They
met for the first time at a hotel in Rancho Cucamonga, a suburb
in the flatlands beneath Mount Baldy across the San Bernardino
County line from L.A. "The minute I opened the door, I realized he
was crazy and he was crazy for me," Sarah said, remembering that
he looked saggy and mottled with age, but also like money in his

Robert Graham shirt, suit jacket, and creamy loafers. "It was just in his eyes—crazy. He was saying, right from the start, 'Oh my God, you are just so amazing!' He was like a schoolboy meeting a celebrity. I just couldn't believe it."

His obsession with her was instant and complete, and it was well-timed. Carmen's money allowed her to ditch Vicky and walk away from the hooker experiment without crawling back home to her parents. The lifestyle Sarah was determined to maintain now included harder drugs, and she needed someone to pay for them. The Warren family settled in a million-dollar town house a few blocks from the water in Huntington Beach, and Sarah scored her first dose of California meth just down the street, from a man she met by the pool at the Hilton. She remembered being immediately taken with him: "He was maybe twenty-five or twenty-six. Cute, charismatic . . . a total loser. He had just gotten out of rehab."

It was probably more about acting out than anything else, but Sarah appeared to have a type.

Mr. Poolside was hardly a keeper, in part because he had a meth-head girlfriend who began stalking Sarah after she entered the picture. One confrontation occurred at a gas station; the girlfriend pointed at Sarah out there by the pumps, got the attention of the cashier, and screamed for all to hear, "This bitch is stealing my man!" Sarah had enough.

She kept Carmen on a string. He was always eager to pay for more of her, but she wasn't ready to become what he would consider his exclusive property. So her next dalliance was a man I'll call Enrique. Enrique was a tattoo artist who was eighteen years older than Sarah but youthful looking, with soft dark eyes and cinnamon cheekbones. Enrique also was on meth. Sarah had crossed paths with him downtown, and he was spellbound. Like Carmen, he wanted every inch of her, except he wanted it for free, including for his work; he had the notion to ink her flesh from neck to toe. "You are my blank canvas," Enrique said. Sarah wasn't into that; she was into meth.

She followed Enrique to his home in the Antelope Valley, in the high desert at the northern edge of L.A. County. Sarah hadn't been there before. The Antelope Valley was a windy plateau gridded with quick-built housing tracts; many of the streets were named for succeeding letters and numbers as if to keep even the locals from getting lost and wandering into rattlesnake country. The winds seemed to never stop; the nerves became tattered. Farther out in the desert, at Edwards Air Force Base, the government designed and tested rocket engines. The space shuttle used to land there. Sarah didn't see any rockets or shuttles, and Enrique didn't work for the government. He didn't live in one of the tract homes, either. Enrique lived in a garage. And he had four cats.

When you find yourself with a guy who lives in a garage with four cats, you've run out of reasons not to get high.

And Sarah loved cats. She did get high with Enrique—he was into heroin, too—but she knew it was only a matter of time before she left him in his L.A. boonies and allowed Carmen to fully bankroll her, so that she would become his round-the-clock sugar baby. Enrique had met Carmen and viewed him as a rival—an old puke who just happened to have money. Enrique was determined to keep him away from her, but he couldn't stop her from leaving. When she bolted, she didn't give him much warning, in case there was a brutish side to him she hadn't seen—junkies weren't always predictable. She returned to Carmen with whatever belongings she remembered to grab from the garage. Carmen didn't hesitate to offer to set her up in an apartment in Pasadena, and she didn't hesitate to accept it, even though Carmen and his wife lived in Pasadena, a short drive from the apartment. Carmen often spoke about his wife: *Janet was her name—and she was a shrink!* He said she understood why he needed a "relationship" with Sarah, and that she "knows all about you . . . even how you look." Okay, that was one thing—if it was true—but it would be another thing if Sarah bumped into her at Whole Foods or Starbucks or just walking down Colorado.

Carmen didn't care about the embarrassment Sarah would feel, even if his wife was fine with some warped open marriage. Maybe having his mistress and his wife in proximity to each other turned him on. It seemed to Sarah that was the sort of thing the rich might find titillating.

The apartment was in a three-story building that crowded half a block of East Del Mar Boulevard; it resembled a hangar except for the rows of narrow balconies cantilevered to the front. Enrique kept calling her. He offered to bring her the clothes she left behind. Where was she staying? She told him, and then he got the devious idea to search for her parents online—and found them through Mary Ann's Facebook profile. He then got her dad on the phone. Enrique claimed that Carmen had kidnapped her and planned to sell her into sexual slavery. He added the touch that it would be sexual slavery in Mexico. He said he knew where Carmen and his confederates were holding her. It was some apartment in Pasadena.

Mom freaked, of course. And then Dad freaked. The next thing you know, he's picking Enrique up at Union Station, and then— can you believe it?—they head out to "save" me. Dad even bought leather gloves, duct tape, and rope to truss up my supposed captors!

Sarah was wasted beyond sentience when her logistics executive father and the druggy tattoo artist turned up at the apartment to take her home. She couldn't remember the drive back to the Huntington Beach town house. She slept—if it counted as sleep—for thirty-six hours. *A day and a half.* And when she woke up, disoriented for a moment, *Enrique was in bed next to her!*

She peeled away from the man she thought she'd never see again and went looking for her father.

"Dad! Are you here, Dad?"

He was at work, so she called him. When he picked up, Sarah unloaded about Enrique:

"You *listened* to this guy? You brought him into our *house*?"

Paul tried to explain: Enrique was talking about kidnapping and sexual slavery. And who knew what this person Carmen was capable of? Paul was her father. He had to make sure she was safe, so he had no choice but to believe Enrique.

Mary Ann was home. Sarah remonstrated with her about Enrique. *He was in her room. Her bed!* "What were you and Dad thinking?" Mary Ann wasn't hearing it. She made the point that Enrique was in the house because he was in Sarah's life, and that was because Sarah had invited him into her life.

And then Paul came home from work and threw Enrique out.

Not long afterward, Sarah disappeared again. Paul and Mary Ann assumed she'd returned to the apartment in Pasadena, but they couldn't be sure. Days and even weeks went by when she didn't respond to their phone calls or text messages. They couldn't reach her when she was away, and they couldn't reach her when she was right in front of them. She drifted in and out of their lives, physically and in every other way. Something had broken in the bright and happy girl they'd watched grow up, and they couldn't get it fixed. Nothing Paul and Mary Ann tried had worked—the rehab in Texas, the move to Southern California, the family therapist. It seemed the more they did to help her, the further they drove her away. They were a sophisticated and successful couple, with three college degrees between them, a substantial income, and a beautiful home—blocks from the beach—new cars in the garage, and money in the bank for whatever else Sarah and her brother needed. But they were failing their daughter, failing as parents. They could not love her more than they did, but their love just turned despair into a form of grief. They were losing Sarah, losing her to drugs, and they were terrified that the drugs could result in the unthinkable loss— and real, unimaginable grief.

And the more Paul and Mary Ann learned about this *Carmen Puliafito,* this fat-wallet dean at USC, the more they feared he would be the means of Sarah's destruction. *This is Carmen, he's paying for things.* That's how Sarah introduced Puliafito to them when she brought him to their home: *He's paying for things*—a man who was old enough to be *their* parent. She didn't have to say what he received in return for paying for things. Their daughter was putting them in their place, letting them know just how independent she had become—independent of *them*—and how little she cared if they didn't approve of how she got there and with whom. She meant it to shock them, and it did.

Paul and Mary Ann had been conditioned to expect underachievers, to use a kind term, when Sarah surfaced with her paramour of the moment. But this overachiever, Puliafito, struck them as far more dangerous. Enrique might have made up the sex-enslavement terror, but he wasn't far off about Puliafito on the whole. Paul and Mary Ann saw Puliafito as a predator without bounds. He gave the impression that money and power guaranteed he would never be held to account for his debauchery, his exploitation of others. Even if his drugs killed Sarah.

The dread that Paul and Mary Ann felt for Sarah's well-being became all-consuming. They were distraught—lost. It reached the point that they consulted a private investigator, an ex-cop who was an acquaintance of a friend. Sarah had pulled another vanishing act and they suspected Puliafito was behind it. The PI confirmed those suspicions and traced Sarah to another apartment in Pasadena that the dean was paying for. When he reported back to Paul and Mary Ann, he wrapped his findings in some advice: Accept Puliafito as part of Sarah's life, and accept him as part of their lives; because if they didn't, Puliafito might abscond with Sarah. He might abandon his job, his wife, his home, everything—and run off with Sarah, run off to someplace distant and anonymous, and they would never see her again.

This keep-your-enemy-close advice shocked Paul and Mary Ann, and then it left them cold. It sounded like an admonition to surrender—to surrender their daughter. The PI used to be a cop. Why wouldn't he counsel them to call the police on Puliafito? Or to report him to the president of USC? To the board of trustees? Maybe he didn't suggest taking those routes *because* of what he'd learned as a cop—because he knew how the system worked, and it worked in the favor of people like Puliafito. His advice made sense to Paul and Mary Ann only because they couldn't calculate the risks in rejecting it. If they did, would Sarah be put in more harm? The PI said Puliafito could keep her out of their lives. Could Puliafito do something even worse? Something of the forever kind?

The Warrens took the investigator's advice.

Sarah had a broom in her hand, and Carmen had her number. He always had her number. She couldn't hide from him, not even in a graveyard. She could be buried under one of these rotting tombstones and he'd still come looking for her.

He would look until he found her. And then he would offer her another escape—as long as the escape was not sobriety. That's why he brought the drugs to her at Creative Care that night. Not once but *twice*. Until it got her booted. The first night, he just knocked on the door of her room, handed her the Xanax and a forbidden cell phone—no phones were allowed in rehab—and told her to keep in touch. He left, but not for long. About an hour later, they were on the phone together. Puliafito had returned to the parking lot. He was waiting for her in the Porsche, with a bottle of champagne and sex toys he had just bought at a gas station. She left her room and trotted across the damp grounds to meet him. Once she was in the car, Puliafito drove down Trancas and parked along the road. Sarah gulped the champagne. She wasn't interested in the toys.

The visit dragged on. The rehab staff making a night meds round found Sarah's room empty. By the time Carmen drove her back to the parking lot, five employees were searching for her with flashlights, the beams steaming through the mist. As the lights swept toward the car, Sarah jumped out, and Puliafito sped away. She had no doubt that she had been spotted and that the staff knew she was with Puliafito. She was right. A staffer asked her about the Porsche. Sarah told him Puliafito was simply checking up on her. Nothing to worry about.

She expected there would be consequences, but they didn't come right away.

So after little more than a day, at around 3:00 A.M. or even later, she called Puliafito on the contraband cell phone. She wanted meth. Any other doctor might have told her no. Any other dealer might have said it was too hairy. But Carmen did not hesitate. He again made the long drive to Malibu. They had arranged that he would leave the meth, a pookie pipe, and a lighter in a sunglasses case on the ground near the driveway. Carmen made the delivery with precision; Sarah found the case after telling the staff she was going for a minute's stroll around the property. As she walked back to her room, the night nurse spotted her. That didn't stop her from firing up the pookie in her private bathroom.

Later that morning, after Sarah joined the other residents in the common area of the main building, staffers noticed the rapid eye movement, the anxiousness, and the other jerky signs of meth. They also knew about Puliafito's second visit. They confronted Sarah and demanded she submit to a drug test. She denied she was high but took the urine cup into the bathroom. Matters came to a head when a staffer saw her diluting the contents of the cup from the sink faucet. The center promptly kicked her out, the counselors terminating her program before it really got started. Sarah didn't blame them.

One of the counselors called Sarah's mother to report that her daughter had been expelled. In a voice taut with malice, the counselor said the "good doctor" had been visiting Sarah again. She said to Mary

Ann that Puliafito was "a menace to society." Mary Ann didn't need to be told that. For nearly a year, she and her husband had been struggling to extricate Puliafito from their daughter's life. Mary Ann knew there was no point in pleading with the counselor to give Sarah one more chance. Drugs in rehab? There were no second chances after that. And the counselor sounded even more determined to be rid of Puliafito than she was to drum out Sarah.

Mary Ann never had a problem convincing a stranger that Sarah was hers. Mother and daughter had the same big personality, the same blazing energy, the same blond beachy look. Paul was the quieter, lower-key counterbalance to his wife. He tried to be the calming influence when they had to confront a threat to their family, a threat like Puliafito. Paul and Mary Ann had hoped that rehab would finally wake their daughter up to the evil that Puliafito was. That's why they chose an expensive place like Creative Care. The Warrens were financially comfortable, but not so much that a five-figure monthly rehab bill didn't hurt. They didn't care about the cost. All they cared about was freeing their daughter from Puliafito's grip.

Now that grip extended even to rehab. Paul and Mary Ann picked up Sarah at the Starbucks where a Creative Care staffer dropped her. They drove their daughter home.

The Warrens understood that Sarah had to leave Creative Care. After all, she broke the rules, and the rules were the rules. But not for everyone. What happened that day was something that happened before; actually, it was something that *didn't* happen: Puliafito was not arrested. In this case, as far as the Warrens knew, no one even called the police or reported him to the Medical Board of California, a failure that also was becoming a pattern. The morning after he delivered drugs to a young addict in rehab, Puliafito was free to return to his job running one of the largest medical schools in the land. He was free to continue evaluating patients and performing delicate eye surgeries. He was free to buy more meth, heroin, Xanax, GHB, Ecstasy, and nitrous oxide for Sarah and the junkies, prostitutes, and other lost souls he collected. And he was free to join them in getting high, which he did with greater and greater frequency.

Carmen spotted her from the cemetery entrance. Standing there under the magnolia trees, in his trench coat and fedora, he smiled and waved. Sarah's escape was waiting there. He knew she always needed to escape.

7

THE CELEBRATION

The white lab coats shimmered in the sun of late spring, a June afternoon. They made the men and women who wore them stand out in the mostly dark-suited gathering at the Keck School of Medicine. The occasion was an invitation-only celebration on the lawn outside a stem-cell research building named for the L.A. billionaire couple Eli and Edythe Broad, whose $30 million gift had helped pay for the glassy structure and the work inside it. A bouquet of jaunty patio umbrellas shaded the sixty or seventy attendees as they sipped wine and settled into folding chairs. They faced a lectern resting on a portable riser that was flanked by loudspeakers.

The celebration was a courtly affair in the manner of the academy. It had not been organized in honor of the Broads.

Nor was it an appreciation for the physicians and researchers in their sparkling smocks.

The man fêted on this Tuesday afternoon was Carmen Puliafito. And the keynote speaker was Max Nikias.

The event was three months after the overdose and two months after I began emailing and calling USC about Puliafito and the events that preceded the end of his deanship. Nikias and the people around him continued to ignore those queries, and the celebration told me the university president believed he had nothing to fear about the *Times*, Puliafito, and a young woman named Sarah. But how could that be? What made Nikias feel confident about publicly—*defiantly*—saluting Puliafito even as the leading news organization in L.A., California, and the West was bird-dogging him?

I had the same thoughts about Puliafito. Why would he want this attention after he learned he was the subject of a *Times* investigation? Did Nikias and Puliafito know something that I didn't know? Something I *should* know? Something I should worry about? And why was this tribute to Puliafito's service as dean happening so long after he resigned the position? Did Nikias wait to stage it until he determined the heat had died down? Could he have intervened with the Pasadena police or their political masters? I had no evidence of that, but I couldn't rule it out.

Maybe the belated send-off was something Puliafito had only recently demanded—as the price of his silence. As bad as the disclosure of Puliafito's involvement in the overdose would be for him, it would be worse for USC. And for Nikias. But, again, I had no evidence to support that theory.

I was at the celebration. I had learned about it when a newsroom source had the invitation forwarded to me. Set in gold borders and topped by the USC shield that featured three torches, the invitation read:

Rohit Varma, MD, MPH
Interim Dean, Keck School of Medicine of USC
Director, USC Gayle and Edward Roski Eye Institute
invites you
to celebrate and honor
Carmen A. Puliafito, MD, MBA
for his leadership and accomplishments
as Dean, Keck School of Medicine of USC

I took in the festivities from a public sidewalk about 150 feet away. Reporters were forbidden to trespass—and the definition of trespassing could be fluid. Keck was a private school with private security, but it was opened to public foot traffic. I did not believe I would be trespassing if I stepped onto the lawn to get closer to the lectern. But it would be another journalism no-no if I passed myself off as an invitee to the celebration, free to make the rounds on the grass without disclosing I was from the *Times.* So I toed the line of the sidewalk, trying to be discreet, and shot photos and videos with my phone.

I had not covered Keck before and had no sources there, but a USC insider who had contacts at the medical school related to me that Puliafito had been disliked, even despised, by much of the staff, although those accounts included nothing about drugs or prostitutes. Puliafito's critics described him as arrogant, egomaniacal, and quick to anger, with little regard for the opinions and sensitivities of others, unless they were useful in ways that reflected well on him. They said Puliafito was like the man who hired him—obsessed with bringing more and more money into the school, especially through the slavish cultivation of donors and the poaching of grant-enriched faculty from other institutions. Perhaps I was looking too hard for it, but I could sense an undercurrent of disdain for Puliafito—or maybe just a lack of enthusiasm—in the throng milling on the lawn. Many of the attendees had the air of the conscripted about them, people with better things to do who joined the assembly to fulfill a disagreeable obligation. That seemed particularly true of the men and women in white.

Puliafito had chosen a nail-gray suit for his big moment. He looked stooped and spongy faced as he shook hands and chatted with similarly dressed men, one-on-one or in groups of three or four. The man of the hour was not swarmed by well-wishers.

In the speeches that followed the wine pouring and handshakes, Puliafito's love of the Boston Red Sox became a refrain, punch-lined with an anecdote of how he had once made a joking offer of free laser eye surgeries to errant umpires. The audience responded with polite laughter. Puliafito sat side by side with Nikias. When Nikias took to the lectern, the listeners appeared to become more serious in focusing on what they were told, on what the boss of their former boss had to impart about Puliafito.

"Today, we have one of the, not just the area's, but the nation's preeminent medical schools and medical enterprises—and, in many ways, thanks to the leadership of Carmen," Nikias said.

From my distance, it was difficult to hear every word because a breeze that kicked up caused an echo from the loudspeakers (my audio recording was also poor). Puliafito opened his remarks by confirming that the "story about the Red Sox is absolutely true." Speaking in the steady, amped-up voice of someone used to addressing crowds, he recounted how quickly he accepted the deanship when Nikias pitched him the job nine years earlier. "I really, really wanted this job," he said. Puliafito declared that USC physicians "really are the best doctors in Los Angeles." And he gave a special thanks to his wife.

I had not seen Puliafito in the flesh before. Several times, I tried to visit him at his home, but the mansion sat behind a high security gate at the end of a long driveway, which put the front door beyond reach. No one responded when I buzzed the intercom outside the gate. The second time, I left my business card on the mailbox near the street, with a note urging Puliafito to call me. He never did—just as he never returned my calls or emails. Staking out the mansion for the chance to catch him coming or going was not practical. There was no parking permitted on either side of the street, so I would have to stand at the curb. I then would have to somehow stop Puliafito before he rolled through the gate. And considering the divorce case, I wasn't even sure he still lived there.

LexisNexis had a second recent address for Puliafito—325 Cordova Street in Pasadena. It was for a large, modern apartment building whose five stories rose straight up from the edge of the sidewalk, with no setback. I drove to the building and parked at a meter. It was an expensive location, around the corner from the Pasadena Civic Auditorium, which was another model of beaux arts architecture and the former venue of the Emmy Awards. If the LexisNexis record was correct—wrong addresses did turn up in the database—Puliafito either had rented an apartment in the building or had some other connection to the address, such as an association with a business operating there or perhaps an investment in the property itself. I bet on the apartment scenario because of the divorce filing. It made sense that he would move out of the mansion while the dissolution of the marriage wound its way through the court.

Puliafito's name was not in the building's electronic directory. I asked a woman in the leasing office if a Carmen Puliafito lived there; the woman said she could not disclose any information about residents and referred me back to the directory. I spent some time on the sidewalk asking residents as they came and went if they knew Puliafito. I showed them a photo of him on my phone in case they might recognize him even if they didn't know him by name.

No luck.

If Puliafito continued to ignore me, I intended to make more runs at him when I got close to filing my story. I planned to brave the Keck security with the aim of cornering him at his office. He saw patients at an office in Beverly Hills that I could try. If those efforts failed, I would have a letter hand-delivered to him by courier and contact any lawyers who represented him (including in the divorce). And I would keep calling and texting his cell phone. I had been prepared to confront him after the celebration, but only if the right opportunity presented itself. Any face-to-face encounter had to be professional. It could not create a disruptive scene that could give Puliafito a legitimate grievance with my editors or get tongues wagging so much that other news outlets would learn of my investigation.

By the end of the speeches, it was evident there would not be a confrontation. My filming had begun to draw looks from the assembled, including Puliafito. And he never strayed far enough from the gathering to give me an opening to approach him. As the celebration wound down, the Keck staffers in white headed back to their clinics and labs, and Puliafito drifted into the shadows of the campus.

I wondered how many of the people who participated in the lawn party knew about the scene that Devon Khan found in room 304. How many were intrigued by the fact that Puliafito surrendered the deanship some two months shy of the end of the school term? How many knew the celebration was a farce? And how many would feel safe confiding that in me?

What I tried not to think about is whether Nikias's temerity in toasting Puliafito said something about his relationship with the leadership of the *Times*. Did he believe he had the fix in at the paper? Was it possible he had no need to muzzle Puliafito or anyone at Pasadena City Hall because he knew the *Times* wouldn't publish what I was chasing? That was hard for me to imagine, even in light of the newspaper's recent history of pulling punches on USC. Maharaj and Duvoisin *were* publishing the stories on Haden. True, the stories were slow-walked, but they were published.

Then I reminded myself of an important distinction: Before the toughest of the stories ran, Haden already had been badly wounded by the tumult in USC's football program, which cost him the support of the boosters and Nikias. Haden no longer had the power and influence he once had. The golden boy no longer was so golden.

Pasadena police chief Phillip Sanchez set a trap for himself. He didn't mean to. It happened when he and his department refused yet again to release information I requested about the overdose. By this point, I had taken my complaints about the unforthcoming chief to Mayor Terry Tornek. In a phone conversation, I asked Tornek for his help shaking loose records and noted that the story was becoming as much about a Pasadena cover-up as an overdose. He did not appreciate that characterization of the city's posture but said he would inquire about my requests.

The latest refusal from Sanchez's department came in response to my request under the California Public Records Act for any written communications among Sanchez and his staff about the overdose, in addition to any they had with USC representatives since the incident. I wasn't surprised that the request yielded little material—regardless of how much there might be. The CPRA was a vital tool for cutting through the heavy curtain government officials pulled down over much of their business. But weaknesses built into the act blunted its teeth. Short of filing a lawsuit under the statute, compliance was based largely on an honor system; journalists and the public were asked to, in effect, trust the government when told that certain records didn't exist or were exempt from disclosure in whole or part.

I had also asked Sanchez to unredact the Call for Service log released to me two months earlier. The log had been stamped in red ink in two places with a reference to the CPRA that said "information deemed non-releasable or confidential has been blocked out or pages removed." Attached to Sanchez's response to my request was another copy of the Call for Service log, this one without the red ink. The identity of the 911 caller—Khan, I knew—remained redacted on the log. That's where Sanchez stumbled into a trap; in justifying the redaction, his letter stated that officers had gone to the hotel "to investigate a possible overdose," and "as this call for service is related to a police investigation, the name of the reporting party is exempt from disclosure."

Wait a minute. *Investigate? Investigation?* All of a sudden, there *was* an investigation. It took me back to the notations of "report" and "RPT" on the Call for Service log. Were they references to a police report?

How could the department conduct an investigation without producing a police report—a *crime* report?

I sent Ibarra a follow-up email pointing out that Sanchez's response "refers twice to an 'investigation,' including for the purpose of claiming an exemption to disclosure under the act. Is the incident, in fact, the subject of an ongoing police investigation? If not, was it ever the subject of a police investigation? And if it was the subject of an investigation, but is no longer, when was the investigation closed?"

Ibarra replied that she had no further information for me and referred my follow-up to the records administrator. I did not hear back from the administrator for several days, when she referred me to the main spokesperson for the city, William Boyer. In the meantime, I emailed Ibarra to again ask for an interview with Sanchez. I wrote that I needed to speak to him because "my reporting has raised larger questions of policy and conduct."

She replied, "Can you please clarify what your questions are regarding policy and conduct?"

I wrote back that the questions would address how the overdose "was handled very differently from similar incidents involving drug possession and use."

Sanchez stood firm in denying me an interview. I could think of no reason for his silence that wouldn't look bad for him. If my inquiries were misguided or misinformed, the chief could straighten me out in an interview; he was in charge of the information. He had everything I needed from Pasadena. But he gave me nothing.

I called Ibarra and put to her the questions I wanted to ask the chief. Why no police report? How could you conduct an investigation without a report? Ibarra told me that the police officer who responded to the overdose had filed a "property and evidence" report, to document the seizure of drugs on the scene.

What? There was a report on drugs seized?

Ibarra said the unnamed woman in the room was under the influence of those drugs. And then the lieutenant said the department *had* filed a police report on the incident. It nearly floored me. I was hearing this four months after my visit to the Pasadena police headquarters to ask for *any* report on the overdose. And all I got was the Call for Service log. I asked Ibarra why the police report had been withheld from me for all that time—and why did she claim back in April that it did not exist.

Her answer marked a first in my career. The lieutenant told me the police report was written *three months after* the overdose and only because of my persistent queries about the events at the Hotel Constance. It was a *retroactive* police report. *Very* retroactive. And for my purposes, the retroactivity was even more pronounced: The report had been created seven weeks earlier, and I was just learning of it. If I had not kept calling and emailing the police department, month after month, the report about an incident involving a prominent person and one of L.A.'s most important institutions almost certainly would have been buried forever.

Ibarra said the police report hadn't been filed the day of the overdose because of a "training issue"? I asked her in multiple ways to elaborate on that, and she did not. I insisted that Ibarra send me the property and evidence report and the police report. Our conversation ended.

The police report—but not the property and evidence report—arrived in my email in-box that afternoon. I opened it, hoping for the best but prepared for the worst. The best would be a compelling account of what happened in room 304—in colorless police jargon, yes, and with holes here and there in the narrative, but packed with enough facts to propel a story into the paper. I got nothing close to that. The report was just two pages. It wasn't a crime report but an Injury and Death Report. That suggested the police remained determined to not label what happened at the Constance a crime. And the report was so heavily redacted that it resembled a test page for the black ink cartridge. The sections for Evidence and Investigation were completely blacked out. So were thirteen other lines, including those identifying the victim.

But a key line was not redacted—the one listing witnesses to the overdose. Entered there was the name of a single witness: "Puliafito, Carmen Anthony." His relationship to the victim was described as "friend," and the rest of the line noted that he was a sixty-five-year-old white male.

Finally.

I now had an official record that placed Puliafito at the scene of the overdose. The most important element of Khan's tip was now confirmed. The pressure on USC and Nikias to tell the truth about the dean was about to become crushing.

Or that's what I told myself.

I wondered why, after all the stonewalling, the Pasadena police had decided to serve Puliafito up to me. They didn't have to; the police could have made a strong argument under the CPRA to withhold the name of a witness so as not to jeopardize an investigation. Law enforcement agencies did that routinely—to maintain the witnesses' confidentiality and, in some circumstances, to protect them from physical harm.

But there was Puliafito's name—the only full one in the report.

It occurred to me that Pasadena City Hall might have determined there was no way to win this one, so whoever called the shots decided to let the *Times* have Puliafito. *Get the newspaper off the city's back. Let USC, Nikias, and his people deal with this. Keep it in the family.*

The Trojan family.

8

WE NEED THE PD

Could a cop named A. Garcia help me?

A box on the Injury and Death Report identified the police officer who responded to the overdose as A. Garcia. I searched a database for government employees in California and got a hit for a Pasadena police officer named Alfonso Garcia. Since the chief himself wouldn't speak to me, I saw almost zero likelihood he'd allow Garcia to do an interview. But would Garcia talk in a private setting—away from police headquarters? Would he speak off the record or on background (the latter meaning I could publish what he said but not name him)? Maybe he'd want to explain why he didn't arrest Puliafito. And why he didn't file a report. He might have thoughts on how the department handled the matter after I began asking questions.

It was another long shot. I scrubbed the *Times*'s databases for a home address for Garcia. The search produced dozens of prospects. I began visiting the most promising addresses to knock on doors. Some of the addresses were out of date or bad to begin with—no Alfonsos or Garcias there. At a few addresses, the residents would not open the door, even though I could see they were home; I left my business card for them. I could not find an Alfonso Garcia who was a Pasadena police officer. I also got nowhere searching social media.

I received no other information of substance from Pasadena. The city expected me to give up and shut up—and move on. It had dished Puliafito's name to me, but only in the innocuous-sounding context of him being a "witness" to the overdose and a "friend" of the victim. I was expected to make do with that. It was five months since the paramedics and police rolled up to the Hotel Constance. I had not been granted a single interview apart from my brief conversations with Ibarra. In terms of records, I had managed to fish out just a handful of pages, the most important of which were muddied with redactions.

But the months of pushbacks I'd gotten only further convinced me I was onto something consequential. The more the shot-callers at Pasadena and USC resisted, the more important the full story must be.

Bad timing had me facing another obstacle in getting that story. I was due for a total knee replacement, the result of an old sports injury. I had put off the replacement for years, but the pain from walking and even sitting had become unbearable. My surgeon said the recovery time would keep me out of commission for many weeks and even months. Which was inconceivable.

Recordings of 911 calls were among the public records that government agencies had become stingier about releasing. The agencies often claimed the calls contained information central to a confidential police investigation or that they included private medical information. I had Khan's blow-by-blow account of the 911 call he made `bout the overdose, but not a recording of it. There was no expectation the recording would differ materially from Khan's telling, whose basic elements were confirmed by the Call for Service log and the Injury and Death Report. But what else might be on the call? Some juicy detail Khan had forgotten? Something interesting the dispatcher said? Maybe there was nothing of substance, but the recording could add in-the-moment authenticity and color to the story.

I sent an email to the Pasadena Fire Department spokesperson requesting a copy of the recording and the paramedic report on the overdose. If the city invoked a medical privacy exemption in refusing to release the recording, I would argue that it was impossible to violate the privacy of someone—Sarah, in this case—whose identity had not been disclosed. The paramedic report was another matter. My request for it was a Hail Mary; the reports are commonly withheld under the exemption.

As I waited for a response, I hoped my back-channel entreaties to Mayor Tornek would pay off on this one. By now, he had to know the *Times* wasn't going away.

Boyer, the Pasadena PIO, responded with an odd request of his own: He asked me to resend every request I made to the city for records and other information, going back to the start of my investigation. He acknowledged that the act did not require me to resubmit requests, but he wrote: "I'm just trying to make this easier and more efficient for everybody . . . one email, all the CPRA requests, old and new, all of the questions . . . just lay it all out in one email . . . send it to me and let's see if we can wrap this up for you."

I had to think about that. What was he up to? Was it a stall? Restarting the clock? Or was he just trying to catch up on all my queries to help move things along? I chose to be optimistic. After noting that I was not agreeing to lift the CPRA deadlines, and after reminding him that I still had not received the evidence report—six weeks after I requested it—I sent him all the email exchanges. The following week, Boyer wrote that he wanted "to re-cap where we are at; provide more/new info per your requests, and to see where we go from here." The email came with ten attachments, most of which were copies of the records I received earlier. Also attached were the evidence report and two audio files of 911 recordings.

Two?

It was after seven in the evening, and I was still in the newsroom. I played the recordings at my desk. The first recording was Khan's call. His voice was easily recognizable. "Hi. I'm calling from the Hotel Constance in Pasadena," he said at the beginning of the call. The rest was how he had described it to me, although the recording abruptly ended after the dispatcher asked him to transfer the call to the room where the young woman overdosed. Did no one pick up on the transfer? That was possible. Or was the city withholding that portion of the call? If so, Boyer should have said that in his email and cited the section of the CPRA that the city claimed allowed it to cut that part of the recording. I made a note to address that in my next exchange with him.

On the second recording, a man who identified himself as an employee of the Constance engineering department asked for the police to be sent to the hotel. He said a woman was "doing drugs" in a third-floor room and was "passed out."

The dispatcher asked if the man meant to call for paramedics.

"We got the paramedic here already," the man replied. "But we need the PD, the Pasadena police, over here, please."

"You know what she took?" the dispatcher said.

Crystal meth, the man answered.

"All right, we'll get somebody over there," the dispatcher said.

Good stuff, I thought. The recording gave me a live account of meth at the scene, confirming the entry on the Call for Service log. And the recording showed that an employee believed a police response was warranted—*We need the PD.* That was evidence that the incident was something more than a medical emergency. Something criminal.

I then read the evidence report. It said the hotel staff recovered 1.16 grams of meth from room 304. I assumed that was the meth Khan said had been found in the room safe. The names of the victim of the overdose, any suspect in a related crime, and the "owner" of the drugs were redacted. The report did list the address of the "owner" of the drugs as 350 East Cordova Street in Pasadena.

Hold on! Cordova? I remembered that Puliafito had an address on that street. I checked my notes and saw that the street number for the apartment building on Cordova I had visited was 325, not 350. And the building did not have *East* in its address. I searched LexisNexis for 350 East Cordova and got no matches. I then checked databases for the L.A. County assessor and tax collector offices: Again, there was no such address—no 350 East Cordova. I tried the roll of registered voters and simple Google searches and got nothing.

Maybe the officer who filed the report—the one named Alfonso Garcia—made a mistake; errors frequently found their way into police reports. Or maybe the "owner" of the drugs gave the officer a phony address.

In any case, this was more good stuff. *Very good stuff.* The 911 recordings added layers of confirmation to Khan's account of what he witnessed, the report placed the meth in the room Puliafito had rented, and Ibarra had said that Sarah was under the influence of that meth. I got nothing more out of Ibarra or Boyer about the Cordova address, but I still had enough for an eye-popping story: The dean of the USC medical school was at the scene of an overdose by a young woman, in a hotel room on a Friday afternoon. The woman reportedly had been using crystal meth. The dean resigned his post three weeks later. He would not speak to the *Times.* Nor would anyone at USC. And the Pasadena police failed to file a report on the overdose for three months, and only then because of the *Times*'s inquiries.

Two days after I received the 911 recordings, the story got even better. Pasadena city manager Steve Mermell sent me an email to follow up on Boyer's. I was not expecting it; Mermell, the city's top administrator, had not emailed me before. He noted in his message that the recording of Khan's report to the dispatcher contained an extraneous conversation from an unrelated call. Mermell also pointed out that the recording included "personal contact information" (including Khan's phone number). The city manager said both the unrelated call and the contact information should have been removed from my copy of the recording.

None of that was relevant to the story. What grabbed me was the line in the email in which Mermell said the city "was able to obtain a better version of this 911 call," and it "continues for longer than the original file."

Able to obtain? Wasn't the recording—and any "version" of the recording—available to the city from the get-go? It sounded like a cleanup operation, like Mermell was trying to correct something that could get city hall in a legal jam.

The new recording of the call was attached to Mermell's email. It was midafternoon on a Friday; the newsroom was in its usual end-of-week doldrums, half-empty and quiet. Outside, the cool of early autumn had settled in. Like the first "version," the longer recording began with Khan's conversation with the dispatcher. Nothing new there. But the longer one didn't end when Khan transferred the call to room 304. The voice of the man who answered the transferred call came on the recording:

"Hello?"

"Hi. This is the fire department. Did you call for 911?"

"Uh, not me, basically. Um, I had, ah, my girlfriend here had a bunch of drinks, and, uh, she's breathing . . ."

"Is she breathing right now?"

"Yes, she's absolutely breathing. Absolutely breathing."

It was the same voice I heard at the celebration on the Keck campus, with the same East Coast inflections, only now the speaker was less sure of himself and agitated. The man on the recording was Carmen Puliafito. I was sure of it. I would have to prove it, but I was convinced it was Puliafito. I listened to him blame alcohol for Sarah's condition, just as Khan had recounted. I listened again: Not only did

I have Puliafito on the recording—I had evidence suggesting that the medical school dean lied on the call about what had caused the young woman's distress.

The story was nailed; I could not *wait* to write it. Sure, I first had to contact all the principals a final time—Puliafito, Nikias, Sanchez, and the rest. I had to give them an opportunity to respond to my new findings, but I doubted that would take long. And my hunch was they would stay mum. As far as I could see, the highest hurdle to a speedy publication was my surgery, which was the following Monday. I knew there would be some delay, but I was confident I could continue to work on the story as soon as I got out of the hospital. I didn't have to walk to write.

Before I left the newsroom that Friday evening, knowing I wouldn't be back for a while, I stopped to chat with Jack Leonard, the law enforcement editor. Jack and I had worked on stories in the past, including when he was a Metro reporter. He was an English-born Irishman whose posh London accent carried echoes of his Oxford education. He also held a graduate degree in journalism from USC. Jack, who was fifteen years my junior, was one of the smartest and most principled journalists I knew. His desk was crammed against the windowed wall of the third floor, though he faced the interior of the newsroom. I stood across from his desk and regaled him with the details of the story I was about to break. I knew it would interest him because, in addition to his alumnus status, Jack had taught a journalism class at USC. He was as steeped in the good and bad of the school as he was in that of the *Times*.

Jack lifted his eyebrows and smiled with a newspaperman's delight as I filled him in on the dean, the young woman, the overdose, the retroactive police report, USC's silence, the 911 recordings—I ran through it all.

"Amazing," he said.

I agreed.

Jack was still smiling when he said, "And you think we'll publish that?"

For a moment, I thought I misheard him. Was he joking? He had a droll sense of humor that sometimes escaped me.

"What?" I said.

Jack nodded toward the offices of Maharaj and Duvoisin on the other side of the room. "What makes you think they'll run it?"

With only a hint of sarcasm, he then riffed on the objections he imagined Maharaj and Duvoisin raising to the story: *Why is this news?* they would say. *Because the dean is involved with a young woman? Who cares? There was no arrest, right? The dean isn't even the dean anymore. And this happened six months ago? How is that news?*

Maybe he wasn't joking. Or he was, but not entirely. I considered myself more cynical than Jack, but I couldn't conceive of the story not being published. Would Maharaj and Duvoisin want to water it down? Given their history, probably—perhaps more than probably. But not publishing it?

"Seriously?" I said to my friend Jack.

He just smiled and shrugged.

9

A PROTECTED PERSON

Henry Huntington was a union-bashing, though cultivated, rail builder and real estate developer in the L.A. of the late 1800s and early 1900s. His name lived on, attached as it was to the cities of Huntington Park and Huntington Beach; the world-renowned Huntington Library, Art Museum, and Botanical Gardens; the palatial Langham Huntington Hotel; and the hospital where Sarah recovered from her overdose. USC's shadow extended to Huntington Hospital. USC-trained physicians were well represented on the staff, and Puliafito had served on its board of directors for several years.

Huntington Hospital was also where, coincidently, I had my knee replacement performed. Before I went under what I thought was just a knife, one of my doctors told me that undergoing a total knee replacement is less like surgery than time spent in high school woodshop—sawing and drilling and hammering. Meaning the recovery could be long and tough. So the night before the surgery, I emailed Lait the 911 recordings and the documents I had received from Pasadena, along with a note about what Khan told me and his contact information. The idea was that, since I didn't know how long I'd be out of commission, Lait could give the material to another reporter to pursue if necessary, particularly in the event a rival news outlet got onto the story. With all the emailing and calling and door-knocking I'd done, it was a near miracle that a competitor hadn't already begun retracing my steps.

The surgery didn't afford much of a break from my reporting. Boyer sent me an email a few hours after I got out of the operating room; it was the familiar refrain—Pasadena had given me all the information I was going to get. He wrote that the release of the second version of the 911 recording "completes City's response to and fulfills any existing CPRA requests." I disagreed but was in no shape to engage him in detail. My wife, Joanna, was in the hospital room, and she said I was an idiot for checking my phone for emails fresh out of surgery.

She had a point, but this was *that* kind of story—I couldn't let up on it. I replied to Boyer, typing carefully in my drug stupor and keeping it brief: "Thanks. I'll be in touch with a few follow-up questions."

Actually, I had more than a few. They included long-standing queries that had yielded no response. I got out of the hospital two days later and left a phone message for Boyer two days after that. I needed to remind him of my repeated interview requests for Sanchez and a more recent one for Garcia and any other officers involved in the overdose call. I also had asked the police department to decipher the abbreviations on the Call for Service log—entries such as CC UR, MR, and DI. I noted that none of the excessive redactions had been removed. And I wanted to know if the police officers reported to the hospital as well as the Hotel Constance and if they had made certain the woman named Sarah pulled through.

Boyer and I connected by phone the following Tuesday, and he emailed the city's responses at close of business that Friday. They were mostly a series of denials. The answer was no to my request for interviews, lifting of redactions, the paramedic report, the IDs of officers, even the explanation of abbreviations.

Matters had descended to a level where the government of Pasadena, an affluent city of international repute—home of the Tourna-
ment of Roses and the California Institute of Technology—refused
to decode for the region's newspaper of record the bureaucratic
shorthand on a publicly available form.

So now, as I had told the mayor it might be, the story was as much
about the Pasadena cover-up as it was about Puliafito and USC.

The mystery address was an irritant: 350 East Cordova. I wondered
if it had slipped through the databases. Maybe it marked one side
of a corner property whose legal address was on the other side. Or
maybe it was a mailing address not attached to a property record.
But then I checked with the U.S. Postal Service, and it had no listing
for 350 East Cordova, either. Since I was still unable to climb into a
car, I asked Nathan Fenno to visit that block of Cordova and look
for the address. He graciously did so and confirmed it was not there.

I could not accept that the appearance of Cordova Street on the
evidence report and in Puliafito's LexisNexis profile was a coinci-
dence. But what did it *mean*? The report listed the address as that
of the "owner" of the meth. Even if the street number on the report
was wrong, and even if he took it down in error, did Garcia actually
determine that the drugs belonged to Puliafito? And then not arrest
him? That was difficult to believe, but then so much of this story
seemed incredible that I couldn't dismiss it.

I came back to whether Puliafito had lied about the street number. I was only assuming the address came from Puliafito because the
woman was unconscious. Puliafito could have given Garcia the address in an interview or the officer might have taken it from the
registration at the Constance, which Khan said was in Puliafito's
name. But why would Puliafito lie about it? How could he think he
would get away with the lie? He had to know the police could find
what I had just found. If the police bothered to check, that is.

The other possibility was the address was Sarah's. She ingested the drugs, and that went a long way to making her their "owner." I checked LexisNexis for any Sarahs or variations of the name at the address. I got just one hit, and the woman did not come close to Khan's description of the Sarah in room 304.

What if Sarah lived in an apartment at 325 Cordova that Puliafito leased for her—in his name? But if that was the case, what were they doing at a hotel a few blocks away? Why chance the discovery of drugs by the police if they could keep the party in the apartment? Maybe she had a roommate and that took the apartment out of play.

Everything seemed to connect, and none of it appeared to add up.

I started to write the story. It was a welcome distraction from the rehab of my surgery.

As I moved from general assignment reporting to investigations later in my career, one of the adjustments I had to make was in the writing. Investigative stories weren't so much written as they were blueprinted and built. They were less a writerly narrative than an exposition of findings—something like an indictment, only easier and more enjoyable to read. My first rough draft of the Puliafito story began:

Last March, in the middle of the academic term, Carmen Puliafito abruptly resigned as dean of USC's Keck School of Medicine, one of the most prestigious and lucrative posts in academia.

The Harvard-educated ophthalmologist had led Keck since 2007. In announcing his decision to step down—effective immediately—Puliafito said in an email to colleagues that he wanted to return to the faculty ranks and pursue outside opportunities in healthcare.

The resignation was not the only dramatic event involving Puliafito that month, however. Three weeks earlier, he was at the scene of an apparent drug overdose of a young woman in a Pasadena hotel room, a Times investigation has found.

It was a working draft to provide Lait with a sense of where I was. As it evolved, I knew I would try different ways to open the story—maybe a hard-news first paragraph that summarized the main findings of my investigation. Or perhaps a more visual opening describing the scene of the overdose. I kept the draft tight—under 1,400 words—but figured it would grow as I added more reporting and context, including about Puliafito's importance to USC. And I believed that when the first story ran, it would generate phone calls and emails from readers who had information about the overdose and Puliafito. I was just as sure that their leads would enable me to find Sarah. I knew the first story would be one of several I would write on the topic.

I sent the draft to Lait on Tuesday, October 25. We both believed the story would be ready for publication by the end of the following week. I started a final round of emails and phone calls to the principals in the story, requesting interviews. I received a quick brushback from Boyer.

"The PPD has been consistent in declining any follow-up interviews and/or in stating the department has no further info to share," he wrote in response to my email. "This remains current today too."

"I will pass along the request for interviews, but please anticipate the answer will be no, unless you hear back from me otherwise by COB Friday."

The answer remained no. I received no response to another interview request I sent to Nikias.

I emailed this to Puliafito:

Dr. Puliafito—

I left a message with your assistant yesterday asking that you call me. I have not heard back.

I am wrapping up a story on your resignation as Keck dean. It focuses on police records and other material that place you at the scene of a drug overdose of a young woman at the DusitD2 Hotel

Constance on March 4. The woman is described as your "friend" or "girlfriend."

I want to give you an opportunity to address all the points in the story. Please contact me as soon as possible.

He did not reply.

A few days later, I tried again—with much more detail, because I believed the story would be published soon and this would be his last chance to engage:

Dr. Puliafito—

You have not responded to my messages. I hope you will reconsider and grant me an interview.

I then laid out for him much of what I had learned about his role in the overdose, including the fact that the police report ID'd him as a witness. I asked him if he used meth or other drugs at the Constance, if he told the hotel staff not to call 911, if that was his voice on the 911 recording, and if he informed Nikias or other USC administrators of his involvement in the incident. I went on to inquire whether his compensation from Ophthotech—a company I learned he recently joined and supposedly was the "opportunity" he'd left the deanship for—was less than what he earned as dean and, if so, why would he give up the USC position. I asked about his current status as a physician at the university and whether he received any extra money to walk away from the deanship. And I asked why USC waited until June to hold the celebration of his tenure at Keck.

I got not a word in response.

As Lait edited the draft, I arranged to have a source who knew Puliafito well listen to the 911 recording. The source verified that the voice on the recording was Puliafito's. I found YouTube videos on which Puliafito spoke—and it was the same voice as on the 911 call.

It was around this time that Maharaj stopped at my desk on the way to his office. I was slouched in my chair to favor my new knee, which made Maharaj appear even taller and more imposing than he normally did. He was a commanding presence in the newsroom, with a regal posture and a confident stride, complemented by a sartorial flair that was uncommon for the male journalists at the *Times*, many of whom dressed as if their wardrobes came from stores that did not specialize in clothing. Maharaj and I chatted briefly about my surgery and family matters. I had long considered him a friend. We were not close, but there had been much to enjoy about him. Maharaj had a cagey intelligence and a dry sense of humor, as well as an inspiring and unconventional backstory; he'd landed at the *Times* by way of Trinidad and Tobago, the University of Tennessee, and Yale University. As we got to know each other, we shared our passions for L.A.'s food scene and sports, and he hosted me and my wife at after-hours events sponsored by the paper. We confided in each other about problems we faced on the job. When Maharaj was editor of the *Times*'s Business section, he tried to persuade me to join him there. And as managing editor, he advocated for my stories when others did not.

But our relationship had become more and more frayed during his five years as editor in chief. Power seemed to have transformed him from the collegial man I had known into someone who was an imperious stranger to me.

The talk at my desk turned to work. Maharaj asked what I had coming. I was surprised by the question; my assumption was that other editors had informed him of the Puliafito story. I wondered if he was just fishing for details. I gave him the rundown on the story, with highlights on how difficult it had been to break through the walls at Pasadena and how complete USC's silence had been. Maharaj's reaction put me on edge. A story like the Puliafito one was the sort editors always reveled in—the sort they lived for. But Maharaj showed no enthusiasm for the tale I was telling. Worse, he narrowed his brow as if I were delivering a piece of bad news that affected him personally. Like I had informed him his car just got towed.

"You should be doing stories that put people in jail," Maharaj said.

I was flabbergasted. "This story *could* put people in jail," I told him. "And it goes beyond that."

Maharaj turned his back and walked toward his office. As I watched him move through the newsroom, I wondered how worried I should be given his comment. And I remembered Jack's words: *What makes you think they'll run it?*

Lait edited the story draft with the care and attention to detail that he was known for in the newsroom. Before moving into editing roles, he had a long and distinguished run as a reporter at the *Times,* exemplified by his reform-generating investigations of corruption in the Los Angeles Police Department. But that was before Maharaj's reign. Like so many of our colleagues, Lait had become frustrated with Maharaj's lack of support for investigative projects, especially those aimed at big targets. Maharaj seemed to approach these enterprises from a standpoint of fear, no matter how solid the reporting and how judicious the editing. It was clear to me and others in the newsroom that the fear was all about Maharaj preserving his position. Investigative stories carried inherent risks—principally the threat of legal action by anyone whose reputation the reporting damaged—to which Maharaj seemed to have an outsize aversion. The risks could be minimized through painstaking fact-checking and a strict adherence to fairness. But they could be eliminated if the stories never ran. Or practically eliminated if the stories were published in a weakened form.

On Maharaj's watch, investigative stories sat for weeks and months as they awaited his green light for publication. They included what became a widely praised series on the opioid crisis, a project Lait directed and edited. Two years passed from the time the series landed on

Maharaj's desk until publication. Throughout that period of mostly pointless delays, Maharaj was often dismissive of the work and insulting to the three reporters who produced it. Two of the reporters left the *Times* for other news outlets before the stories saw print.

So Lait knew he would again have his hands full with Maharaj on my story—perhaps more so than with the opioid investigation. The drug series focused on OxyContin manufacturer Purdue Pharma, which was based on the other side of the country. The USC story was not only in the *Times*'s backyard but involved someone Maharaj knew personally and openly admired: Max Nikias.

The trepidation Maharaj conveyed on investigative stories seemed to have bled into the upper management team he had assembled. Masthead members like Duvoisin and his subordinate, California editor Shelby Grad, often appeared to edit those stories for an audience of one—Maharaj. Not so Lait, whose edit of the Puliafito draft was purely a journalistic labor—an effort to make the story bulletproof to any challenge of the facts and to sharpen the composition for the reader. I had no problems with the changes Lait made to the story, even if they were not my first preference.

He then sent the draft to Grad, his immediate supervisor. As I suspected he might, Grad made significant cuts in the story, nearly all of them of material that might have embarrassed USC or Pasadena.

Fear. That was my initial reaction.

The story did not need trimming for length; it had remained short for an investigative piece. Grad inserted no notes for us to read that explained the cuts, and he raised no concerns about the accuracy of the reporting. Instead, he simply crossed out the sentences and paragraphs. He even axed what was known in journalism jargon as the "nut graph"—a paragraph high in the copy that told the reader why the story was news and why it was important. In the Puliafito draft, the nut graph was the one that said that the circumstances of the overdose painted "a murkier picture" of his resignation as dean than

USC's official version. It also said experts questioned whether Pasadena handled the incident appropriately.

Gone along with that paragraph was the reference to the celebration USC threw for Puliafito three months after the overdose. Gone, too, was most of the criticism of the police and of city hall's withholding of information. Sanchez no longer appeared in the story at all.

In my view, the cuts had nothing to do with the journalistic merits of the story; they all came down to fear. It was not that Grad was afraid of riling USC or Pasadena, I believed, but that he feared Maharaj would do even more damage to the story if it were not softened by the time it reached him. Many of us in the newsroom had become aware that Maharaj regularly bullied Grad, including in the presence of others, and typically when Grad challenged him. On the cuts, I was willing to accept that Grad hoped they would make the story publishable in Maharaj's eyes. But that didn't mean I could live with them. I was preparing written responses when I and much of the newsroom got diverted to coverage of a tragedy 370 miles north in Oakland: thirty-six people were killed when a fire raced through an old warehouse that had been illegally converted into an artists' residence and concert venue. That occupied most of my time for the next several weeks. And it was now *nine months* since the overdose.

Lait persuaded Grad to restore most of the cuts. My take was that Grad had needed Lait's support, in the sense that two frontline editors would be better than one in the coming fight to get the story past Maharaj. First, however, it had to go through Duvoisin. So I braced myself for the rough treatment that had become customary for non-positive USC stories as they moved up the editing ladder. One of Duvoisin's early edits resulted in cutting a description of the story as a "*Times* investigation." The term was routinely used in stories of this type. It informed the reader that the paper was reporting findings of an original nature that had been unearthed through, well, an *investigation*. My reporting on the overdose checked every box for an investigative story. What else could the piece be? A breaking news story? A feature on drug abuse at architecturally distinctive hotels?

I walked into Duvoisin's office and asked why he objected to labeling the story an investigation.

"It implies wrongdoing," he said.

Implies wrongdoing? The story didn't *imply* anything. It reported the facts to the degree that USC and Pasadena disclosed them. In terms of any criticism in the draft, it came from experts, on the record, and was directed at the actions of the Pasadena police and city hall.

"Wrongdoing?" I asked. "By whom?"

"USC," Duvoisin said.

But of course. If an exception to the standard use of "*Times* investigation" was to be made, it would be in a story on USC.

I later said as much to Lait, profanely. He also was incensed. We tried to change Duvoisin's mind, with me laying out all the investigative steps I had to take to get the story. Duvoisin did not budge. And in a separate conversation, he volunteered—virtually blurted— that the story was not worthy of the front page. I took that to mean that another USC-only standard had been laid down. Because otherwise the story met every metric for page-one play. It then struck me that Duvoisin's insistence on removing "*Times* investigation" from the draft would make it easier for him, appearances-wise, to keep the story off the front page, where investigative stories almost always ran.

Duvoisin and I had joined the *Times* within a few months of each other, fifteen years earlier. He was city and projects editor of *The Philadelphia Inquirer*, and I was the West Coast bureau chief for *The Dallas Morning News*. We both were hired as editors, a position I took somewhat reluctantly (my bureau was closing, and I'd have preferred to remain a reporter). He was in late middle age, bespectacled and indoorsy, and he had become known to many staffers as a socially awkward manager whose smiles and compliments could not always be taken as sincere. His lack of people skills was not reflected in his ambitions. Duvoisin openly coveted the managing editorship, which remained vacant for months after Maharaj was elevated to editor in chief. Once Maharaj gave him the job, Duvoisin reciprocated with an abiding loyalty.

For a non-investigative, non-front-page story, Duvoisin spent an inordinate amount of time on the Puliafito edit. He dragged out the process for another month, dipping into the copy now and then to make cosmetic changes that added nothing of substance for the reader. He could not challenge the reporting, because it was anchored in government records and statements from government officials, and it had been thoroughly fact-checked. So he tinkered and dawdled. In one of our initial sessions, late on a Friday afternoon, he told Matt and me that I should try to visit Puliafito and Garcia at their homes. I informed Duvoisin that I had already attempted that, more than once, and had reached out to them by other means as well. I said a potentially more fruitful door-knock at the last minute would be at the USC presidential estate in San Marino. I made the obvious point that Nikias could address the most important unanswered question about USC: Did he strip Puliafito of the deanship because of what happened at the Hotel Constance? The prospect of me dropping in on Nikias at home seemed to alarm Duvoisin. He shook his head and said I should instead try Puliafito and Garcia again. Duvoisin was adamant about it. Lait and I glanced at each other in disbelief.

A few minutes later, Lait and I were in Lait's office, and he suggested we visit Nikias's together over the weekend. "Sure," I said. It often was preferable that a cold call at someone's home be done by two reporters. The presence of two reporters showed the interview subject that the paper was especially serious about the story. And if the subject was uncooperative or hostile, it was good to have a second reporter on hand as a witness to anything that might become a matter of contention. On the positive side, sometimes the subject hit it off with one of the reporters more than the other and thus was more likely to talk.

Lait sent Duvoisin an email informing him of our plan. As soon as the email arrived, Duvoisin read it on his computer, slammed his hand down on his desk, and said, "No!" Duvoisin then replied to Lait's email with a firm directive that we were not to visit Nikias *before clearing it with him!*

Never in my career had an editor tried to stop me from knocking on the door of the subject of a story. Nor had an editor ever required that I get clearance to do so. Editors are supposed to *make certain* that reporters knock on those doors if all other attempts to reach the subject failed.

I resolved in Lait's office that Duvoisin would have to fire me to stop my visit to San Marino. And to create a paper trail for myself, I sent Lait and Duvoisin an email the next day with "Nikias" in the subject line. "If I'm going to knock on his door," I wrote, "the weekend offers the best chance of success."

It was a Saturday afternoon, but Duvoisin replied in twenty minutes: "The cop and the doc are much more important, in that they were both in the hotel room."

Lait responded to him first, ten minutes later. In reference to Puliafito, Lait wrote that Nikias "would know whether the university pushed him out over the incident and explain why he remains a faculty member. We have left numerous messages for him and his designated public affairs people with no response whatsoever. I think it's more than fair to knock on his door at this point."

I replied to Duvoisin a few minutes after that, before seeing Lait's response:

"I thought the main 'unknown' is whether Puliafito was removed because of what we have already documented about the hotel incident. Nikias is the ultimate authority on the reason for the dean's departure. We have Puliafito's version of that."

Duvoisin did not reply. Lait told me Duvoisin asked him why we were "escalating" with Nikias.

It seemed Duvoisin was bent on eliminating any doubt that C. L. Max Nikias held special status with the leadership of the newsroom. That he was a protected person who had the number two news executive at the *Times* running interference for him on a weekend.

Duvoisin wasn't quite finished with me that afternoon. Grad called my cell to reinforce Duvoisin's dictate that I concentrate my efforts on Puliafito and Garcia. I was in a hardware store looking at power saws when I answered the call. I let Grad go on for a while and then stopped him by raising my voice.

"Shelby, I smell newsroom corruption!"

I said it again, at a volume that caused customers to turn their heads toward me.

Grad uttered some words in defense of Duvoisin, but the waver in his voice told me his heart wasn't in it.

"Newsroom corruption!" I repeated.

I said I was going to Nikias's house whether Duvoisin liked it or not.

Grad relented. He agreed that Nikias required a visit. The following morning, he emailed me to say, "It's a really important story."

10

SPIKING THE STORY

A misty drizzle veiled the boughs and streetlamps along Oak Grove Avenue, a well-tended lane graced with the serene stillness that came from money. Night had just fallen. I parked across from the gated driveway that led to the rambling estate where Nikias resided as the eleventh president of USC. The property would later sell for *$25 million.* As large as it was, the home could not be seen from the street. This was San Marino, a place where people with means could thoroughly insulate from the noise and hustle and changes of the larger city around it.

I arrived at the Oak Grove address with a gambler's notion. I believed there was a chance of persuading Nikias to invite me into the grand quarters for the frank discussion we should have had months before—for a coming clean on the downfall of Dean Carmen Puliafito. But I hedged my bet by preparing for the outcome of not getting through the door. I had typed up a note on *Times* letterhead to leave for Nikias. It read:

President Nikias—

I hope we could have a confidential conversation about the circumstances surrounding Carmen Puliafito's resignation as dean of the Keck School of Medicine. Publication of my story on Dr. Puliafito is imminent. I am reachable at all hours.

I closed by listing my work and personal phone numbers. I believed Nikias might finally see the futility of ducking me and, at minimum, confirm on background—that is, as an unnamed source—that Puliafito did indeed get the sack because of behavior associated with the overdose. I sealed the note in an envelope.

The sidewalks were empty as I hobbled across the street on my still-smarting new knee. The driveway split a row of mature olive trees with serpentine trunks that stood sentry in front of the estate. An intercom on a stone pillar guarded the spiked iron gate. I pressed, and no one answered. I pressed again. More silence. I tried a third time, and a faint, staticky voice—I could not tell the gender—came over the speaker; I identified myself and asked if President Nikias was home. The speaker went dead. I had been hung up on. I limped back across the street to retrieve the note from my car, intending to leave it on top of the intercom. Just as I returned to the driveway, a car pulled up (in the dark, it looked like a Mercedes, but I couldn't be sure). I recognized the driver and lone occupant as Nikias's wife, Niki. I smiled and waved in greeting, and she lowered her window. I introduced myself and asked if her husband was home. She said no.

I showed her the envelope. "Could you give this to him, please?"

She eyed me as if my sheer presence was an affront. But she politely accepted the envelope. Then the gate opened, and she drove onto the estate grounds.

• • •

The next morning, a Monday, my note to Nikias arrived at the *Times* by courier—still in the sealed envelope. Nikias hadn't even bothered to read it. The note was accompanied by a letter addressed to Maharaj from Brenda Maceo, USC's vice president for public relations and marketing. (Maharaj did not share the letter with me; I did not see it until weeks later, when I learned of its existence and demanded a copy.) Maceo wrote:

Davan

As you may know, President Nikias is travelling out of town for the CFP. He has posted from his trip on his Instagram account.

Last night, Pringle, who follows Dr. Nikias on Instagram, showed up at the Nikias' residence after dark and asked Mrs. Nikias to deliver an envelope (enclosed, unopened) to her husband. When Dr. Nikias called me last night to let me know what had happened, I assured him I would deliver the envelope to you and express our profound disappointment in the situation.

Needless to say, Pringle has again crossed the line. We understand he is doing his job, but we also expect a degree of respect and professionalism between our organizations.

Thank you

I did not follow Nikias (or anyone else) on Instagram and had no idea he was at the College Football Playoff. It was a fact I had visited the residence around five thirty or so in the evening, after it had grown dark. Beyond whatever Maceo was implying on those two scores, I found the letter to be very instructive, just as I did Nikias's refusal to read my note. The tone of the letter told me Nikias and his lieutenants expected a measure of obeisance—something close to servility—from the editor in chief and publisher of the *Times*. I had to wonder if Maharaj had created that expectation through his words and actions. The reference to me by only my last name suggested that I had been the topic of earlier and perhaps ongoing communications—unpleasant ones—between Maharaj and Maceo, if not Nikias. So did the statement that I had *again* crossed the line.

I wasn't sure when or where those previous line crossings occurred or even what constituted a line. I had not been to Nikias's home before. So did I make one too many phone calls to him or others at USC? Did I send one email too many? Or did one or more of my stories on USC step over Nikias's line? Was it the Haden story, for which I was still reporting follow-ups? Some of the Coliseum coverage? The stories way back on Carroll and the NCAA scandal? Were they all uncrossable lines in Nikias's view? Most striking was that he apparently felt so secure in his dealings with the *Times* that he didn't see the need to even glance at a hand-delivered note from one of its investigative reporters.

If I had seen the Maceo letter in real time, rather than weeks later, I might have been better prepared for what was coming from Maharaj, although nothing could have steeled me enough.

At last, Duvoisin's circular edits came to an end. The facts central to the story had not changed nor been challenged in the three months and three weeks since I'd filed the first draft. It was now mid-February, close to the anniversary of the overdose. Nikias and his people were as closemouthed as ever. Puliafito continued to ignore my queries. And the identity of Sarah remained elusive.

But the story was ready to go. In normal circumstances, if the bosses at USC and Pasadena—and later the *Times*—had treated the story like the routine journalism endeavor it was, publication would have been a memory by now. Lait and I were just relieved it was running, along with photos of the principals, graphics of the documents, and a video built around the 911 recordings. It was a compelling package. Late on a Wednesday, sometime after he sent the story to Maharaj, Duvoisin emailed me this:

"Davan's going to think on it overnight and will meet with us in the morning."

I had to read that a couple of times. *Maharaj had to think on it? Overnight? Sleep on it? Sleep on what?*

The story was unassailable on every front—records, interviews, experts, 911 recordings. It was so cautious and scrupulous in its presentation that we weren't even identifying Puliafito by name as the man on the recording, simply because the police refused to verify it. The story did point out that the caller referred to himself as a doctor and described the woman as his girlfriend. It also noted that the police records did not mention any other doctors or friends at the scene. And anyone who knew Puliafito would recognize his voice.

The draft had been through four editors (not counting the copy desk), including the one responsible for page one, Scott Kraft. Duvoisin no longer spoke of the story as undeserving of the front page. He even ordered up a second piece to run the same day in which I explained to readers how I had arrived at my findings, which is something rarely done for anything but a page-one story.

The newsroom lawyer had reviewed the story for any legal problems and cleared it.

Everything was set for publication that weekend. I approached Maharaj as he left his office that evening. "What's up with the story?" I asked. He mumbled something about being late, and he hurried past me.

"We'll talk tomorrow," Maharaj said over his shoulder. He disappeared into the elevator lobby.

In his email, Duvoisin had not invited Lait to the meeting with Maharaj, which made me suspicious. Why wouldn't the lead editor on the story be included? I called Lait. And he confirmed my suspicions:

"Marc told Shelby Davan is going to sleep on whether to kill the story or not," Lait said.

I swore, but I still did not believe Maharaj would spike the story, if only because doing so wouldn't be in his personal interest. I was sure that my colleagues would be outraged, and Maharaj's support among the staff was already at its lowest point ever. *Los Angeles Magazine* had recently published a long takedown of his management of the newsroom, with a focus on his handling of the OxyContin investigation. (I was one of the sources for the *Los Angeles Magazine* piece—unnamed, because I likely would have been fired if I'd gone on the record.) I was banking on Maharaj knowing he could not afford the criticism that would come from stopping the Puliafito story.

I replied to Duvoisin's email: "Why isn't Matt in the meeting?" It was about 9:00 P.M. An hour later, Duvoisin responded, "I'll ask him to come."

It occurred to me that I needed Lait there as much as my witness as my editor.

The meeting did not get underway until midafternoon. It was in Maharaj's office, the largest of the "glassholes." Lait and I sat facing Maharaj and Duvoisin, our backs to the newsroom. Maharaj began the discussion not with a review of what he considered the strengths and weaknesses of the story, not with questions about my reporting and sources, not with anything of a journalistic nature. Instead, he remarked on the successes I've had at the *Times*, the number of important stories I had worked on, and how he had always "supported" me. It was bizarre, but I knew where he was heading—and I tensed.

"We are not going to publish this story," Maharaj said.

My face grew hot—flush with anger. There was a ringing in my ears.

"What?" I said, more as a curse than a question.

Maharaj came back to the line that I should be grateful for all he had done for me. I didn't know what he was talking about. I brought good stories to him year after year; I suppose he expected me to be indebted to him because he didn't kill them. Maharaj mentioned the time off I took for my surgery—implying, it seemed, that he could've denied me the sick leave I had earned. Did he forget how quickly I returned to work from the surgery and that I had continued to do interviews and write during my recovery at home?

Then Maharaj made a reference to the two and a half weeks I had taken off more than two years earlier after the suicide of my daughter's fiancé. Now I feared my anger would turn to screaming rage. The suicide was a tragedy wrapped in a deeper tragedy. Jeremy Adler was a sweet and brilliant young man who had been born with one of the worst and rarest brain disorders known to medicine, congenital central hypoventilation syndrome. People with CCHS lose the ability to breathe when they sleep. They must use a mechanical breathing device to stay alive when not awake. The syndrome damaged other functions of the brain, including its response to anxiety. The less delicate name for CCHS was Ondine's curse, from the spell that caused the unfaithful husband of a mythical water nymph to stop breathing if he ever fell asleep. CCHS was incurable, but Jeremy conquered it long enough to become a dazzling scholar and attorney. He had been an adored part of our family for seven years. I had joked that I won the lottery when Jeremy became my future son-in-law. We did everything together. After he died, I spent those two and a half weeks comforting my daughter, helping to plan Jeremy's funeral, writing his obituary, emptying his apartment, and beginning the process of launching a college scholarship in his memory—and grieving. I had since become a patient advocate for Jeremy's twin, Pierre, who also had CCHS.

That Maharaj would drag this pain into the meeting was as telling as it was heartless. It signaled that he found it necessary to use every weapon to back me off the story.

I heard myself nearly shouting as I demanded to know what was unpublishable with the story. Maharaj admonished me to "settle down," but he did not point to anything in the piece that was wrong or unfair or unimportant. He said he would not publish the story because of "what we don't know."

I wasn't sure I heard him right. "About what?"

Maharaj's response was halting and vague. In essence, though, he said we could not report conclusively that Nikias removed Puliafito because of the overdose. That was like saying we couldn't publish a story on the occurrence of a crime without first solving it. Or that we couldn't report that a lightning storm preceded a wildfire unless we determined that it sparked the fire. It was a dodge, evidently the only one Maharaj could muster.

I looked at Duvoisin, who was stoic. I insisted that he tell me what in his mind had changed since the day before that made the story unpublishable—after he had worked on it for six weeks. He said he had thought it over and agreed with Maharaj. His voice was toneless, free of conviction.

Lait was the picture of composure on our side of the room. He leaned back in his chair and asked Maharaj what we could add to the story to get it into the paper. Maharaj was evasive, but Lait kept pressing and the bottom line emerged: Maharaj expected us to get Nikias or Puliafito to state on the record that Puliafito lost the deanship because of the overdose.

And for me, the last of the clouds parted: Nikias was essentially *in charge* of the story. Everyone in the room knew that Puliafito would never discuss his role in the overdose with the *Times.* That could finish his career in medicine. So that left Nikias. If he talked, the story might run. If he didn't, it wouldn't. It was a cover-up artist's dream.

I needlessly reminded Maharaj that Nikias had been given every opportunity to go on the record and say whatever he wanted, but he declined. I asked Maharaj if he would publish the story if I got one or two sources close to Nikias to confirm that Puliafito was forced out of his job. I had no sense I could pull that off but proposed it to get Maharaj's reaction. He said he could not commit to that.

Of course not. Because if he had called the meeting to sort out how to publish the story, he would have started it with suggestions of his own—or at least asked us for ours. I then offered one: How about Maharaj reach out to Nikias, since he had a relationship with him, to get the confirmation about Puliafito? Maharaj had used his position on the masthead before to aid in the reporting of a story. He once boasted to me how, in his previous role as managing editor, he contacted Schwarzenegger's lawyer to help a reporter confirm that the former governor had fathered a love child with his house-keeper. So why shouldn't he use his Nikias connection now?

"I'm not the reporter on this story," Maharaj said.

"You've done it before," I said.

"I'm not the reporter on this story," Maharaj repeated.

The longer the meeting went on, the more apparent it became that his decision to spike the story was final.

My anger did not abate. I pointed over my shoulder.

"The whole newsroom is watching," I said.

I meant it as a threat—that Maharaj would get blowback from the staff for killing the story. He told me again to calm down, but he looked unnerved.

"I'm not closing the door to further reporting," Maharaj said.

And I thought, *The editor in chief of the* Los Angeles Times *should be insisting that I do whatever reporting was required to get this story published—a story about a scandal involving an institution on the scale of USC and the people who run the city of Pasadena. And in-stead, he makes it sound like he's doing me a favor by not forbidding more reporting.*

I also thought, *"Leaving the door open" to that reporting did not mean the reporting would ever be published.*

I told Maharaj and Duvoisin that I no longer trusted them, so much so that I would not be represented by the same lawyer as they had in a legal challenge of the paper. I said to Maharaj that his re-lationship with Nikias and USC, including in his role as publisher, created at least the appearance of a conflict of interest. I asked him why I shouldn't believe his decision to kill the story wasn't influenced by that relationship.

"Why shouldn't I be concerned?" I said.

Maharaj cocked his finger at me. "That's not cool," he said. "That's not cool."

But he didn't give me a reason.

And I was convinced that the scandal that I had been chasing for months outside the Times Building had now crept into the newsroom.

11

SECRET REPORTING TEAM

The hours that followed the killing of the story were a seething blur. As I walked out of Maharaj's office, reporters and editors at the city desk looked over in my direction. The meeting had become heated enough to draw their attention, and it was known to many in the newsroom that I had expected trouble from Maharaj on the story. I was tempted to shout across the room what had happened, but I held my tongue until I reached Grad's office. The door was open, and he was at his desk, his back to me, gazing at his computer screen.

"He killed it," I said, nearly snapping at him.

Grad swiveled around. He looked as if I had smacked him in the head.

"He *killed* it?" he said.

"He fucking killed it," I said.

Grad seemed to struggle for words, then began uttering something about speaking to Lait about it—or was it Duvoisin? I wasn't listening—I couldn't.

I took my rage home to my wife and older daughter. For months, they had listened patiently to my dinner-table groaning about Maharaj and Duvoisin and USC, until it had become something like therapy for me, even if it disrupted our nightly *Jeopardy!*-watching ritual. On this evening, they reacted to the news that the story was killed with an anger that rivaled my own. They told me I could not give up, I could not back down. I retreated to my home office and began writing a memo to Maharaj. I needed to do something constructive. I drafted the memo in the manner of establishing a record of what occurred in the meeting. I included material on earlier clashes with Maharaj and Duvoisin, such as the effort to stop me from visiting Nikias's residence.

I wrapped it up with the line, "It is heartbreaking that I had to write this memo." My plan was to send it to Maharaj the next morning or no later than the following Monday.

Fury kept me awake for most of the night. The morning brought rain. We lived on a hillside, where storms turned the streets first into streams and then into rushing rivers. I went back to the memo and expanded it to include more ethical lapses by Maharaj, among them false statements he tweeted about the *Los Angeles Magazine* piece. Then I emailed the killed USC story to a half dozen colleagues, along with a note on what had happened before and after the meeting. They replied with expressions of outrage and disgust and sympathy—but not surprise. They had known for a long time that less-than-flattering stories about USC were at best an unpromising venture.

I debated whether to stay home for the day—to cool off to the point where I could plot my next step and know that it was a rational one. It was a brief debate. I was only in the mood to fight. I could not let the story stay dead.

By the time I started my drive to the office, the rain had become loud and hard—one of those L.A. downpours that thumped in the high canyon areas before softening over the city basin. The peaks of the taller downtown towers were hidden in the roil of low clouds. Greasy lakes formed in broken pockets of the pavement on Broadway, where I pulled into the *Times* parking structure. In the newsroom, I stopped first at the office of Jeff Glasser, the newsroom lawyer. He knew the story had been killed. I told him I could not trust Maharaj and Duvoisin in any matter of ethics and honesty, and for that reason could not be represented by the same attorney as they had—meaning him. Glasser suggested I reconsider, saying I might be making things worse. I insisted, and he acknowledged I could be entitled to my own lawyer if I believed I had a conflict with Maharaj and Duvoisin. Glasser later arranged for me to be represented by an attorney with our outside law firm.

Then I remembered the complaining letter from USC that Lait had told me about. I emailed Duvoisin: "I would like a copy of the complaint made about my visit to Nikias' house."

He replied, "I have it right here, on my desk."

I walked to his office, counseling myself to say nothing to him— knowing that if I restarted the face-to-face battle over the story, it would get ugly and I might give him what he would claim were grounds to discipline me. As I stepped into his office, he nudged a large envelope on his desk toward me. I barely met his eye before taking the envelope and walking out.

Lait had informed me of the complaint and its contents shortly after it arrived. But Maharaj and Duvoisin did not give him a copy, so Lait could not do it full justice from memory. Now, as I settled in my chair and read it, the condescending language that Maceo, the university vice president, used toward Maharaj leaped off the page. Maceo's words were a declaration that USC had come to regard the editor and publisher of the *Times* as someone in service to the university. They reminded me that the broader relationship of USC and the newspaper had changed. A balance of power that existed between USC and the *Times* for generations had been subverted—so that it had become tilted in USC's favor. Numbers-wise, this was no revelation—not for the past ten years or so. As the *Times* reeled from sharp declines in print circulation, revenues, and the size of its staff, USC had enjoyed a boom decade. The university was erecting more and more buildings as it expanded its campus, while the newspaper could no longer even claim title to its headquarters: Tribune had spun the *Times* and its other papers into a separate company; it kept the Spring Street landmark in the original company and then sold it. And as layoffs at the *Times* became as regular as the seasons, USC's remained one of the largest employers in L.A.

But this was about something more than numbers—something other than money and real estate and connections. In its modern era, the *Times*'s power had always flowed principally from the robustness and incorruptibility of its journalism. Its power came from being a *check* on power—on any institution or individual whose misuse of power made them fair game for the paper's reporting.

And it was that power that I was convinced Maharaj and his enablers had surrendered to a rising and emboldened USC.

I still hadn't sent my memo to Maharaj when Lait phoned me with a proposition: How about we put four more reporters on the story? If the bar we had to scale was to get someone close to Nikias to talk—although Maharaj said even that might not be enough—why not flood the zone with door knockers? Five reporters could hit up a long list of USC administrators in a short time.

"I want to force the issue," Lait said.

It was my call. I could insist on continuing to pursue the story on my own. Most of my bigger investigations had been solo efforts; it was my nature to work alone. But when I did team with colleagues, including on the Coliseum and Haden projects, I had enjoyed the experience, and the reporting benefited from it. And what Lait was suggesting made sense: *Let's cover as much ground as quickly as possible and maybe we'll get lucky.* I agreed within a couple of minutes and had a suggestion of my own: Two of the reporters should be USC graduates. My thought was that they would bring to the undertaking both a personal expertise about the school that I lacked and the moral weight that only an alum could claim when encouraging a fellow Trojan to be forthright. (I had brushed up against Trojan tribalism in my reporting on Pete Carroll; some USC faithful accused me of writing the stories merely to avenge the Trojans' defeat of my alma mater, Penn State, in the 2009 Rose Bowl.)

Lait and I agreed we would do this quietly—that is, without telling Maharaj and Duvoisin. We were certain they would not approve of the added reporting firepower, even though editors routinely threw more staffers at stories that had the potential to deliver a significant impact.

So the expanded USC team would be kept secret from the top editors of the newspaper, on a story of considerable importance to them and the city. It was beyond extraordinary and a sorrowful sign of the distress the *Times* had fallen into.

And it was risky. Maharaj and Duvoisin could view our actions as insubordinate, and I had heard of instances in which they apparently punished those they perceived as disloyal, critical of their decisions, or in any way a threat to their positions. Maharaj and Duvoisin ordered a Pulitzer Prize–winning reporter in the Sacramento area to relocate almost immediately to L.A. after she raised an ethical concern about their acceptance of a grant from an organization that had a conflict of interest with her reporting. For weeks, the reporter, Paige St. John, was forced to drive 430 miles to L.A. on Sundays and sleep on colleagues' spare beds and even in her car during the workweek, then drive back home on Friday evenings. And after he took the beating in *Los Angeles Magazine*, Maharaj overruled other masthead editors in ordering that the *Times*'s Pulitzer Prize nomination of the opioid series be submitted as a "staff" entry, rather than as the work of the three reporters who produced it. That meant the reporters' names would not appear on the prize if the series won (it did not). This was widely seen in the newsroom as a particularly cruel act of retribution; I believed Maharaj suspected the reporters cooperated with the *Los Angeles Magazine* writer, even though there was no evidence of that.

Only one of those reporters remained at the *Times*—Harriet Ryan, who was Lait's first choice for the USC team. Harriet was in her early forties, a Pennsylvania native and graduate of Columbia University. She came to the *Times* from Court TV and previously wrote for the *Asbury Park Press* in New Jersey. I had known Harriet for most of her nine years at the paper. She was a graceful writer who had acquired a taste for investigations. Many times, we had lamented together about the direction of the paper. I became a confidential source for the *Los Angeles Magazine* piece because I was appalled at how Maharaj and Duvoisin had treated Harriet and her two partners on the opioid story, Scott Glover and Lisa Girion.

The other three staffers Lait and I wanted for the team represented a de facto youth movement on the staff that sprang from waves of buyouts that targeted older, higher-paid journalists, most of whom were happy to take the money and jump off the Tribune ship. The oldest of the three was Adam Elmahrek, thirty-two, an L.A. native and California State University, Fullerton, graduate whose Jewish mother and Palestinian father emigrated from Israel. Adam had been at the *Times* for just seven months, arriving at the paper from the Voice of OC, a nonprofit news organization in Orange County. His desk was next to mine, so we had gotten to know each other during his short time on the staff. He was a close and quiet watcher—the type who took everything in, who listened before he spoke, and who could read people as if they telegraphed signs visible only to him.

Two twentysomethings Lait and I hoped to recruit for the assignment were graduates of USC's master's degree program in journalism—Sarah Parvini and Matt Hamilton. I didn't know them well on a personal level but had been greatly impressed with their reporting two years earlier for the paper's Pulitzer-winning coverage of the San Bernardino terrorist attack that killed fourteen people. Sarah, whose parents were from Iran, grew up in San Diego and earned her bachelor's degree at the University of California campus there. She wrote for several print and broadcast outlets before joining the *Times*. Matt's family was based in Delaware, and he moved west after finishing his undergraduate studies at Boston College. He was stringing for *The New York Times* and working for a trade publication for California attorneys when the L.A. paper hired him. Sarah and Matt were alike in a fundamental way: Their youthful plunge into big-city journalism made them wise and suitably hardened beyond their years.

I had no doubt my four colleagues would bring whole stores of talent and energy to the assignment, but I had to ask myself: Why should they agree to help? Why should they invite the wrath of their bosses? Why jeopardize their careers? The newspaper industry was in free fall. The next round of buyouts and layoffs was always just around the corner. And job protections that were common at other media shops did not exist at the *Times*. The newsroom had no union representation and never did, unlike most major papers in the nation. It was a patrimony of the *Times*'s original publisher, Harrison Gray Otis, who fought organized labor with a fervor that seemed inflamed by a creed—and even more so after a radical unionist bombed the newspaper building in 1910 and took twenty or twenty-one lives (historical accounts differ on the number). As the last publisher from the family, Otis Chandler, Harrison's great-grandson, kept the newsroom nonunion with a gentler approach. Chandler pampered his journalists with generous salaries and perks and otherwise treated them well—so well that the paper became known in the business as "the Velvet Coffin," a comfy place to work until you retired or died.

Tribune had begun stripping away the velvet soon after it acquired the *Times*. Salaries stagnated, benefits were cut, and job security became a pipe dream. The Chicagoans who now ran the company had recently compounded those injuries with the insult of a name change: They dropped *Tribune* in favor of the lowercase *tronc*—short for *Tribune online content.* Apparently, they thought this rebranding evoked a digital future, despite the disco-era font they selected for the tronc logo. To the newsroom and much of the world outside of it, the name sounded like something heard during a Heimlich maneuver.

And so, in this environment, why should my colleagues involve themselves in the potential disaster of trying to revive the USC story? Would that be worth getting fired over? What were the chances of finding another decent-paying job at a newspaper? Although the firings would have been for doing the honorable thing, that might not mean much to a prospective employer. That's something Devon Khan had understood: People might love the *idea* of a whistleblower, but that was not the same as wanting to hire one. At the end of the day, isn't a whistleblower just another breed of troublemaker?

Sarah and Matt were just beginning their careers. Harriet and her husband had two young daughters and a mortgage. And Adam had by far the least seniority among the four reporters. He and his wife, Crystal, had a newborn and were looking for a home closer to work, with money as tight as ever. When Adam told his wife about the USC assignment and the risks it entailed, she was nervous—even scared. She knew that if Maharaj and Duvoisin were bent on reprisal, her husband would be the first. *He's the new guy, and if they go after somebody, it will be the new guy.*

No two ways about it, the smart move for Adam would be to take a pass on the USC story. I wouldn't blame him; no one would.

But he chose the other move.

"I saw it as an opportunity to take a stand for the principles of our profession," Adam told me later. "I was proud to do it."

So were Harriet and Sarah and Matt. My four colleagues didn't become journalists for job security. Journalism was their calling—a calling that required something more than merely a passive adherence to the principles Adam cited. Sometimes it demanded the courage to defend those principles, regardless of the personal cost. Not every journalist was up for that, but these four were.

Maharaj and Duvoisin didn't see them coming.

At the beginning, the team took unheard-of precautions. We were careful not to gather as a group anywhere Maharaj or Duvoisin or their allies could see us. We stuck to the recesses of the newsroom or to the cafeteria downstairs. Or we spoke by phone. And we decided for the time being to use our private email accounts for any communications that could tip off Maharaj or Duvoisin to what we were doing. That's how upside down things had become. None of us had ever imagined that we would have to sneak around in the Times Building and go dark on company email to report a story. It was the type of stealth insurgency against corporate management that we covered in other industries. We didn't engage in it. But now here we were.

The plan was that we would fan out across L.A. to find the one USC insider who could confirm the true circumstances of Puliafito losing the dean's post. I compiled a list of USC administrators who might know something. Contacting them by phone or email to ask them to speak to us against Nikias's wishes was not a good option. We needed to visit them at their homes; in-person conversations left no phone logs or digital fingerprints, which might put the administrators more at ease. And we planned to go in pairs whenever possible; again, two reporters were often better than one. But before we knocked on a single door, the younger folks on the team turned to cyber-sleuthing, the form of reporting that was more instinctive to them than it was to me. They mined the Web for any Puliafito connections to a Sarah, something I had not done in earnest since Lait and I began fighting to get the story published. Matt found a couple of fresh Sarah candidates, and one seemed a good bet—a woman named Sarah More who was Facebook friends with Puliafito. She wasn't a solid match for the description Khan gave me, but she came much closer than the Sarahs I had found earlier. This Sarah appeared to be roughly the same age as the woman who overdosed. In some of her Facebook photos, her dark hair was bleached blond. But she was heavily tattooed up to her throat and had an inked splash of hard-to-read lettering above one cheekbone. Khan had not mentioned tattoos. He said Sarah was dressed only in a bra and panties, so he would have noticed if she were a human cave painting. Could she have had the work done in the past eleven months? Possibly.

Matt sent me two photos of a second Sarah who was Facebook friends with Puliafito. She had black hair and otherwise appeared to be a woman of color. Her sole similarity to the Hotel Constance Sarah was her age.

I called Khan and said I was about to text him photos of prospective Sarahs and they would come from my personal phone. Until then, I had texted him on my work cell, which I no longer trusted for sending texts and images. They could be accessed without my knowledge by the company, meaning Maharaj and Duvoisin. I sent Khan three Facebook photos of the first Sarah—she was blond in two of them—and two of the second Sarah. As I waited for his reply, I drummed my desk with a pen in anticipation.

Khan texted back quickly. The second Sarah wasn't even close. What about the first one? The blond one?

"Sorry, not her," Khan said.

Just to make sure, I sent him a link to her Facebook page so he could view other photos of her. He did and then texted back:

"I'm pretty positive that it's not her."

I thanked him, crestfallen.

The next morning, I was back at it. I had the *Times* library scrub our databases again for records on Puliafito, and this time with Sarah More or Sarah Moore as cross-references. Those names didn't score a hit, but another Sarah turned up for the first time as an "associate" of Puliafito on LexisNexis. An "associate" could mean just about anything—business partner, lover, roommate, or relative. The key was that she was linked to the same address as Puliafito. That suggested LexisNexis had recently found a record that contained her name and at least one of his addresses. Maybe some sort of property transaction, or a voter registration, or a professional license—whatever could be harvested from a database. This Sarah's last name was Warren; she was twenty-two and appeared to have a family in Huntington Beach, a family that had moved there from Texas, according to the records. She was probably another dead end, but the age was right. I asked the library to go deeper on the Texas front and the family, while I began searching social media.

As I'd expected, the list of Sarah Warrens on Facebook was endless. There also was no scarcity of young ones with blond hair. So I scrolled and clicked for a numbing amount of time.

Until I found a Sarah Warren who said she was from Pasadena.

Who very much resembled the woman Khan described.

I texted Khan one of her profile photos. She was looking at the camera with Kewpie eyes, not quite smiling. She looked even younger than twenty-two.

"Could this be her?"

"Yep!" Khan replied.

I stood from my desk. I wanted to whoop, clap—make some noise. *Yep!*

It was about five in the afternoon on a Wednesday. And 355 days since the overdose, 320 days since the tip came to me, and 120 days since I'd filed the first draft of the story that was killed.

For a moment longer, as if to dispel some superstition that he might retract his confirmation, I studied the text from Khan, below the image of the doll-like woman with untroubled eyes. I told myself it just got more difficult for Maharaj and Duvoisin to keep the story killed.

But first, we had to find the woman in the photo.

12

SARAH'S ESCAPE

Sarah Warren found herself sitting on the roof of the Balboa Bay Resort, a hotel on the Newport Beach waterfront. *On the roof.* It was a summer evening in 2016, and Sarah was alone, her feet dangling over the edge. She was clutching a pink monkey doll. The roof was not designed for visitors.

The view through Sarah's methamphetamine haze was of yachts and sailboats tucked into the slips of a brightly lighted marina, the water off Newport dusky beneath drifts of clouds. Sarah had been in the throes of a meth freak-out, a drug psychosis, when the impulse struck her to find a way out of her room—the window, the balcony—and spider onto the roof. By that time, Puliafito had left the hotel, and so had Warren's latest boyfriend, Don Stokes, who had given her the stuffed monkey. The get-together at the Balboa was a send-off for Sarah, a last bit of fun before she carried through on her promise to return to rehab. Puliafito paid for the room and the drugs and a new bong with a bowl the size of a grapefruit. The Balboa was his kind of place—expensive, exclusive, and discreet.

Discreet, that is, until the staff found it necessary to call the cops. After the meth took over, it seemed to Sarah that she was screaming.

Don had begged her to stop, but she could not. Did it start with her yelling about the room service? It was something like that—something that just caused her to erupt. Then she was screaming about the demons that were coming after her, tormenting her, making her do things she didn't want to do. She screamed that she was like Harry Potter: *I'll use my powers to save the world!* She screamed out on the balcony and then the roof, and she had kept screaming even after Don told her the racket would bring the police. He was on parole and being in the room with the bong could send him back to prison.

"I'm out of here," he told her. "I've got six years hanging over my head."

And he was gone.

The cops arrived with the paramedics. It was like a repeat of the Hotel Constance, except she was mostly conscious and Carmen wasn't there. As she would remember it, she was back in the room when the four men approached her—and then they were forcing her into restraints and trying to sedate her. *That's what they were saying—sedate her. But were they really trying to kill her? Was that a lethal injection they had for her?* She fought them, determined to break free of the restraint, twisting and whirling. She might have spit at one of the paramedics. It was no use. They bundled her out of the room.

Here comes jail.

Stokes was waiting for a taxi on a corner in front of the hotel when he saw the cops and paramedics haul Sarah out of the building. If he had stayed in the room just a few minutes longer, they would have rolled him up right alongside her. It was smart to leave Sarah to her screeching and wailing, but he didn't feel good about it—especially now as he watched the cops fold her into the paramedic van. He had known her only a short while, yet he believed their connection was timeless in a way, that it existed long before they actually met, and that it had a larger purpose than romance or sex. Stokes was a spiritualist.

He also was a DJ in Huntington Beach, hosting karaoke nights at Tumbleweeds Bar & Grill, a neighborhood hangout with billiards and darts and live bands when Stokes wasn't onstage. He met Sarah there when she was staying in the Huntington Breakers apartments just down Beach Boulevard from the bar. Stokes was seventeen years older than Sarah, but he had an enduring innocence and youthful abandon about him that was both appealing and a sign of trouble. He was making the same destructive choices in his late thirties that Sarah was making in her early twenties. And like Sarah, Stokes was a junkie.

He was determined to be Sarah's protector, including from the drugs that he was trying to kick himself. But when Sarah drew him into her world, she dragged him into Puliafito's as well. And Stokes was no match for the fancy doctor with the Mercedes and Porsche and enough cash to keep half the addicts on the Orange County coast afloat in meth and heroin. He knew Puliafito didn't like him. Once, the old man threatened to cut off Sarah's drugs and rent money if she didn't dump him. Sarah ignored the ultimatum, and then Puliafito was forced to keep her happy by welcoming Stokes into the running party. He became a source of free meth for Stokes, plus weed. He paid for Stokes's motel room, his iPhone, and even his storage unit. Dinners and massages were always on Carmen. And there were gifts of cash.

If Sarah was hooked on Stokes, Puliafito would have to get Stokes hooked on him—hooked on his drugs and money. To mollify Sarah and to control him.

The hook got so deep that after Stokes moved into a sober-living home, in another attempt to get clean, he knew Puliafito would be waiting for him to fail, waiting with the drugs. And he was. Stokes visited Sarah at her apartment, and Puliafito was there. He had his usual supply of meth. Stokes asked Puliafito for the drug. Puliafito knew Stokes was struggling to kick, and he knew he was living at the sober house. But the physician gave him the meth anyway.

"As an addict," Stokes said later, "it's hard not to ask."

How could he protect Sarah from Puliafito? How could he do that when he couldn't protect himself from him?

Stokes watched the patrol car and the paramedic wagon pull away—driving off with the would-be love of his life. His guilt at leaving Sarah to fend for herself nearly drove him to his knees. Would he ever see her again?

The frolic and scuffle at the Balboa occurred at least four and a half months after Puliafito learned I was investigating him. By then, if he wasn't convinced I'd given up on the story, he obviously felt confident that I would soon enough. Why shouldn't he have? He'd already managed to stay outside the reach of law enforcement. Why would one reporter make him sweat? It certainly wasn't enough to end the partying at places like the Balboa. Or to stop providing Sarah with the drugs that could end up killing her, even with a fall from a roof.

He seemed unperturbed in almost a sporting way that the *Times* was sniffing around. And he hadn't dismissed the possibility I might find her. So he warned Sarah that "a scumbag named Paul Pringle" was looking into him. Puliafito told her to never speak to me and to make sure her family didn't either. She promised him they'd all keep quiet.

And that was funny, Sarah thought, because she and Kyle, her heroin-dealing boyfriend at the time, used to talk about blackmailing Puliafito by going public about him being a drug supplier to young people and a dope fiend himself. So did another member of their group, who was an Amish girl from Pennsylvania, believe it or not. Dora Yoder was a few years older than Sarah and Puliafito's "number two girl." Yes, they talked about shaking down Puliafito, but they were never really serious about it. Besides, Sarah explained later, "I didn't think I could win against him. He implied that he knew people and he'd always be okay in the end."

On the day she was taken from the Balboa to the Newport Beach jail, I'd just begun to write the first draft of the story that would be killed five months later. I still had no idea who Sarah was. And the Pasadena police remained incurious about the physician who had drugs in his hotel room and a ludicrous story about his relationship to the unconscious woman in his bed. The Newport Beach police booked Sarah on charges of possession of a controlled substance, possession of nitrous oxide, being under the influence of a controlled substance, and battery on the cops and paramedics. It was arrest number three in the six months since the overdose at the Constance.

Carmen never got busted. If he had been locked up after the overdose—who knows?—that might have done the trick: She might have been clean by now.

Instead, after she woke up at Huntington Hospital, and after she listened for a few minutes to a social worker there, a nice woman who encouraged her to get into rehab, Sarah was free to go. She called Carmen, and he picked her up and they drove right back to the hotel to resume the party. The drugs were waiting for them there. Carmen told her he had hidden them in the stairwell two floors below their room—the meth and the heroin, with a bong and pookie. He was very proud of that. *Clever, right? It was very "street" of him.* They retrieved the bag of goodies from the stairwell and checked into a room. Sarah vowed there would be no sex. Even when she wasn't recovering from an overdose, she couldn't stomach him anymore, couldn't bear to have him on top of her. Their first night at the Constance, the night before the overdose, Carmen hired a male prostitute for her. He liked to watch her have sex—to watch it and to film it. And she preferred sex with a stranger, as empty as it was, to another romp with Carmen. They had planned a second night with a male prostitute when she overdosed. She had taken way too much GHB—a whole vial. Carmen watched that, too.

Two days after they checked out of the Constance, Sarah was arrested in the San Fernando Valley. She was driving around with

Kyle. He was still sort of her boyfriend then, which Carmen hated. He had many reasons to hate it: Kyle was young and handsome and exciting, everything Carmen wasn't, no matter how much he tried to be. Kyle also had become one of Carmen's heroin dealers. The drug business didn't keep Kyle in much money, so he dabbled in identity theft and other types of larceny. After they got pulled over in the San Fernando Valley, a male cop kept an eye on Kyle while his woman partner took Sarah aside. It was like she knew Kyle was the criminal in the relationship and she felt sorry for Sarah.

"It's just you and me here," the woman cop said to her. "Tell me now—are there drugs in the car?"

"No," Sarah lied.

And then they found the drugs, and off to jail she and Kyle went. The charges for her were possession of a controlled substance and possession of drug paraphernalia. Kyle got rung up for more of his thievery. They didn't stay behind bars for long, and the arrests didn't slow them down much. The movable bacchanal that Carmen financed kept Sarah and Dora and Kyle and the rest of the doctor's young crowd in drugs and money. Sarah partook as much as she could. She used and used until there seemed to be no bottom, no hole too deep for her to fall into. Carmen didn't mind. As long as she stayed close and came to him for her drugs, he had no complaints.

But she reached a point where she couldn't tolerate herself. She went back into rehab. For this go-around, her choice was Monarch Shores, a place down the coast in Dana Point. Sarah had the same trouble going cold turkey at Monarch Shores as she did at Creative Care. Again, Carmen found a way to deliver drugs to her—and without getting both of them caught.

He called it "Skittles surgery." Once a week—or maybe more often, Sarah remembered—Carmen mailed a gift package to her at Monarch. The package contained a bag of Skittles candy. An occasional bag of candy was okay by the staffers who screened the mail.

What they didn't know was that Carmen had carefully opened the package—taking pains, with an eye surgeon's precision, not to tear it beyond the seams—and replaced the colorful buttons of candy with Xanax. He then reglued the bag and mailed it off to Sarah.

She looked forward to the bags of Skittles. They made the thirty-day stay at Monarch a little easier. And when she got out, Carmen was waiting for her with more than just Xanax. The drugs flowed again, and it was like she had never left the party. And she met a new guy in Huntington—Ryan, who was a former police officer, of all things. He was pretty young to be an ex-cop, maybe ten years older than she was, except that he now worked in security and still carried a gun. She shacked up with him at the Hilton, the one on Pacific Coast Highway by her parents' place. Sarah was staying at the hotel on Carmen's tab. She had told Carmen about Ryan and expected him to have the usual jealous reaction, but she didn't expect him to drive all the way down from Pasadena and bang on the hotel room door at six in the morning. He was yelling her name, demanding to be let in.

Ryan opened the door, and Carmen leaned in and shouted toward her: "Sarah!" She was standing by the bed when Ryan kicked him in the balls. Then he whipped out his 9mm pistol and stuck it in Carmen's bug-eyed face.

"Get out of here!" Ryan said.

Carmen staggered back and ran down the hallway. They were up on the seventh floor. Two cops arrived within minutes. The questioning took place outside the hotel entrance. One of the cops brought Carmen over to Ryan to make an ID.

"Yes, that's him," Carmen said.

He complained of the pain in his groin.

Ryan tried to explain himself to one of the cops, saying this man he didn't know was pounding on the door and screaming into the room. He had to protect Sarah and himself, Ryan said, so he kicked the man and pulled the gun. Self-defense, he said. But the cops didn't buy it. They told Ryan he was under arrest.

And they were sitting there on the curb, in the thin dawn light, Ryan in handcuffs, when Sarah's dad rode by on his bicycle and saw them. Paul Warren happened to be on his way to the gym for his morning workout.

When does it end?

Ryan was booked at the Huntington Beach jail for exhibiting a firearm and battery on a person. Luckily for him, Carmen had no interest in becoming ensnared in a criminal case, not at the risk of the cops poking into his relationship with Sarah, especially if the *Times* was still on his tail. She had already told the cops that she met him when she was a prostitute. They asked him if that was true, and he confirmed it. He eventually told the police he did not want to pursue the charges. No hard feelings.

Getting her lover's gun jammed in his face didn't dissuade Carmen from paying the rent on a new apartment for Sarah. She had burned out on Pasadena and wanted to move closer to home. Carmen got her the place at the Breakers, a breezy spread of pastel-colored buildings that was right across the street from her parents' town house. Less than a month after the incident at the Hilton, Sarah decided to unwind at Huntington Beach's weekly street fair. She visited its petting zoo and texted Carmen a photo of her posing with a deer. Then she got drunk, poured herself into her car, and promptly slammed it into a median, breaking the axle. She was waiting for a tow truck when the cops arrived. She recognized the two patrolmen as the same duo who'd arrested Ryan. They recognized her, too.

"This girl's a troublemaker," one of them said.

They took her in for driving under the influence, and she spent the night in jail. Carmen retained a lawyer for her. He said long afterward that he had found it "touching" that she had visited the petting zoo.

"I felt fantastic for her," Puliafito said.

• • •

Sarah's brother, Charles, smoked weed in high school. Who didn't? But he stayed away from the harder stuff. And then Sarah introduced him to Carmen, who, again, was happy to entertain anyone important to her. The seventeen-year-old Charles and the dean became freeway buddies, driving all over L.A. Carmen chauffeured him to smoke shops to stock up on meth pipes and nitrous oxide, to a liquor store for a keg and whiskey, and to the apartments the dean rented for Sarah. Sometimes other young women whose companionship Puliafito was paying for would be there. He offered Charles sex with one of the women, who was in her early twenties and heavily tattooed. Charles declined.

By then, Charles had become Puliafito's meth-smoking buddy, too. Puliafito had turned him on to meth. It was on a day when Charles dropped by the Pasadena apartment Puliafito rented for Sarah. They were both smoking meth, and Puliafito offered some to him, Charles recalled. After that, just about every time he got together with Puliafito—Carmen, he called him now—the doctor gave him meth or Xanax or nitrous oxide or pot. Carmen bragged that the meth he bought was biker meth—the best.

"Very pure," he told Charles. "Very clear."

Carmen gave him "teeners" of meth—sixteenths of an ounce—which could cost more than a hundred dollars each. The doctor even had the meth Ubered to Charles and Sarah at their parents' home. One time, all three of them smoked it up in the kitchen when Mom and Dad were away. Meth was on the menu when Carmen drove Charles to the Keck campus and showed him around his office. Charles was impressed with the degrees on the wall. Carmen ordered his secretary to treat his guests to Trojan T-shirts and other gear from the bookstore. The secretary, a slight woman of middling age, looked frightened of Charles. They left Charles alone in the office, and he fired up the meth pipe. He and Carmen also smoked meth together in the Keck parking garage.

Carmen acted like he could out-party anybody, never mind

that he was old enough to be Charles's grandpa. He tried hard to appear young to Charles, including when it came to women. One day when they were driving, Carmen took a call and told Charles it was a woman—Dora—who "wants to suck my dick." *Wants? Yeah, if the price is right.*

When Charles turned eighteen, Carmen threw him a party that started at one hotel and ended the next day at another hotel. The booze and drugs were on the doctor.

That wasn't long after I got my first good look at Puliafito during the celebration USC threw for him on the Keck campus. And it wasn't long after the Pasadena police wrote a retroactive report on Sarah's overdose and then buried it.

All the running around with Puliafito was already taking a toll on Charles.

He started to fall behind in school; he blew the PSAT, missed the SAT, and got bounced out of his acting lessons. And he no longer felt like the healthy, strapping boy who met Carmen months before. It wasn't easy, but he finally broke off any contact with Carmen. He couldn't get his sister to do the same. Carmen exploited her in every way. He even used her as a mule, having her carry their drugs on their flights to Vegas and the East Coast. And it seemed that every time Charles visited Sarah, Carmen was with her and they were doing drugs. She had become an addict, and Carmen didn't care. The doctor was slowly killing her.

The last straw was when Sarah called Charles in fear for her life: Carmen learned she had been seeing another man, so he burst into her apartment in a jealous rage. He was there now tearing the clothes from her. "I paid for these!" he was shouting. Charles sprinted across the boulevard to the Breakers, a folding knife in his pocket. When he reached Sarah's apartment, he could hear her screaming inside. Charles burst through the door, and Carmen was still ripping her clothes away. He spun around, and Charles slapped him in the head. Then he kicked him hard in the knee, and Carmen collapsed with a yelp. For good measure, Charles unfolded the knife and threw it into the door, the blade biting into the wood. It was a warning to Carmen. *If I ever see you with my sister again, I'll kill you.*

Later, he heard that Carmen flew to Boston to have his knee repaired—maybe because he didn't want to explain to anyone in L.A. medical circles what caused the injury. Charles also heard from his mother that Carmen had told her he had mob connections and could have them "disappear" her son the next time Charles got rough with him.

Charles did disappear from Puliafito's stomping grounds. Paul and Mary Ann Warren became so alarmed at their son's worsening condition that they persuaded him to enter a detox center and then rehab. Charles completed the program, and afterward, he did his best to stay sober. But the treatment didn't take. Over the following months, and then years, he lurched from one rehab stint to hospital stay after another. College didn't happen. A good job wasn't possible. And he wondered how different those months and years might have been if he had never met Puliafito—if the Medicare-aged party animal had never plied him with the endless helpings of drugs and alcohol that the high schooler thought he could handle but could not.

My brothers were around Charles's age when drugs and alcohol began to unhinge their lives. As hard as they fell, they would have fallen harder and faster if they'd had a millionaire like Puliafito financing their addictions. As Charles put it:

"When you have carte blanche for just about everything, it's easy to lose your way."

Sarah did not go into rehab after the impromptu roof rave-up at the Balboa. Carmen moved her to yet another apartment, to put more distance between Sarah and her parents. The apartment was at the open-air Bella Terra mall farther inland in Huntington. Around Thanksgiving, after she had settled into Bella Terra, the drugs had sunk Sarah to a level physically and emotionally where she would be willing to pay *him* just to leave her alone—just to get him far away from her. Carmen must have sensed this, because suddenly he was talking about them getting married. He said he wanted to divorce his wife and marry Sarah. Did he really believe she would consider marrying him? Was he that delusional? That arrogant?

Sure, he was. Wife would be just the latest role he expected her to play for him. In the past, Puliafito tried to pass her off as his assistant at USC—or as his niece. He even had her attend receptions for his students at his mansion, with his actual wife there. Another time, he asked her to be his date at the black-tie opening of the Broad museum, the hottest social event in L.A. The museum was named for Eli and Edythe Broad, the billionaires who built it, and the opening was full of types like Kamala Harris, the mayor, Gwyneth Paltrow, and other movie stars—*Chrissie Hynde was the musical guest, for God's sake.* Sarah had refused to go.

"Carmen, I'm a twenty-year-old drug addict," she said. "Are you crazy?"

It's more than a year later, he's still here, and now he's asking me to marry him.

I can't do this for another ten minutes! I have to get back into rehab!

But how could she? How would she pay for it? She was still on her parents' insurance, but that wouldn't cover everything, and she couldn't ask them to pay more, not after all the pain—and expense—she had already caused them. And if Carmen offered to pay again, that would keep her tied to him, which could not happen. There was no getting clean and staying clean with him around.

And what about her cats? Through all this, she had somehow managed to adopt three cats. She loved them, and she could not just abandon them. She was trying to make that point with her dad. They were at the town house, and he was insisting that he would pay whatever it cost to cure her addiction, to save his daughter. She was grateful, *so grateful.* But the cats—what about the cats? She said she could not leave them to go into rehab.

Then her dad started to cry.

"You cannot put the cats over your own health," he said, pleading with her.

His tears closed the deal. Sarah packed her bags for Ocean Recovery. The cats would be fine.

And now Carmen was at Magnolia Memorial Park in his trench coat and fedora. He was standing in front of his tangerine chariot of a BMW, which could be the means of her escape from the drudgery and boredom of rehab. But Sarah had already made her escape—from him. She pointed out Carmen to the nice old man in charge of groundskeeping at the cemetery. Sarah told him the guy in the trench coat was looking for her and she wanted nothing to do with him. The groundskeeping chief walked over to Carmen and ordered him to leave.

That was the last time Sarah saw Puliafito.

But he had more in store for her and her family.

The same month that Sarah checked into Ocean Recovery, Hollywood actress Lori Loughlin and her fashion designer husband, Mossimo Giannulli, arranged to have sent by FedEx the first installment of a total of $500,000 in bribes to get their daughters admitted into USC as fake athletes. The money went to a college admissions adviser from Newport Beach named William "Rick" Singer and to USC athletics administrator Donna Heinel. The FedExed check would make Loughlin and Giannulli the highest-profile people—rivaled only by another famous L.A. couple, actors Felicity Huffman and William H. Macy—in the unfolding "Operation Varsity Blues" scheme.

At that time, in November 2016, there was no indication that the news media or the government knew anything about Singer's sophisticated swindle that corrupted the college admissions process for the purpose of enriching himself and his coconspirators. There was no outward sign that higher-ups in the Nikias administration—those ranking above Heinel, who was the number two administrator in athletics—knew, either.

Singer's multimillion-dollar scam targeted universities such as Stanford, Yale, UC Berkeley, and Georgetown, but none to the degree that it did USC, where the subsoil for payoffs and cheating was particularly fertile. And so in the fall of 2016, a third major scandal was lurking beneath the surface at USC.

13

NO SNITCHES

Cordova Street T-boned off the Arroyo Parkway, a stretch of Historic Route 66, and coursed east past the columns of a Masonic Temple and then the glassy-faced Pasadena Hilton and rows of apartment buildings just north of the California Institute of Technology, until it came up just short of the baseball field named for Jackie Robinson at Pasadena City College.

Adam and I drove out to the building at 325 Cordova, with photos on our phones of the woman Devon Khan identified as the overdose victim and whom LexisNexis and Facebook identified as Sarah Warren. We were hoping that, if we couldn't find her, we'd at least happen upon someone who knew her. There was still no Sarah Warren listed on the building directory and likewise no Puliafito. None of the residents we showed her photo to recognized her. And the staffers in the rental office stuck to the rule of not releasing any information about tenants. The cell number LexisNexis had for her went straight to voice mail, suggesting the phone was powered off. We decided not to call the numbers listed for the couple who appeared in LexisNexis to be her parents; cold-calling parents about a child in trouble is never the preferable first step. We planned to try contacting them in person.

And for the moment, the reporting team was having better luck in the *Times* newsroom than on the street. Harriet had recognized Puliafito's name from a legal dispute she once considered writing about: In July 2015, the University of California sued USC over its poaching of an Alzheimer's disease researcher and his grant-rich laboratory. The lawsuit was still being fought out in the courts. It accused USC of civil conspiracy and aiding and abetting breach of fiduciary duty in luring Paul Aisen away from UC San Diego. The Aisen lab was expected to receive more than $340 million in grant funding. That was a windfall for USC and a large feather in the cap for Puliafito, who described himself as the "quarterback" in the effort to score Aisen. As such, the dean was a key witness in the lawsuit, and it would not help USC's case if it became publicly known he abused street drugs and gave them to others. So we had to consider: Could the school have more than 340 million reasons to cover up Puliafito's actions and refuse to cooperate with the *Times*?

As we weighed that possibility, and as we went deeper into online public records and her social media connections, a fuller digital profile of Sarah Warren was beginning to emerge. An email address associated with Warren led to the Humaniplex prostitution website, where we found her listing; it was easy to confirm through the sultry photos she posted. Warren's arrest record surfaced in the form of case numbers and brief descriptions of the charges. Those leads took us to paper records at courthouses in each jurisdiction where Warren was taken into custody. The case files spawned more leads, and they extended our search to a convicted drug dealer named Kyle Voigt, who had been arrested with Warren in the Valley. Matt took a break from the court records to look up Puliafito on Venmo, and he found that Voigt was one of the former dean's "friends" on the money-transferring app. It wasn't proof that the two used the app to exchange money, but as Matt wrote in an email to the team, the find "brings this other figure closer into Carmen's orbit."

Wow.

Puliafito not only was at the scene of Warren's overdose—his "girlfriend's" overdose—but he also had a possible money link to a drug dealer who had been arrested alongside her. This was the type of discovery that, normally, reporters would be eager to share with the top editors in the newsroom. But we continued to keep our work secret.

Voigt's rap sheet was a strong argument for the courts to go paperless. We found fifteen cases over the past seven years. Many involved multiple offenses, most of them drug-related in one way or another. He had pleaded guilty or no contest to possession for sale of meth, heroin, oxycodone, fentanyl, and Ecstasy. He had cases pending on charges of possession, identity theft, burglary, and probation violations. And he was currently sitting in Men's Central Jail downtown.

Sarah Parvini pulled Warren's rehab history from court records. During the past thirteen months, there were stays at Michael's House in Palm Springs and Monarch Shores in San Juan Capistrano and, most recently, Ocean Recovery in Newport Beach, where Warren was admitted on December 7, 2016. That date was past the typical thirty-day program for rehab, but Sarah noted that Ocean's website stated that it offered a ninety-day program as well. "There is a CHANCE that she is in fact still there and that's why her phone is off," Sarah advised the team in an email. It was certainly worth a drive down to Newport Beach, so Sarah and I took the trip together. The thought was that if Warren wouldn't speak to both of us, she might speak to one of us. Sarah was close to Warren in age, and sometimes interview subjects were more comfortable speaking to a contemporary, especially one of the same gender. Then again, younger people who get caught up in a story like this might prefer to speak to an older and more experienced journalist (like me). Sarah and I had our fingers crossed for the Newport trip, because we had come up empty on visits to two Pasadena apartments that we linked to Warren—different ones from the Cordova address.

Nine years earlier, I had written a story about the "cottage industry" of expensive rehab centers in Malibu and how they often were rule-breakers and a rip-off. The industry had since outgrown the cottage category, and the class of rehabs housed in converted seaside villas had exploded in number up and down the Southern California coast. But Ocean Recovery wasn't the type that offered sumptuous accommodations with ridgetop views, although it was within steps of the sand and looked toward the tall masts of a marina. It was in a beige-bland two-story apartment building—it appeared to be a fourplex—on busy Balboa Boulevard. Sarah and I parked across the street and walked over: Three young women were hanging out near the entrance, two of them smoking cigarettes. We asked if "Sarah" was there.

The women gave us the once-over, and then one of them said, "Oh yeah. She's in B."

"She's here now?" I said.

"Uh-huh."

We found her.

We walked into the building, and a woman who seemed to be in charge greeted us. We identified ourselves as *Times* reporters and asked if we could speak to Sarah Warren. The woman said she could give us no information about residents of the center. And she asked us to leave. We did.

On the way back from Newport, Sarah and I made a stop in Huntington Beach, five miles up the coast, to check out another address LexisNexis linked to Puliafito. It was an apartment in a large complex on Beach Boulevard called the Huntington Breakers, which was across the road from the address we had for Paul and Mary Ann Warren. Could Puliafito be living in the apartment there to be close to Sarah? Or maybe Sarah had been living there and he paid for it.

There were more than three hundred apartments at the Breakers, whose three-story buildings were arranged in barracks-like rows. Puliafito's name was on the directory in the main building; his apartment was on the first floor. Sarah and I found it and knocked. There were packages outside the door, but they weren't addressed to Puliafito or anyone else whose name we recognized from our records searches. The LexisNexis listing was four months old, so Puliafito could have moved, and management might have neglected to update the directory. Whatever the case, there was no sign of him.

The next morning, Matt Lait announced that he was leaving the *Times* to head an investigative unit at CNN. This was another body blow to the paper—the latest loss of a first-rate journalist who was departing because of what had become of the *Times* under Tribune and tronc. It also did not augur favorably for the USC team. Lait was the principal advocate for the story on the editing staff. He was the editor who would not relent when Maharaj killed it. We had two weeks before he was gone. All we could do was press on.

Security gates thwarted the reporting at Puliafito's mansion, at Nikias's estate, and now at the town house development off Beach Boulevard. If our information was correct, Paul and Mary Ann Warren lived in one of the town houses, which were built about a dozen years ago in a private community of trimmed palms and spotless sidewalks. With Sarah incommunicado in rehab, I decided it was time to reach out to her family. So Matt and I made another trip to Huntington Beach. And we encountered the gate. As a general rule, journalists were barred from entering a gated neighborhood unless they had a resident's permission. We could not walk in simply because the gate was briefly left open or, worse, by misrepresenting ourselves to a security guard, such as by claiming to work for a delivery service. Gates took away the element of surprise in door-knocking, and much of the human element as well. Asking a fearful person to speak to a newspaper was much easier face-to-face than over an intercom. But the latter was what Matt and I were left with. When I punched in the code for the Warren residence on the intercom panel, the call seemed to be forwarded to a cell phone. I didn't leave a message—too impersonal for this task.

Matt and I couldn't see the Warren home from outside the gate, so we were left to stake out the gate itself. If someone reasonably resembled the mother or father of a woman who looked like Sarah Warren, maybe we'd get the chance to approach him or her at the gate. Or we might catch a break and encounter another resident who would give us permission to enter. We stood there in the sea air and watched the town-housers come and go, most driving but a few walking. One woman behind the wheel looked old enough and blond enough to be Sarah's mom, but she drove out too quickly for an approach.

Just when it seemed hopeless, an older gentleman invited us to walk in with him. Another dash of luck would have one or both of the parents home. The two-story town houses were of contemporary design with hints of Mediterranean revival. The grounds around them were decked with flower beds. The neighborhood was not the type one would associate with street drugs and prostitution. Much of what we had found in social media and public records—setting aside the court dockets—suggested that the Warrens were an archetypical middle- to upper-middle-class Southern California family. They had moved here from Texas a couple of years ago, when Paul Warren began working as a vice president at a logistics company in Long Beach. Mary Ann Warren earned a master's degree from Pepperdine University and had worked in real estate and as an aesthetician. Sarah apparently had attended the University of Texas before the move, and it seemed a safe assumption that her younger brother, Charles, was either in college or college-bound. And they lived in a seven-figure town house a short stroll from the beach.

We knocked on the Warrens' door. No one answered, but then

a young man appeared in the doorway of the attached garage. He looked at us guardedly.

"Hi," I said. "Is this the Warren residence?"

"Who wants to know?" the young man said. He told us he was Charles Warren.

Matt and I said we were from the *Times*. That made Charles roll up the sleeve of his T-shirt to show us a tattoo. The ink read: "No Snitches."

Charles stayed true to the motto and wouldn't talk, but he promised to give our business cards to his parents. He seemed sincere. We had at least made contact with a member of the family. And since Paul and Mary Ann Warren would now know we wanted to speak to them, I called the numbers I found for them in LexisNexis and left voice messages. My calls weren't returned, although it was possible the numbers were bad. By the next day, the business cards we'd left with Charles had not yielded anything. So I headed back to the beach—Long Beach for this trip, and the company Paul Warren listed as his employer on LinkedIn. If Paul were a public figure or otherwise the subject of a story that involved his job, his workplace would have been one of my first stops. But, for the purposes of this story, we had no basis to believe that he was anything more than the father of a troubled young woman. We hadn't any way of knowing if he was even aware of Sarah's overdose, arrests, or ties to Puliafito and Voigt. That made a work visit tricky; I didn't want to embarrass Paul in front of his bosses. My hope was that I could discreetly ask for his help in communicating with Sarah.

The logistics company was in downtown Long Beach. It took security seriously; a guard presided over the lobby. Without identifying myself, I asked him if he could direct me to Paul Warren's office. No dice. He asked for my name and said he would let Paul know I was there. I did not tell him I was a reporter. As I waited for Paul, I stepped a few feet away from the security post to get a better view of the office layout. There wasn't one. But then Paul appeared, stepping off an elevator, a brown-haired man in his fifties, with a youth-ful countenance and posture; I recognized him from his LinkedIn photo. I introduced myself as a *Times* reporter, lowering my voice so the guard wouldn't hear me. Paul's face sagged with resignation; his eyes took on a mournful cast. He led me to an area near a stair-well, where we wouldn't be seen by the guard or anyone entering the lobby. I told him why I was there, that it was about Sarah, and he nodded and sighed as if he had known what I was going to say but still did not want to hear it. He said he had a good idea what I was after—*Did he know we were investigating Puliafito?*—but that he couldn't tell me anything and that this was a bad time for Sarah and for his family. I felt a pang of empathy. I thought again of my own daughters. I apologized to Paul for my presence, but I asked if I could pose just a few questions. I said we could speak confidentially. He thought about it for a moment and then agreed.

"Do you know a Carmen Puliafito?"

Paul looked down and shook his head—in a way to signal rancor, not to indicate he did not know him.

"Yeah, I know Carmen," he said. "I know who he is, too."

"What's his relationship to Sarah?"

Paul smiled slightly in disgust. "I guess Carmen would say she's his girlfriend. Or was his girlfriend."

He paused, and the smile vanished. "We tried everything to get that guy out of Sarah's life. Everything. I can't even tell you—for two years, we've tried. Rehab, thousands of dollars for rehab. She's in rehab now."

I nodded in sympathy. He seemed to be getting things off his chest.

"Really, I shouldn't be talking about this. Sarah's doing better now. That's all I care about."

I asked him about the overdose. His eyes saucered, and he shook his head again, this time in sorrow. Paul told me his daughter had been through hell but was doing well in rehab and that was his only focus.

"I have to get back to work," he said.

I gave him my card and asked if we could speak again. He said he would think about it.

I watched as Sarah's dad—he could be anyone's dad—walked slowly toward the elevator, his head low.

Paul's account was a breakthrough. It not only confirmed Puliafito's relationship with Sarah but characterized it as a long-standing one—two years, Paul said—that spanned the period of all her California arrests. The dean was sexually involved with a young, wayward addict who had a tendency to end up in jail. Through her, Puliafito was connected to an inveterate drug dealer, and we still had more leads to chase down. The circle of addicts and criminals that fanned out from Sarah to Puliafito was widening.

Our scrubs of court files, social media, and Venmo linked Sarah and the dean to a nude model named Dora Yoder, who had an arrest record for petty theft and drug possession. She appeared to have a boyfriend who was arrested for possessing heroin, a scale, and plastic baggies. We would try to locate and interview them, but Voigt came first. That required a visit to Men's Central Jail, where Voigt was being held on burglary charges. Talk about a captive audience. The jail was a mile from the newsroom, and Sarah Parvini and Adam drove over on the off chance Voigt would accept a visit from two strangers. Men's Central Jail looked suitably forbidding—a fifty-four-year-old pile of concrete slabs that seemed designed to repel the sun. Its sour innards were lined with old-fashioned tiers of cells. No wonder Voigt agreed to meet with Sarah and Adam; any visitor meant a break from the dungeon.

Voigt was thirty-seven, good looking in a wholesome way, with reddish-brown hair and blue eyes. He was staring down the likelihood of a multiyear sentence for his outstanding offenses. Voigt's criminal record dated to 2009 and followed his service in the navy as a photographer in Iraq and his years at the University of Illinois, where he earned a bachelor's degree. One of Voigt's former lawyers

told Adam that his client's descent into lawlessness was triggered by the post-traumatic stress disorder that stemmed from his time in the military. In the jail visiting room, Adam and Sarah sat on stools facing Voigt on the other side of thick plexiglass and spoke to him over the intercom phone. He acknowledged knowing Puliafito and referred to him alternately as "Tony" and "Carmen." Voigt also called him a "monster," particularly in terms of his relationship with Warren, which he described as "toxic."

Sarah and Adam asked about the other young women whom we determined Puliafito knew through social media, and Voigt confirmed that they all hung out together. "Carmen's always there," he said. But he clammed up when Sarah and Adam turned to questions of whether Puliafito bought drugs. Voigt did say that he and Warren's mother had compromising photos of Puliafito. He refused to describe the images further, although he said he might share them with the reporters when he got out of jail.

Voigt told Sarah and Adam the story they were after was "bigger than you probably know."

On the same day of the Voigt interview, I decided to poke Nikias again. I wrote an email for him with the 911 recording attached. My idea was to send it and then have Sarah and Matt, the Trojans, confront Nikias at his office an hour or so later. They were eager to do so. I'd showed a draft of the email to the team for their suggestions, and Harriet replied with this: "My only concern is that our work will be shut down internally before we can nail it completely if Nikias complains anew."

A good point. We'd been working for two weeks without the knowledge of Maharaj and Duvoisin, as far as we could tell, and I had to assume the email and the unannounced visit by Sarah and Matt might well generate another Nikias complaint, which could get the story killed again. But I was confident we now had enough, with Sarah's identity and her arrests and rehab stays, that Nikias would

see the wisdom in finally talking. I was confident but not certain. And as I mulled the prospect of Nikias cooperating, rather than complaining, I had to reflect again on how unreal and disturbing it was that I had to worry about the editor and managing editor of the *Times* getting in the way of the story.

Screw them. I sent the email a few minutes after nine on a Thursday morning. I wrote:

President Nikias—

Let me say once more that I hope you will make yourself available for an interview about the circumstances surrounding Carmen Puliafito's resignation as dean of the Keck School of Medicine.

My colleagues and I are reporting that, three weeks before he quit, Dr. Puliafito was a witness to the drug overdose of a 21-year-old woman in a Pasadena hotel room registered to him. This was on a weekday afternoon during the school term.

A Pasadena police report identifies Dr. Puliafito as the woman's "friend." A man recorded on a 911 call about the overdose, who sounds very much like Dr. Puliafito, describes himself as a doctor and the woman as his "girlfriend." (The 911 recording is attached.)

The woman was passed out and unresponsive. Paramedics took her to the hospital, where she recovered.

A police report states that methamphetamine was seized from the hotel room. The police confirmed to me that the woman overdosed on the drugs found in the room. As we have come to understand, the woman has a history of drug abuse and other problems, and her troubles escalated in the months after the overdose.

I have firsthand information that another witness to the overdose called your office and demanded that action be taken against Dr. Puliafito. Shortly afterward, Dr. Puliafito resigned.

I filled out the email with questions about the overdose, any contact USC had with Pasadena, and the celebration for Puliafito at Keck. I closed with: "Also, for the record, I have never followed you on Instagram, and I have no interest in your travel schedule."

If an email like that didn't persuade Nikias to engage with us, especially after it was punctuated by a visit to his office by two products of his own journalism school, then I was at a loss as to what would.

Sarah and Matt then headed to the campus. Once inside the bricked and towered confines of the Bovard Administration Building, they could not get past the layers of human buffers outside Nikias's door. Nikias's chief of staff, Dennis Cornell, emerged from the office to send the reporters on their way.

"President Nikias will not be speaking to the *Times* about this subject," Cornell told them.

And Nikias never responded to my email.

The following Monday, Grad emailed the team instructing everyone but me to return to their "regular knitting" and to send to me whatever material they had so I could write a new draft of the story. Then, Grad wrote, we would "regroup." *What the hell did that mean?* The team was on a roll; our reporting was opening the story up, making it bigger and better. We had more leads to pursue— the other young people around Puliafito, the photos Voigt mentioned, the UC San Diego case. But Grad's email suggested that the team had been discovered and, as Harriet feared, was about to be disbanded.

The email arrived just after Sarah and I made a stop in Altadena, a mountainside town on Pasadena's northern boundary. We were visiting the place that property records listed as the residence of Yoder, the nude model. It was a cabin-size house on Ventura Street in need of repairs and a front-yard cleanup. A woman who answered the door said Yoder was not there. She said she did not know where Yoder was and did not know when she would return. Sarah and I concluded we'd be making more than one visit to the house.

On my drive back to the newsroom, I called Lait to express my suspicion about Grad's directive to, in essence, break up the team. Lait was in a difficult position; he was a manager being asked to discuss another manager. But he confided that he'd learned Maharaj found out about the team and was pressuring Grad to take everyone off it except me. We didn't know if this resulted from a Nikias complaint, but the timing could hardly be more suspect. (Later, through his lawyer, Maharaj denied that he had Shelby remove reporters from the team.)

The next day, Matt excavated an October 2015 court record in which Voigt listed as a contact address the location of Puliafito's home in Pasadena. Matt informed the team in an email with the subject line, "Bingo." Yes, we had another link between the drug dealer and the dean—one that told us Voigt was so comfortable in his relationship with Puliafito that he felt he could use the doctor's address on a public document.

But then the following afternoon, after asking me to concentrate on writing a new draft of the story, Grad sent another email reinforcing the command for the other reporters to stand down. We ignored it—and continued digging. We were no longer a secret reporting team. Just an insubordinate one.

14

ECSTASY BEFORE THE BALL

amily therapy and the FBI. The FBI and family therapy.

Not a normal pairing. But in their grapple with Carmen Puliafito, normal for the Warrens was on the run.

I gave Paul Warren several days to get in touch; when he didn't, I called him and left a message, but I got no response. Then I heard from Mary Ann Warren. She was meeting with a family therapist, and it was actually the therapist who called my number and asked if Mary Ann could speak to me in confidence. I said yes, and she handed the phone to her. Mary Ann asked what I had planned to write and, in particular, how Sarah and the family would be portrayed in the *Times*. I replied that we were still reporting and wanted very much to hear the Warrens' side of the story. Mary Ann then began describing the trauma that Puliafito's relationship with Sarah had inflicted on the family. The therapist confirmed Mary Ann's account of trying repeatedly to extract Sarah from Puliafito's hold, including by informing the Pasadena and Newport Beach police that he was giving her drugs. With Mary Ann's permission, the therapist said, she reported Puliafito to the FBI; an agent followed up on the phone, but then Mary Ann got cold feet about speaking to her. Mary Ann told me she feared that the FBI, like the cops, would do nothing about Puliafito, and he would find a way to hurt the family if he learned she spoke to the agent. She agreed to meet with me the next day.

What I didn't mention to Mary Ann is that I had made contact with her husband. And since she didn't mention it to me, I assumed he hadn't told her. I had to maintain Paul's confidentiality, even from his wife.

We met at the Hilton in Huntington, whose twelve stories banked cliff-like above Pacific Coast Highway. I parked at a meter just across from the sand, a midafternoon wind snapping off the surf. Mary Ann was waiting for me in the lobby lounge, at a table near the back of the room. Her personality filled the space as soon as I introduced myself. She said Sarah and her husband did not know she was speaking to me, and over the next two and a half hours, she had me filling my notebook with the tale of Carmen Puliafito and the Warrens—a story that was, as Voigt hinted, far wilder than what we had imagined in the newsroom, and much more sordid than the court records and prostitution websites conveyed. Mary Ann spoke in electric torrents as she recounted how her A-student daughter had careened from the usual alcohol-drenched foolishness of late adolescence into a state of chemical-charged, risk-taking rebellion. She related how Sarah had run away from home, only to reappear with an addiction to methamphetamine and a boyfriend who was the sixty-four-year-old dean of the Keck School of Medicine.

She told me about the arrests and Sarah's failed attempts to get clean. And then she leaned in close to describe the time Puliafito delivered drugs to Sarah while she was in rehab in Malibu. I had to stop her there.

"You're saying he actually gave her drugs while she was *in* the rehab center?"

Mary Ann nodded fiercely. "And they caught him, and they kicked Sarah out."

"They *caught* him?"

I needed many more details about that, but Mary Ann was already on to another riveting episode. And then another and another. There were the times Puliafito Ubered meth and heroin to Sarah at their home. There was the time Mary Ann witnessed the dean himself using drugs. There was the time her son, Charles, wrecked Puliafito's knee.

"Carmen got him hooked on meth," she said of her son.

And there were the photos and videos—everything was on the photos and videos, she said. The drugs, the sex, *everything*.

"Wait—photos?" I said. "Videos?"

Mary Ann said she had found them on Sarah's computer—maybe hundreds altogether—and Puliafito was either in them or appeared to have shot them. She said she was so distraught at seeing the images of Sarah having sex with Puliafito that she called her husband at work and insisted he come home immediately; Paul did rush back from Long Beach, and she yelled at him to do something about the photos and videos—that he should *beat the shit out of Puliafito*. And when Paul reacted with less rage than she did, Mary Ann said, she screamed louder at him and slapped him. She said the noise caused a neighbor to call the police, and they arrived within minutes and arrested her for domestic violence, even though Paul begged them not to.

The cops weren't moved by what she had to tell them about the dean of USC's medical school, Mary Ann said.

I remembered we had found the domestic violence arrest during our search for court records on Sarah. Mary Ann was going on about how ridiculous it was, but I wanted to bring her back to the photos and videos—specifically, the ones portraying drug use. If we could get images of Puliafito doing illegal drugs or even being in the presence of Sarah doing them, Maharaj and Duvoisin would *have* to publish the story.

Right?

I made my pitch to Mary Ann about how important it was for me to see at least some of the drug images. I asked if there was any way she could get access to them again.

Mary Ann nodded. "I jacked Sarah's phone and computer and made copies."

I'm sure I failed to mask my excitement. I gave another little speech on the critical need for me to examine the images. I said I would conceal her identity as the source of them.

Mary Ann was silent for a moment.

"I'll think about it," she said.

Over the next three days, I kept in touch with Mary Ann by phone, nudging her to send me at least one of the most incriminating photos or videos. My nudges were gentle but persistent: "I know this is difficult, but it would really help us get the story out." And in her reluctance, Mary Ann wrestled out loud with her fears that if she gave me the images, Sarah would feel betrayed and violated—*How dare you, Mom! They belong to me!*—and Puliafito would seek retribution in some ghastly form.

To break the deadlock, I proposed that the *Times,* in addition to maintaining her anonymity, would merely describe the images and not publish them. Mary Ann was satisfied with that arrangement. She said she would search the cache of photos and videos for a "good one." I didn't hear from her again that day and reached out the following morning. Late that afternoon, we spoke by phone, and she said she sent a photo to my work email. It didn't arrive. I asked her to resend it to my phone.

A few minutes later, *there it was:* a photo of Puliafito using a butane lighter to fire up a large white meth pipe, which was pressed against his lips like a hungry squid. He wore an elaborately flowered, open-collared shirt and appeared to be enjoying himself. And the markings on the photo showed it was a still shot from a video.

I asked Mary Ann to send more from the video. She delivered six more stills; in the last three, Puliafito was languidly exhaling meth smoke. The video itself would follow, Mary Ann promised—and it did.

I shared the images with the team. We all had the same reaction: *Holy shit!*

And I thought, *How could the* Times *not publish this story ASAP?*

I sent my beginnings of a draft of the new story to Harriet for her to do what we call *rewrite*, meaning that she would craft the narrative from the reporting of the other team members (in addition to her own). We all tossed around ideas for how to lead the piece, to quickly illustrate the stark contrast between Puliafito's exalted station in his profession and his secret life; USC's website helped with photos of him attending glitzy soirées for Keck. Harriet's first take:

> *Carmen Puliafito, the dean of USC's Keck Medical School, arrived at the gala fundraiser at the Beverly Wilshire Hotel a year and a half ago with the confidence of a man totally in his element.*
>
> *He moved through the crowd of celebrities such as Pierce Brosnan and Don Henley and wealthy school donors like Dana and David Dornsife, shaking hands, posing for photos and delivering the message that had become a refrain in his eight years in office: USC was climbing into the ranks of the country's most elite research institutions.*
>
> *In the less refined setting of the Van Nuys courthouse a few days earlier, a convicted methamphetamine and heroin dealer named Kyle Voigt was told to write his contact information on a court form. The address he scrawled was a sprawling $5 million mansion in one of Pasadena's toniest neighborhoods: Puliafito's residence.*
>
> *The Oct. 5, 2015 Superior Court record hinted at a troubling side of Puliafito, 66, rarely seen. A Times investigation found that while Puliafito was running the medical school and collecting a*

salary of $1 million a year, he was using drugs and associating
with a group of much younger drug addicts and criminals. Pho-
tographs and videos reviewed by The Times show him smoking
from the type of pipe commonly used to smoke methamphet-
amine.

And then Mary Ann called me to say that Puliafito had contacted her. He wanted to meet her—*Lunch tomorrow?*—so they could talk about Sarah. Mary Ann said he mentioned in a dark way something about the *Times.* I could hear the apprehension in her voice as she speculated that Puliafito had somehow learned that she had spoken to me. Should she be afraid?

Each time she and Paul turned to a third party for help in dislodging him from their family, Puliafito had prevailed. The Huntington Beach police had taken no interest in him. Neither did the Pasadena cops—and not just after responding to Sarah's overdose. Mary Ann told me of a second incident in Pasadena: Sarah had dropped from sight again but then let Charles know where in Pasadena she was staying. It was another apartment Puliafito had rented for her. Paul and Mary Ann drove up from Huntington in hopes of persuading Sarah to return home. They worried that she would refuse to even speak to them, so they brought Charles along as "bait" to get her to at least open her door. That worked—and what they found terrified them. Sarah appeared to be strung out on drugs. Kyle was there, and Mary Ann spotted a bag of heroin and a scale on a table. Sarah told them to get out. *Leave now!* No one had to tell Kyle that; he dashed out the door with the heroin and scale like the felon on parole he happened to be. Sarah locked herself in a room and screamed at them to go. Paul and Mary Ann were beside themselves. They called the Pasadena suicide hotline and pleaded for help; they believed they'd get a quicker response from the hotline than from the police. But then two police officers arrived with a man Paul and Mary Ann were told was a nurse. Paul and Mary Ann told them about Kyle and

Puliafito and the heroin and the meth. The nurse was sympathetic, the officers not so much. A third cop showed up and persuaded Sarah to let him into the room so they could talk. After some minutes, he emerged from the room and told Paul and Mary Ann their daughter insisted that they leave and they should do just that.

"The problem is you and you," the cop said, pointing to Paul and Mary Ann.

They left without Sarah.

Was it any surprise Puliafito was confident enough—cocky enough—to now propose a meeting with Mary Ann, even knowing the *Times* was circling?

"What do you think I should do?" she said to me.

But even as she asked, Mary Ann seemed to be talking herself into it. She felt she could convince him she was not speaking to me. He was arrogant, she said, and that made him susceptible to believing whatever he wanted to hear, including that someone as powerless as she was wouldn't dare betray him. And maybe she could learn what his intentions were for Sarah once she got out of rehab. Mary Ann believed he would be waiting for her daughter with drugs.

After she decided to meet Puliafito, I considered the possibilities for the story. I could confront him before or after the lunch with a few questions, maybe take a photo or two. That might yield a bit more color for the story, but it was unlikely Puliafito would impulsively spill his secrets. I could stay out of sight and leave it to Mary Ann to ask certain questions—particularly about providing her children with drugs—with the aim of eliciting incriminating statements from him. They would be natural questions to ask, and I believed Mary Ann could pull it off, but then whatever he said would come from her as a secondhand account. Not ideal for publication. Of course, in the perfect scenario, Mary Ann could surreptitiously record their meeting; in California, though, it was illegal to record someone in such a situation without the person's permission. There were narrow exceptions to the prohibition, including ambient recordings made in a public place where a person did not have a reasonable expectation of privacy. A restaurant was a public place. Could I legally record the lunch from an adjoining table? Just let my phone pick up Mary Ann's conversation with Puliafito along with the other sounds in the restaurant? Would my intent to home in on that conversation remove any legal protections? That seemed like a risk, so I consulted Glasser, the newsroom attorney. He didn't like the idea.

Okay, but what if I just *overheard* the conversation from that table? Eavesdropped? And took notes? There was some discussion of that, and we all agreed it would be within the law.

But I couldn't be the one with my ears trained at the next table. Puliafito knew that I was investigating him; I had to assume he'd googled me and found my photo. If he recognized me, that could be bad for Mary Ann. But he had no reason to suspect anyone else at the *Times* was on his trail. None of the other reporters had contacted him, the Warrens, or anyone else close to him, except for the visit with Voigt, and he was still in jail. So I came up with a plan to have Sarah Parvini and Adam do the listening—if it was logistically possible. They could pose as a couple out for a leisurely lunch. As always, two reporters were better than one in case there developed any dispute over what was said.

First, I had to get Mary Ann to agree. That was the easy part—she was *enthusiastic* about it. Now, if we had any hope of success, Puliafito would have to let her choose the place and time. That would allow us to set things up. The restaurant would have to be large enough to ensure there would be many tables available and the lunch would have to be unusually early—say, eleven thirty—to guarantee that two adjoining tables would be empty.

Mary Ann came through on those counts. Lunch was at eleven thirty at Bluegold, a cavernous steak-and-seafood restaurant in a higher-end Huntington Beach mall called Pacific City. Sarah, Adam, and I got there at eleven. I drove separately and parked outside the mall, a block from Pacific Coast Highway. As I awaited reports from my colleagues via texts, I ran through all the things that could go wrong: Puliafito could smell a rat as soon as he walked into the dining room. Or as soon as Sarah and Adam sat down within earshot. That was if a table close enough to hear anything actually was available. The mall seemed busy for a weekday morning. And what if Mary Ann got nervous and said something that blew everyone's cover?

But it was St. Patrick's Day. I had to bank on the luck of my Irish heritage.

Mary Ann texted me a few minutes before 11:00 A.M.: "He msg he'll be there at 11:45—druggie," she wrote, meaning Puliafito was running late and probably because he was wasted. "I'll meet ur pp in Bar—leaving in 10."

She did connect with Sarah and Adam in the restaurant bar. "Here," Mary Ann texted me. "Made contact . . . Have booth next to us—it's rounded so they can hear."

Beautiful.

Sarah and Adam took the booth and sat side by side with their backs to Puliafito, nearly close enough to bump heads with him. Puliafito had the bleary, washed-out appearance of someone coming off a bender. Sarah and Adam ordered shakshuka and shared it, as a couple would. Mary Ann and Puliafito seemed to be sticking to drinks.

And the plan worked perfectly. The lunch stretched out for *three hours*. Mary Ann was masterful in steering Puliafito to subjects he would have been smart to avoid. He was evasive when her questions backed him into a corner, but he copped to more than enough to establish that he'd had a long-term relationship with Sarah that centered largely around drugs that he paid for.

When Mary Ann said that he gave her daughter drugs, Puliafito said, "I gave her the money. I could have cut her off."

He said he still wanted to "help" Sarah: "I thought, she's so nice, she's so smart . . . and then I couldn't stop helping her."

My two colleagues kept pace with their notes.

"Guess what? I did stupid things with Sarah," Puliafito said. "Sarah had a hold over me."

As the lunch went on, he said, "I was in love."

Mary Ann prodded him about the overdose. He said he found Sarah passed out when he went to the Hotel Constance to check on her.

"When you see someone passed out, you call 911," Mary Ann said, in the manner of an accusation.

"I'm glad I did what I did," Puliafito said vaguely, "and I didn't try to make a big deal out of it."

Then he added, "Reporters think that's why I stepped down."

Mary Ann told him that Sarah had overdosed five times in his presence. He didn't deny it but said, "Sarah was one to never blame somebody else for her problems. She never blamed me for anything. She was grateful to me."

Returning to the overdose at the Constance, Mary Ann said, "You and the Pasadena Police Department, man . . . they've given you a lot of grace."

She paused. "What did they say when they called you?"

"You can make restitution," Puliafito said. And then: "Some reporter said I tried to cover up the 911 call."

Sarah and Adam were texting me bits and pieces of the exchanges. I was rapt as I sat alone in the car. They also texted a selfie of them with Puliafito visible in the background.

Mary Ann told Puliafito the staff at Creative Care said he brought Sarah drugs there: "Carmen Puliafito came at 4:00 A.M. and delivered meth." Again, he didn't deny it. She returned to that topic a little later, and he acknowledged that two or three people were kicked out of the rehab center because of it.

Puliafito vented now and then and indulged in self-pity. He told Mary Ann he didn't make Sarah an addict and "should get some freaking credit for sending her" to rehab. And he warned her about reporters from the *Times* chasing after him. "Never talk to 'em," Puliafito said. His voice barbed with suspicion, he added, "Are you sure you aren't talking to them?"

"Why would I throw my daughter under the bus?" Mary Ann replied.

15

HAZEL AND WILLY

Another weapon we could use in our fight for publication was evidence that Puliafito's behavior was part of a pattern. That meant tracking down more of the people he and Sarah consorted with. Our search of court records and social media had told us that the real name of the tattooed woman from Puliafito's Facebook page was not Sarah More. I'll call her Hazel here because identifying her might only compound the upset in her life. She was twenty-four when we found her, and she had a nineteen-year-old husband I'll call Willy. Hazel's public records footprint belied her young age. She had been arrested for possession of meth in a lockup, grand theft auto, and a variety of prostitution offenses. Willy also had an arrest sheet for assaulting an uncle with a rake and twice battering Hazel. Somehow, the couple knew Puliafito even though they lived way out in Riverside, more than fifty miles away. The idea of the Harvard-educated dean driving that far to hook up with two small-time criminals would have seemed unbelievable not long before. Adam had gotten their address from a Riverside cop, who said Willy had been arrested at the house three times. We drove out for an unannounced visit.

Willy answered our knock at the door. He was thin and pale and marked with his own full inventory of tattoos. After we introduced ourselves as *Times* reporters, Willy smiled in the way people do when they sense trouble.

"What's up?" he said.

When we said we wanted to speak to him about Puliafito, Willy stepped out onto the porch and kept smiling. Hazel appeared behind him and peered over his shoulder; she was instantly recognizable by the carpet of tattoos. And she was visibly pregnant.

The interview that followed was a sad little feint and parry. Hazel and Willy did their best to cover for Puliafito, but with enough jailbird wisdom to understand that if they denied knowing him or painted too rosy a picture of him, nothing they said would be believed. So they acknowledged that the dean of the big medical school up in L.A. was their pal and that Hazel had met him maybe four years earlier.

"He's one of my best friends," Hazel said.

Every week or two, she said, Puliafito made the hour-plus drive from L.A. to pick her up in his Porsche. They'd go to the local Coffee Bean for some conversation, Hazel said. Sometimes, she said, he'd drive her to Pasadena, where she would house-sit for him or stay a couple of nights at the Hilton. We asked if she knew a Sarah Warren, and Hazel said yes—they had met at that same hotel.

Hazel and Willy said Puliafito spent generous amounts of money on them—more than $10,000 altogether. They told us they really needed the help because they had been living in a dry riverbed before they managed to rent this house. Puliafito also bought them marijuana, they said.

We asked if Puliafito ever bought them hard drugs or paid Hazel for sex. They said he never did. It was just a friendship, they assured us.

There wasn't much point in pressing them. We had confirmed what we had come for—that Puliafito's arrangement with Sarah was not an isolated rendezvous with prostitutes and drugs. And while Hazel and Willy had criminal records, as Sarah did, they were sympathetic in a broader sense: Puliafito exploited them for his rank pleasures, and they were willing to let it happen for the cash and gifts they took in trade. But the cash didn't last, and the flash of the gifts faded soon enough. And when he was done with them, Puliafito returned to his million-dollar job and his mansion in Pasadena, and Hazel and Willy had to keep hustling to stay out of the riverbed.

The next day brought another breakthrough. Mary Ann agreed to show me the rest of the photos and videos she'd found on Sarah's laptop and phone. She said she would meet me at the Hyatt Regency in Huntington Beach that evening. I was profuse in my thanks and said I would bring along Sarah Parvini. Then Mary Ann said she had told her husband she was speaking to me, only to be told the same thing by him. *Awkward.* I apologized for the surprise and explained that I had to maintain confidences, even between spouses.

Later in the day, Mary Ann texted to say Paul and the family therapist would also be in the meeting. A conference room—the Pelican Room—was booked for us.

"We just want to do what's right," she wrote.

Sarah and I drove down together. The Hyatt was a short block from the Hilton on Pacific Coast Highway. The cool of the evening was settling in, the sun low over the water and dimmed by streaks of clouds. When we entered the Pelican Room, Mary Ann and the therapist, a middle-aged woman who wanted to remain anonymous, were seated at a table. Paul was pacing back and forth. After we exchanged greetings, Paul said, "I just found out today you and Mary Ann have been talking. It's a little embarrassing." I offered the same apology I gave his wife, except now it had a rueful quality. We got down to business: On the table were the laptop and hard drive. The meeting was off the record, and we could take the devices with us to examine the images, but we did not have permission to publish them. The therapist reinforced how difficult the situation was for the family, how agonizing the past two years had been for them, and how our reporting might be their best hope for keeping Puliafito away from Sarah and Charles, since nothing else had worked.

Paul told us about Charles's attempts to protect his sister, including the time he smashed Puliafito's knee. To demonstrate, Paul thrust his foot into my knee, the one still healing from a replacement; the kick wasn't hard, but the pain it caused had me guzzling air. I explained the reason for my gaspy reaction, and it became funny, a mood lifter. Sarah and I sat down to ask questions and take notes. The session went well, and we left with the jackpot of images. Sarah and Adam began scrolling through them that night—there were dozens and dozens—and Matt pitched in the following morning.

It was all there in the photos and videos. One video showed Puliafito and Sarah in a room at the Hotel Constance the night before the overdose; it was date-stamped, and we pinpointed the location by reviewing promotional photos online of the hotel's rooms. In the video, Sarah asks Puliafito to help her crush some meth to prepare a "hot rail," a method of snorting the drug.

"Absolutely," Puliafito says. Warren later bends over lines of white powder on a tray.

A video shot the day after the overdose, at another hotel, features Sarah saying she overdosed on GHB at the Constance. "Carmen saved my life," she says. In another video, Sarah and Puliafito "shotgun" meth—she takes a hit from a pipe, and as she exhales, Puliafito sucks in the smoke that streams from her mouth.

A photo time-stamped around 3:00 A.M. shows Voigt and Warren in Puliafito's office at Keck. Voigt is wearing an inflatable Trojan hat and a lab coat embroidered with the dean's name. Voigt and Warren are holding pieces of aluminum foil that were blackened from smoking heroin. In other photos, Voigt is behind the wheel of Puliafito's vintage Mercedes, with a piece of foil in his lap; the doctor is behind him in the back seat.

The brazenness and recklessness Puliafito displayed in allowing himself to be filmed and photographed was gobsmacking. These were not recordings made without his knowledge or when he was incapable of consenting. He was smiling in many of the images, sometimes in a provoking manner—daring whoever might be watching to try to do something about his behavior.

He apparently did not object when, in one filmed bit, Sarah looks into the camera to say that she and Puliafito were making a "good old-fashioned doing-drugs video."

One filmed sequence stood out in the way that it bridged the two lives Puliafito was leading. He is dressed in a tuxedo, ready to head off to an event where he would mingle with other moneyed elites—a museum opening or another USC fundraiser, such as the ones where he posed for photos with Warren Beatty and Jay Leno and Pierce Brosnan and tech billionaire Larry Ellison. In the video, Puliafito eyes the camera with aplomb, shows an orange pill plopped on his tongue, and says, "Thought I'd take an Ecstasy before the ball."

And he swallows: The dean of the Keck School of Medicine of the University of Southern California. The stamp-collecting sugar daddy of a troubled young woman named Sarah Ann Warren from Spring, Texas.

Two days later, on a Saturday, Paul Warren called me. He was driving with his daughter, during a day trip from Ocean Recovery. Sarah was ready to speak to me, Paul said. On the record.

I grabbed my notebook, Paul gave Sarah his phone, and we started from the beginning.

16

DISAPPEARING THE WHISTLEBLOWER

A blockbuster.

That's what the Puliafito story had become by the last week of March in 2017. Sarah Warren held nothing back in her interviews with me. She recounted in granular detail her twenty-one months of drugging with Puliafito and of trading her body for the narcotics he provided to her. The photos and videos were a visual documentation of her story. More corroboration came from the interviews with Sarah's parents and the eavesdropping mission at Bluegold. I found Don Stokes through Mary Ann, whom he had contacted to check on Sarah's well-being. Stokes also went on the record about Puliafito. And so did Charles Warren. Charles's statement that he was a minor when Puliafito first gave him drugs appeared to be the most damaging allegation for the dean and USC.

Harriet rewrote the draft to include the new material. Grad edited it and sent it to Duvoisin. I had added a couple of lines from my interviews with medical ethicists who commented on Puliafito's bad behavior. Two of them happened to say during the interviews that the *Times* had an obligation to disclose the information we had about Puliafito as soon as possible because he was still treating patients. They were right. I couldn't tell them of my concern that the story might sit unpublished for weeks or months under Maharaj and Duvoisin, if they ran it at all.

I was also mindful that the Warrens were still dealing with Puliafito and that they were worried that Kyle Voigt might cause them trouble when he got out of jail. And I kept worrying that another media outlet would beat us on the story.

So I sent this email to Duvoisin on April 6, 2017:

Marc—

The ethicists I interviewed made the valid point that, because Puliafito is still treating patients, we have a responsibility to share our findings with the public as soon as possible. So I hope we can avoid any further delays in publishing this important and shocking story.

There are other reasons. I have earned the trust of the Warren family, beginning with Sarah's parents, and they see publication of the story as the end of their two-year nightmare with Puliafito.

Lately, Puliafito has been calling the Warrens late at night, warning them not to speak to me. They are worried he could go off the rails. In the past, he has made threats of violence.

The drug dealer in the story, Kyle Voigt, posted bail a few days ago (Puliafito probably paid for the bond), and is on the loose. The family considers him a threat as well.

I filed the original story more than five months ago. If it had run within any reasonable length of time, the deeper findings in the new story—and likely much more—would have been published by now in the form of follow-ups. I would have heard from the

Warrens after the first story landed, and Puliafito would have been out of business in short order.

Also, it's either a miracle of luck or just a sad commentary on the state of our competition that no other news outlet has reported at least a piece of the story, considering the number of cages we've rattled.

Duvoisin replied about two and a half hours later:

Paul:

The new and much-improved story was given to me a few days ago. I read it last night, will it [*sic*] again tonight, and will follow up with any questions.

Best,
Marc

And from that point on, Duvoisin went back into delay-and-dilute mode. He effusively complimented our work (which we had learned did not necessarily mean anything in terms of publication) and returned the copy to Grad peppered with his questions and suggestions. We addressed every issue he raised quickly and thoroughly, and Grad sent the draft back to him. And then days passed with no word for the reporters from Duvoisin, although Grad had dealt with a few more questions from him and told us the story was close to the "final lawyering" stage, the review by Glasser that typically was the last major step before publication. I wasn't convinced of that, and I told Glasser that I feared the story would remain buried for months like the one that was killed. If that happened, I said, I would complain formally to Tribune's corporate office—specifically, the general counsel and HR—and highlight the concerns I laid out in my email to Duvoisin. I said this to Glasser knowing that he would inform Duvoisin and Maharaj of my intentions, as he should. Glasser didn't tell me he would do that, but he didn't disappoint.

The result was this email from Duvoisin:

Paul:

After receiving a copy of the story last week, I read and returned it to Shelby. He gave me a new version, and I returned it to him over the weekend with some questions.

Last night, he delivered to me some supporting materials I had asked to see.

The story is vastly improved with all the new reporting. I am very excited about publishing it. I have briefed Davan, and he is very excited.

No one is ignoring the story or trying to keep it from being published. But it is a complicated story, with a large quantity of new material, and it needs close scrutiny and careful editing.

I'm willing to commit the effort but first I need a reciprocal commitment from you. Drop by at your convenience, and I'll explain what it is.
Marc

I wanted to believe that he and Maharaj were excited about publishing the story, but the taunting line about it requiring "close scrutiny and careful editing"—which story wouldn't?—read like Duvoisin was laying the ground for something I and the other reporters would not like. Worse was his stating that his commitment to the story was *conditional*, that it depended on whether he received some unspecified reciprocation from me. I couldn't believe he would put something like that in writing. Duvoisin's commitment to publishing a story of significant importance to our readers should be based solely on the soundness of the journalism.

I walked into his office as soon as he was free that day. Once the door was closed, he all but shouted at me, and I learned what he expected in return for committing himself to the story: my promise to never take any ethical complaints to HR. He said he respected me a great deal, but that I had violated some sort of trust by threatening to go to HR about a newsroom matter.

"The newsroom handles its own problems," Duvoisin said, his owlish face blanched with anger. "We do not involve HR."

I told him it wasn't smart to pressure employees not to report ethical concerns to HR, which company policy required us to do. Duvoisin was unmoved. He brought up the demand I'd made for legal representation separate from Maharaj and him after they killed the original story. In doing that, Duvoisin said, I had created a "toxic relationship" between me and them.

Long ago, I had become used to Duvoisin's passive-aggressive behavior, his way of using hollow praise to set you up for a negative experience. But I had never seen him like this—his voice on the edge of a scream as he slapped his desk and jabbed his fingers and denounced me as a traitor of sorts. I wanted to give it back to him at full volume; I didn't because I believed that would only imperil the story further. He had summoned me in expectation of a trade-off: essentially my silence in exchange for his promise not to put the brakes to the story. So I told him I did not intend to complain to HR. That appeared to placate him, and the meeting ended.

And then Duvoisin took the story away from Grad and gave it to the paper's newly hired investigations editor, Matt Doig. Duvoisin was restarting the editing process *from scratch*. I and the other reporters protested, noting that Grad had been shepherding the story since Lait had left, that he knew the material inside and out, and that the story had already been edited four or five times. Duvoisin replied that Grad was "too busy" to handle the story, which was news to

Grad. It seemed evident that this was Duvoisin's way of punishing me for raising the ethical concerns. And if that meant our readers would be denied timely publication of the story, and if it meant Puliafito and his enablers at USC could carry on without public exposure for more weeks and months, that appeared to be okay with Duvoisin.

In the midst of the fight over the story, and with the knowledge and support of a few colleagues, I mailed a letter on *Times* stationery to Dr. Patrick Soon-Shiong, expressing the hope that he would become the next owner of the newspaper—that is, Ferro and tronc had to be run out of L.A. if the *Times* were to survive.

Soon-Shiong was a billionaire physician on the strength of his advances in cancer-treating drugs. He had been interested in buying the *Times* in the past and controlled the second-largest number of shares in tronc stock after Ferro. The year before, Ferro had invited him to invest in the company to fend off a takeover by the Gannett newspaper chain. But the relationship between the two men soured after Soon-Shiong took exception to Ferro's lavish spending of shareholder money, including on his private jet. Ferro had recently maneuvered to have Soon-Shiong kicked off the company's board of directors.

The letter I sent was unsigned—I was certain tronc would fire anyone associated with such a gambit—but I wrote that its sentiments reflected those of the vast majority of the newsroom staff, which I and others believed to be true. Those sentiments included a lack of faith in Maharaj.

I had no way of knowing if the letter had reached Soon-Shiong personally or if he had received similar missives and pleadings from inside the *Times.* Meanwhile, another effort to save the paper was unfolding: a covert campaign to organize the first-ever labor union in the newsroom. It was launched by three staffers in their twenties— graphics reporter Jon Schleuss, data journalist Anthony Pesce, and business writer Natalie Kitroeff. They then brought me into their core group because I had organized a newsroom union at the start of my career.

Much like the USC reporting team in the first weeks, the leaders of the union drive proceeded in secret because of fears they would face retaliation if their efforts became known to the *Times* bosses and tronc executives.

It was apparent that Maharaj and Duvoisin hired Doig because of the hits they took in the *Los Angeles Magazine* piece. To Maharaj and Duvoisin, the problem with the number and pace of *Times* investigations wasn't them but the staff, and Doig seemed to approach his role as someone brought in to whip us into shape. In my first meeting with him, he told me the USC piece was "a good story but not a great story." *What?* I asked him why, in his view, it fell short, and he said it was because Puliafito wasn't an elected official. That threw me, and I suggested to him it was even worse—and more newsworthy—for the dean of a prominent medical school to be using and trafficking in dangerous drugs than for a politician, especially when the dean was performing delicate eye surgeries between meth binges. Doig assured me I was wrong.

Our relationship went downhill from there, and his dealings with the reporting team overall became strained with his first reedit of the story. It was actually a rewrite more than an edit, and he would do many more. Normally, edits are done in close collaboration with the writers, but that wasn't Doig's method, at least not on the USC story. He behaved more like an enforcer than a colleague—again, someone whose principal task was to correct deficiencies among the reporters. He was quick to lash out when we disagreed with him; he snapped at me to "knock it off" when I offered the opinion that his rewrite of the first paragraphs of the story diminished its scope. And while assessing the quality of writing is inherently a subjective exercise, and there is always more than one way to artfully craft any story, we found Doig's work on the USC piece to fall below the *Times*'s standards for publication. We complained in writing to Duvoisin about that as well as Doig's uncollaborative behavior. Duvoisin ignored the complaints but did not propose that Doig's re-rendering of the story was fit for publication.

The more we exhorted him to restore the draft to acceptable form and get it into the paper, the more Duvoisin engaged in his signature form of insincerity: He assured us that he and Doig were committed to publishing the story, but he did little or nothing to advance it week after week. Instead, he emailed us questions on occasion. Most of them could have been asked and answered within minutes or hours of when the first draft was filed back in late March. Others had been answered in material that Doig cut from the copy. None posed a fundamental challenge to any of our reporting. Duvoisin returned to his robotic line that the story had to undergo a "careful edit" and "legal review," which was like noting that it would need a headline.

We reminded him repeatedly that Puliafito was still treating and operating on patients and remained a threat to the Warren family. Duvoisin responded with silence. And by injecting Doig into the edit, and through his own tactics, Duvoisin did a favor for USC, deliberately or not, because the resulting delays guaranteed the story did not run during the *Times* Festival of Books, which the paper staged on the university campus, or during May commencement, which featured Will Ferrell as the main speaker. The Nikias administration would not have wanted those events tarnished by our findings about the former Keck dean. Tommy Trojan, my insider source, told me that word had circulated among Nikias's lieutenants that an embarrassing story might be coming, but not until after the end of the school year. How anyone at USC could know that was beyond me. It did not come from the reporters. I had to wonder if someone on the masthead was leaking information about the story.

The calendar bedeviled us as the edit, or this perversion of an edit, devolved into daily combat as we tried to inch the story toward publication. It was easy for us to forget that in a healthy newsroom, the situation would've been the opposite, with the reporters and editors working collegially to get the best possible story into print as soon as possible. But so much of that had become a quaint memory at the *Times*—nostalgia. All we could hope for is that the story would be published someday and in a state that would not mortify us. Our world was upside down.

Not once during those months of edits did Duvoisin meet with us to brainstorm ways to make the story stronger, to heighten its impact and importance—to look beyond Puliafito's conduct for evidence that his superiors, including Nikias, knew about his behavior and covered it up. That was what editors typically do and what Duvoisin had done on other stories. This was another break from the norm.

And from the time Duvoisin turned it over to Doig, not a single change had been made to the copy that we believed improved it in a significant way. Substantive deletions imposed on the draft benefited Puliafito, Nikias, and USC. First, the section on Puliafito's success in poaching grant-funded researchers from other schools and USC's dogfight with UC San Diego over the Alzheimer's lab—the potential motive for the Nikias administration to protect Puliafito—was cut in half. Next, the paragraphs on Hazel and Willy, which showed that Puliafito's relationship with Sarah Warren pointed to a longer-term penchant for associating with young criminals, were excised in full.

Then Duvoisin deleted the passage about the unnamed whistleblower—Devon Khan. Gone was the fact that Khan called Nikias's office to report that Puliafito had been at the scene of the overdose. Just like that, Duvoisin let Nikias off the hook: As far as the reader would know, the call had never happened. It was telling that Duvoisin made the deletion without following the newsroom editing protocol of marking it with strikethroughs so that the reporters would see it and perhaps question it. He just disappeared the whistleblower.

The reporters decided immediately that this was something we would refuse to accept, no matter the consequences. We demanded a meeting with Duvoisin and Doig to raise our objections. And if we didn't prevail at the meeting, if the whistleblower's call was not restored, we were prepared to withhold our bylines from the story in protest, which none of us had done before. Pulling our bylines would signify to our colleagues in the newsroom and our peers in the news business, in addition to media-savvy readers, that the reporters did not approve of the published story.

The meeting took place in Duvoisin's office the following day, and it became contentious almost before we could take our seats. Adam, the rookie on the reporting team, with less than a year at the paper, looked Duvoisin in the eye and said, "Cutting the whistleblower is unethical."

Duvoisin glared at him, but Adam did not flinch. The level expressions of Harriet and Sarah and Matt likewise offered Duvoisin no refuge. The managing editor was boxed in. Doig couldn't help him. From the start of his involvement in the edits, Doig had said the whistleblower was vital to the story. He retreated from that position only after Duvoisin's deletion.

And next, Duvoisin changed the rules. He said Khan had to be removed from the story because he was a single anonymous source. I was dumbfounded. The *Times* had a written policy about such sources, and my use of Khan landed squarely within it: He had a legitimate need to remain anonymous (he would be fired if identified); his information was firsthand; he had proved truthful on other, related matters; and nothing else in the reporting had cast doubt on his reliability. I had lost count of the number of times I interviewed him, going over his story again and again, and he never veered from even the smallest detail of the events and actions he recalled. And whenever I had documentation to check his information against—such as the Pasadena police and city attorney records, as well as the 911 recording—it supported him 100 percent. In his flailing attempts to defend eliminating the whistleblower, Duvoisin pointed out that the documentation did not include a phone record. I said I would get it. But what cut through the back-and-forth about the whistleblower and sourcing were comments by Duvoisin that suggested we ease up on Nikias—because the story, without the whistleblower, was already damaging enough for him.

"As it is, Max Nikias is going to have a bad day," Duvoisin said. "It will be the worst day of Max Nikias's life."

He seemed to be pleading for leniency for the president of a powerful institution who may have covered up wrongdoing that posed a threat to the public.

Harriet stood from her chair and gave Duvoisin a lacerating look. "What you just said is very disturbing," she told him.

She spoke for all of us. The meeting was over. As we left his office, we advised Duvoisin that we would explore our "options," the implication being that we were considering a complaint to the corporate office. He said nothing.

We regrouped in Grad's office and returned to the discussion of withholding our bylines from the story, presuming it never would be published. Grad implored us not to pull our names, because that would give Duvoisin and Maharaj an excuse, however dishonest, not to run the story. We saw Grad's point.

The next day, Duvoisin ordered Harriet and Adam to his office and more or less disciplined them for raising the ethical issue about the whistleblower, saying they were "out of line." But Duvoisin must have taken to heart the implicit threat of a corporate complaint because he restored the whistleblower the day after that. He offered the laughable explanation that he had now realized how central Khan was to the story. It so happened that I had secured from Khan the phone record showing his six-minute call to Nikias's office. But that seemed to no longer be a priority for Duvoisin.

Summer was approaching. We had sent Grad the draft of the story in the second week of spring. The Warrens were on the verge of giving up on the story. They were considering hiring a lawyer to take a complaint to USC about Puliafito, who still hadn't been exposed in the pages of the *Times*. He could be back in their lives at any moment. He already was in touch about paying some of Sarah's lingering bills from her crash-and-burn months with him. What if he started bothering her again?

I'd hoped the Warrens would not get an attorney until after the story ran. Lawyers frequently counseled their clients to not talk to reporters. But I couldn't fault the Warrens if they retained an attorney and cut me off; they had been more than patient. And since I could not share with them any of the internal newsroom conflicts, they could not fathom what was taking so long. All I could do was appeal to them for more time.

17

PULIAFITO STORY EXPLODES

Anger was now my routine, the stamp of my personality. I woke up angry, I arrived at the newsroom angry, and I came home angry. Editors who were supposed to be my colleagues, who were supposed to support me in pursuing the paper's journalism mission, had become a barrier to that mission. I knew the other reporters felt the same way. I hoped it didn't grind at them as much as it did me, especially after hours, but there was no minimizing it.

And I continued to allow my anger to tax the patience and understanding of my family. Then one night, during another dinner made less pleasant by my ranting and raging, my daughters, Rachel and Mariah, told me to stop bitching about what was happening at the paper and *do* something about it. I mentioned, again, the possibility of filing a formal complaint to corporate.

"So why don't you," Rachel said. She didn't frame it as a question. Mariah concurred with a sigh of exasperation.

That night, I began writing the complaint. I worked on it off and on for nearly three weeks and showed drafts to the USC reporters and a few others in the newsroom for feedback. There was no guarantee that filing a complaint against the top editors would not backfire at the cost of my job; tronc's corporate leaders weren't winning plaudits for their commitment to journalism. I consulted a lawyer about what I should expect. He said it would not be uncommon for the company to stand behind Maharaj and Duvoisin and treat the matter as a "personality conflict," one best resolved with my departure. Perhaps I would be offered a healthy severance payment, the lawyer said, or perhaps not.

July was just ahead when I sent the complaint to Tim Ryan, who was tronc's president of publishing, and the company's chief legal counsel, Julie Xanders. It read in part:

> This is to report actions by Davan Maharaj and Marc Duvoisin that I believe have harmed, and could further harm, The Times and the corporation. Our Code of Ethics and Business Conduct requires me to make this report.
>
> In part, my situation reflects a serious problem that has persisted in the newsroom since Davan and Marc assumed control—their inability or unwillingness to publish investigative stories in anything like a timely manner. . . .
>
> For many months, Davan and Marc have unconscionably delayed publication of my reporting on a dangerous, drug-abusing former dean of USC's medical school. He provides methamphetamine, heroin, and other drugs to young people; bails drug dealers and drug users out of jail; and continues to treat patients. He has a history of threatening people with violence.
>
> I believe he could be a threat specifically to a family that helped me expose his monstrous behavior. I have earned the trust of the family and others who turned to The Times to do the right thing. That trust has been betrayed.

I addressed in the letter the killing of the original story, and I wrote that the actions of Maharaj and Duvoisin could expose the *Times* to allegations of a conflict of interest, a reference to the ties between the paper and USC. I cited several passages from our ethics code. Ryan replied in writing the next day to say he had turned the complaint over to the HR director, Cindy Ballard, for a formal investigation. Two days later, I met with Ballard and her assistant in the HR offices on the sixth floor of the Times Building. As a preface, I told them I was prepared to be fired for what I was doing, and I chose my words in such a way to suggest I would go public if that happened. I added that I did not require anonymity in making my complaint, which *Times* policy allowed, and that they were free to take it directly to Maharaj and Duvoisin with my name attached.

Ballard assured me I would not be fired. She also sold me on anonymity from the standpoint that if I faced retaliation from Maharaj and Duvoisin, other staffers might be afraid to come forward during the investigation. So once again, I retreated into the shadows of my own newspaper to tell a story.

The same week I met with Ballard, the Warrens folded. They decided they could not wait for the story any longer. Paul Warren left me a voice mail saying the family had retained Mark Geragos, the high-profile, camera-loving attorney who had represented famous clients such as Michael Jackson and Winona Ryder.

"He took us immediately," Paul said.

I had no doubt about that, and it was what I had feared. Now, Geragos could hold a news conference to reveal the bombshell allegations of his new clients, and the *Times* story would be compromised. We would be competing with other media *on our own material.* All these months after we got the story! Geragos himself was a CNN contributor; the Warrens described for me how he showed off the mini studio in his law office during their visit. And in his hands, the story might come off as just another looney legal dispute.

Harriet and I knew Geragos from covering his earlier cases. We

both called him to ask that he not go public until our story was published. He agreed to hold off but said he wouldn't wait long.

I told Duvoisin—with urgency—of the Geragos complication. He
acted entirely unconcerned.

Duvoisin's next assault on our work came out of nowhere. He decreed
that we could not report that Puliafito regularly used drugs, even
though we had three firsthand, on-the-record sources saying so—and
with a frankness that implicated themselves in the illegal conduct—in
addition to three other sources who provided corroboration. Duvoisin's "reasoning" was that Puliafito was seen doing drugs in just a few
of the photos and videos we had of him with Sarah Warren and the
other young people. *Ridiculous.* I had pointed out repeatedly to Duvoisin, based on my interviews with Sarah, that the photos and videos
were shot to satisfy Puliafito's voyeuristic desires; they were mostly
of sex scenes. We happened to get lucky that he allowed a few frames
to capture him indulging in street drugs, and we had those, too.

But Duvoisin said he would not allow us to describe Puliafito as
a regular drug user, regardless of what our sources said, unless we
found *more* photos and videos showing him smoking meth or heroin or the like. It was a first in all our careers—we were required to
obtain images of misconduct witnessed by our sources if we were to
publish on-the-record accounts of that misconduct.

It was a patent violation of the *Times*'s standards for reporting.
As usual, we pushed back, we dug in as much as we could, but Duvoisin would not yield.

I was keeping Ballard informed of our face-offs with him. She
understood the threat Geragos's presence posed to the *Times* maintaining exclusivity on the story. Ballard and her staff also had begun
interviewing other reporters and editors for the HR investigation,
starting with my colleagues on the USC team. The inquiry was expanded beyond the particulars of the USC story to other problems
with Maharaj, Duvoisin, and some of their allies on the masthead. It

remained a confidential undertaking; Ballard said Maharaj and Du-voisin were not aware of it. She brought Glasser, who reported to corporate, into the investigation and swore him to secrecy as well. I learned later that Glasser told Maharaj that if Geragos revealed our findings before the story was published, that would be bad for the paper and for Maharaj personally. Maharaj, I was informed, reacted angrily to Glasser but took the warning seriously. (Later, in an email to Maharaj, I wrote that I had been told that he and/or Duvoisin received such a "stern message" from corporate; I did not name Glasser. Maharaj's attorney responded by saying my query reflected "a predicate that is utterly false.")

Glasser's admonition boosted my spirits. For the first time since the original story was killed, I believed the paper might actually report what we knew about Carmen Puliafito.

But the ride was not yet smooth. Duvoisin did tell the team that the story was set for publication the following Monday. That timetable was another gift to USC: Major investigative stories like this typically appeared in the Sunday paper, because it is our showcase edition with the largest circulation by far.

And then came the final blow. On the Friday before publication, Duvoisin went back into the copy and deleted all but one of the references to Puliafito supplying drugs to others. The provision of narcotics was the worst of the dean's alleged crimes and potentially the most legally perilous to USC as his employer. It's one thing for a physician to use illegal drugs, but it's quite another for a physician to give them to others, especially to a minor and to someone in re-hab. Duvoisin also deleted references to Puliafito drugging on the USC campus, including Charles Warren's account of smoking meth with him there. A passage that survived was the one describing Pu-liafito giving Don Stokes meth in Sarah Warren's presence. I won-dered later if Duvoisin had allowed that to remain only in his haste to make the cuts or because it wasn't as damaging as the reporting that was deleted.

All the material was first placed in the story more than three months earlier. Duvoisin made the cuts without discussing it with us. He let me know after the fact with an email, saying:

> Jeff and I have gone over the story again and consulted with Davan, and we're going to make some further edits to [*sic*] in response to concerns Jeff has raised. . . .

> The edits will touch parts of the story that deal with him buying drugs for others, providing drugs to others, where we don't have corroboration and are relying on a single source's say-so.

> Bottom line: We're going to be able to publish a very hard-hitting story but it's not going to have in it everything that you want.

> I appeal to you to maintain a professional demeanor today as we work through the edits, and not personalize differences of opinion, or impugn the motives of editors and colleagues.

> Please do not call Jeff. He is on his honeymoon, and anyway, I am handling the story. . . .

> This is a personal message to you; please do not forward it. If you want to let the other reporters know what the general plan is, that's fine.

I was so furious I couldn't think straight. I reread the email two or three times: Nearly as enraging as the declaration that the most damaging material had been erased was Duvoisin's statement that *"we don't have corroboration and are relying on a single source's say-so."* That was not true. None of the material was based on a single source without corroboration. And I found it hard to believe that Glasser would take the initiative to raise last-minute "concerns" about our reporting. *He had already signed off on the story after giving it an excruciatingly lengthy and detailed review.*

Duvoisin's admonishment to me to remain "professional" echoed the upbraiding he had given Harriet and Adam after they objected to the deletion of the whistleblower. Gaslighting.

I allowed myself to simmer down for an hour, and then I sent this response:

Marc—

We do not have a single source for his providing drugs to others—we have five on-the-record sources. We have three other sources who were given contemporaneous accounts of him doing so. And we have from his own mouth that he gave money to Sarah to buy drugs. We have no denials from him.

I have always behaved in a professional manner. This is not the first time that you have accused me or other members of the USC team of behaving unprofessionally because we raised ethical concerns, as company policy requires us to in such situations.

I ignored Duvoisin's directives to not forward the email to my colleagues nor contact Glasser, who was not on his honeymoon. Those orders alone were evidence of something rotten. The other reporters were as disgusted as I was about the deletions. I learned that Maharaj had ordered Glasser to go into the copy and come up with "the most conservative version of the story possible"—that is, a weaker version—by flagging lines and paragraphs for cuts.

So Glasser identified those findings of ours that were most injurious to Puliafito and USC, and the two top editors of the *Times* made them go *poof*. I wanted to doubly confirm the untruth about Glasser's role, so I asked Duvoisin about it. Matt and I were in Duvoisin's office at the time, going over edits by the copy desk.

"So it was Jeff who asked for the cuts?" I said. "Jeff initiated it?"

Duvoisin eyed me coolly. "Yes," he said.

He would not consider our arguments to restore the material.

We would have to settle for getting the watered-down version of the story published.

In our last discussion with him before publication, late on a Sunday, Duvoisin asked Matt and me if we had any follow-up stories in mind. He posed the question with no enthusiasm—as a throwaway query to break one of the awkward silences that increasingly punctuated our sessions with him. Matt and I replied that all of us, the five reporters, had plans for more stories on the subject. There was much to uncover for our readers: What did Nikias know, and when did he know it? Had there been warning signs at Keck of Puliafito's behavior? Were there complaints by his colleagues or patients? What more could we learn about the Pasadena Police Department's handling of the overdose? Why didn't the cops in Pasadena and elsewhere ever take the Warrens' reports about Puliafito seriously? Did the FBI open any kind of inquiry after the family therapist contacted the agency?

Duvoisin's enthusiasm needle stayed at zero.

The story appeared in print and online on July 17, 2017, one year and three and a half months after I got the tip about the overdose, nine months after I filed the initial story, and three and a half months after the team filed the second story. In all that time, no holes in the reporting of either story had delayed publication, nor did any denials by Puliafito, nor did any conflicts in the accounts of our sources.

The article that ran that Monday did not measure up, in content or the writing, to the draft we completed in late March.

But it still exploded on the Web.

The online version drew more readers in a matter of hours than other popular *Times* stories garnered in a month. The wire services and television networks jumped on it. So did other large newspapers around the country, along with media outlets as far away as England and Australia. Emails of praise filled our in-boxes, followed by queries from several Hollywood production houses and agencies interested in the rights to the story.

In the early afternoon, the reporting team got together in Grad's office, figuratively catching our breaths, to plan the next day's coverage. Suddenly, Maharaj appeared in the doorway. He had a nervous, almost frightened look on his face. I knew him long enough and well enough to discern what was happening: The reception the story received kneecapped him. Now he had to find a way to rewrite his history with it to protect his job and salvage his reputation.

When he spoke, his voice was creaky—this was not easy for him. "It's the story of the year," Maharaj said.

Those were his first words to me about the story since the day in February when he killed the original version and pressured me to move on to something else.

Nobody was in the mood to engage with Maharaj now. I turned my back to him. After a moment, he walked out of the office.

18

PURGING THE MASTHEAD

A few hours after the story appeared, Carmen Puliafito's four-decade career in medicine effectively came to an end. USC's media office issued a statement the day of publication saying that Puliafito had been placed on leave and would no longer see patients. That was followed by an announcement by the Medical Board of California that it was opening an investigation of Puliafito based on our findings.

The USC statement said nothing about the details of our story and included no expressions of concern from university administrators about the welfare of Sarah Warren or the other young people Puliafito cavorted with. But it did offer tender words for Puliafito himself, while raising the possibility that our reporting was false:

"If the assertions reported in the July 17 *Los Angeles Times* story are true, we hope that Carmen receives care and treatment that will lead him to a full recovery."

The statement didn't go over well with the USC community or our readers. They wanted to know what the university intended to do about the failings in the administration that allowed Puliafito to lead his second life for so long. So the next day, Nikias sent out a statement of his own, which said in part that the "university categorically condemns the unlawful possession, use, or distribution of drugs." But then he returned to the theme of the first statement: "We are concerned about Dr. Puliafito and his family and hope that, if the article's assertions are true, he receives the help and treatment he may need for a full recovery."

The reporting team had expected that USC would try to downplay the whole affair as simply an individual employee struggling with addiction. It was likely the best damage-control strategy the Nikias administration could devise once the story ran, and it was enabled by the deletion of our reporting about Puliafito being a purveyor of drugs, not just a user. We had not given up on getting that material into the paper, particularly the accounts of Puliafito delivering drugs to Sarah in rehab and giving them to her brother when he was a minor. But we could not see how that would happen as long as the editors who ordered the deletion, Maharaj and Duvoisin, remained in charge of the newsroom.

The city of Pasadena also had a tough time absorbing the story's blow. City manager Steve Mermell sent a memo to the mayor and city council acknowledging that the article "reflects poorly on the City and the Pasadena Police Department." Mermell wrote that Alfonso Garcia, the officer who responded to the overdose, had been disciplined for not filing a report on the incident until two months after I started asking questions. *Say again?* The city had never revealed anything about Garcia getting punished—not since my first visit to city hall in April 2016. The cover-up had been broader than I had known; Mermell and Police Chief Sanchez still refused to say what form the discipline took (Garcia was not fired).

The city did release an audio recording Garcia made of his encounter with Puliafito at Huntington Hospital—after Adam pushed for it. Mermell's office should have given it to me more than a year earlier. The recording featured Puliafito lying about his relationship with Sarah, his stay at the Constance, and the drugs he brought to the room. It showed that Garcia and a social worker at the hospital were highly skeptical of Puliafito's statements, but the officer didn't press him much.

Key exchanges:

Garcia: And were you staying [at the hotel] there with her?
Puliafito: Ahh, no.
Garcia: No?
Puliafito: No.
Garcia: But the room's registered to you?
Puliafito: Correct.
Garcia: Under your identification and . . .
Puliafito: I visited her in the room, but I did not spend the night.
Garcia: Okay. . . . And do you know about all the stuff that was found in the room?
Puliafito: Uh, no.
. . .
Garcia: How do you know her?
Puliafito: Family friend. . . . Friend of her dad.
Garcia: You're a friend of her dad?
Puliafito: Yeah.
Garcia: You guys have a romantic relationship between each other?
Puliafito: No.
Garcia: Just friends?
Puliafito: Just friends.

A few minutes later, Garcia and the social worker, who identifies herself as Lauren, move away from Puliafito to discuss the dean's story:

Lauren: So, uh, you buy it?
Garcia: No.
Lauren: [laughing] "Old family friend." . . . Lascivious activity.
Garcia: I'm thinking that's probably why he's so concerned.
Lauren: Yeah, yeah. And a friend of the father? Uh, excuse
me. . . . It's just funky.

Maharaj and Duvoisin warmed themselves in the glow of the story's huge readership. They wanted a chunk of the credit when outlets such as *The New York Times, The Washington Post,* and National Public Radio spotlighted our reporting. Maharaj insisted that the team meet regularly with him and Duvoisin to discuss the follow-up stories we had in the works. Suddenly, the two were keen on going deeper on the subject of Puliafito and USC, after undermining our reporting for all those months. The meetings were workshops in jaw-tightening and tongue-biting; it was hard not to call out Maharaj and Duvoisin for the hypocrites they were, which we feared would turn them against the story again.

But we called out plenty in another set of meetings three floors above Maharaj's office—in Cindy Ballard's HR department. Her investigation was expanding rapidly, even as she kept it a secret from its subjects. Ballard told me the company hired a law firm to examine thousands of emails and text messages by Maharaj and Duvoisin; the idea was to look for any incriminating exchanges between the editors and USC. I had doubts that any would be found, because Maharaj had confided in me that an earlier HR investigation into his conduct included a scouring of his emails. I didn't know if he shared the same information with Duvoisin, but it seemed likely. I couldn't see them being so reckless as to communicate with Nikias or anyone else at USC in an email that contained compromising material about their handling of the story. Ballard also asked me for phone numbers for Nikias and others at the university so the inquiry could check for calls made or received by Maharaj and Duvoisin. Again, I wasn't confident that effort would yield anything. The editors could have legitimate reasons for phoning the USC people, such as planning for the Festival of Books. Or they could at least claim as much if records of the calls turned up.

Because my complaint cited the company's conflict-of-interest policy, a main prong of Ballard's probe was aimed at determining if promises or concessions were made to USC about the story because of the university's relationship with the paper and the editors. If that happened, it would be a fundamental corruption of our journalism principles.

But I believed there was another form of corruption that could be just as damaging to the *Times*'s mission, and that was the type that flowed from cowardice—a fear of taking on powerful institutions and their leaders in a story that was as hard-hitting as the facts warranted. The cowardice would be rooted in the editors' desires to avoid any potential risks to their careers by shying away from stories that would rile people with unlimited access to money, lawyers, and political connections. That was never supposed to happen in a newsroom—and if it did, proving it might be difficult. An editor could protest that it was merely a high level of journalistic caution, not cravenness, that got a story killed or weakened. The line between the two could be hard to draw for an HR investigator.

As more and more staffers took the elevator to the sixth floor, however, it seemed less and less likely that Ballard would need to draw such a line. The complaint about the USC story lit the fuse to a rebellion in the newsroom. Ballard had to schedule interviews after hours and on weekends to accommodate the crush of employees who came forward with their own tales of the abusive and dysfunctional Maharaj regime. The foot traffic into her office became a stampede after Maharaj and Duvoisin did something that I had warned Ballard they would do: target Grad for his support of the story. They removed him as California editor and assigned him to a vaguely defined project that looked to me and many others to be a demotion and perhaps a last stop until he was shown the door. I immediately sent Ballard an email from my private account and labeled the action against Grad retaliation. The USC team then emailed Ryan, the tronc head of publishing, to ask him to intervene. It worked. Ryan and Ballard ordered Maharaj to pause Grad's removal while HR looked into it. We knew then that Maharaj and Duvoisin would soon be informed of the ballooning investigation into their conduct (if they hadn't been already). I wasn't worried about that. I believed HR already had enough grounds to fire or demote Maharaj and Duvoisin. I shared that with Grad after I learned he was scheduled for an HR interview the next day. I sent him a pep-rally email, urging him to tell all:

> Shelby, the bottom line is that Davan and Marc are finished. They cannot survive this. Publication of the USC story and the great play given the follow-ups will not save them. Corporate gets the hypocrisy in Davan's and Marc's late conversion to the story.
>
> Davan and Marc are done. It's only a matter of when, in the short term.

I also wrote: *This is about the future of the* Times. *This is a decisive moment.*

Grad replied with a simple *Thanks.*

I don't know what Grad said in the HR interview, but the investigation continued to accelerate. And when it became known to Maharaj and Duvoisin, they mounted a counterattack. In conversations with other editors and reporters, they denied that the move against Grad was retaliatory, said it had been long planned, and defended their actions on the USC story, including by disparaging my original work. Colleagues related to me that Maharaj told them he killed my story in February because it was "unpublishable."

Several dozen staffers had walked into HR to give negative statements about Maharaj and Duvoisin and other managers who supported them. As the investigation neared its conclusion, some of Maharaj's masthead editors joined in a letter to tronc CEO Justin Dearborn and executive chairman Michael Ferro to complain about the inquiry. "We ask you to meet with us today, as a group, to discuss a Human Resources investigation that has disrupted our workplace for more than a month," the letter said, according to a story in *Variety*. "We are concerned about the repercussions for the news organization."

But the real disruption was coming.

A strange cool marked that Friday in August, the temperature barely topping eighty degrees downtown. I stayed late in the newsroom. The reporting team was wrapping up a story on USC's latest attempt to bind the Puliafito wounds to its reputation: The university's fundraising chief issued a statement that sought to diminish Puliafito's past achievements as a diviner of dollars—an apparent attempt to assure prospective Keck applicants and donors that all was fine at the medical school. Our story on the statement carried a photo of Puliafito at a Keck benefit with Beatty, Annette Bening, and Shirley MacLaine. *The Washington Post* also reported on the statement that day, under the headline, THE BLESSING AND CURSE OF FUNDRAISING FOR HIGHER EDUCATION. The *Post* story likened the Puliafito scandal to a "Hollywood drama."

By around 7:00 P.M., a churchly quiet had settled over the newsroom. Then I heard voices coming from the elevator lobby and looked up from my desk; it was Maharaj and Duvoisin. I knew they had met with HR. Now they had to walk right past me because my desk was on the aisle.

Maharaj's eyes were slashing. "Hello, Paul," he said in a voice an octave higher than normal.

"How are you?" I replied.

"Oh, I'm great," Maharaj said.

Duvoisin was silent, but his expression sent venom in my direction.

I watched them walk in tandem to their offices—Maharaj in front, his posture plank-straight as usual, but his gait a bit slower. Duvoisin trailed him by a step or two, kneading his hands, following the man who might have led him astray.

It didn't occur to me that it was the last time I would see them.

On Monday, August 21, 2017, the *Times*'s website was dominated by stories on the arrival of the "Great American Eclipse," which blotted out the sun from Oregon to South Carolina. The eclipse and the war in Afghanistan would blanket much of the front page of the next day's print edition. A spot on the lower-right corner of the page was reserved for news about the *Times* itself.

Around noon, my colleagues began texting me that something was brewing. Maharaj hadn't appeared in the newsroom. Duvoisin turned up, but then went missing. I was driving to the building when one of our political reporters called me to say he'd heard from a source that Maharaj would be fired. I told him I wouldn't be surprised, and I shared with him the scene of Maharaj and Duvoisin returning to the newsroom the previous Friday evening. I received more calls and texts as I parked in the Broadway garage, all of them about rumors or half-confirmed reports that Maharaj was out. By the time I reached my desk on the third floor, the calls and texts included speculation about Duvoisin's fate. One unsettling question making the rounds: *If Maharaj were fired, the company wouldn't place Duvoisin in charge of the newsroom, would it?*

No, it wouldn't. The official announcement came a few minutes after 1:00 P.M. in a staff-wide email from tronc CEO Justin Dearborn: Maharaj, Duvoisin, and Doig were "leaving" the paper. So was deputy managing editor Megan Garvey, who was a key member of Maharaj's masthead. Also out were Duvoisin's wife, reporter Jill

Leovy; and Maharaj's executive assistant. The announcement gave no reasons for the firings (it didn't mention Leovy or the assistant), other than they were part of "important management changes" that would help "drive our transformation and further position our-selves for long-term growth as a media organization."

Oh.

Dearborn's email actually led with the news that Ross Levinsohn, a peripatetic media executive who served briefly as interim head of Yahoo!, had been named CEO and publisher of the *Times,* and that Jim Kirk, former editor in chief of the *Chicago Sun-Times,* had been appointed interim executive editor of our paper.

The masthead purge was stunning, particularly for those who hadn't been clued in to the HR investigation. Even I needed time to grasp the enormity of the firings. Supporters and friends of the six who got sacked were stiff-faced and whispery; the word *bloodbath* was uttered in anger. But the overwhelming reaction of the staff to the dismissal of Maharaj and Duvoisin was a blend of relief and grat-itude. The scene in some corners of the newsroom resembled an awards celebration, with reporters and editors hugging and shak-ing hands and taking photos to memorialize the event. Word of my role in the HR investigation had leaked out of the building; media writers covering the firings emailed me interview requests, which I declined.

The *Times*'s story referred to the firings as a "dramatic shake-up" and focused on the appointments of Levinsohn and Kirk and the financial struggles the paper faced. The HR investigation was ad-dressed deep in the article, which noted that Maharaj and Duvoisin had defended their editing of the USC piece as appropriate for such a sensitive subject. The story also said that the company's inquiry had found no conflict of interest with USC.

Fair enough. As I expected, the investigation did not find a smoking-gun email or text message showing an unethical alliance between the editors and Nikias. Nor did I expect the company to throw any more of its dirty laundry into the story, although it would have been the journalistically proper thing to do. The story included this statement from Maharaj: "During the last 28 years, it has been an honor working with the best journalists in a great American newsroom. . . . I'm proud of the work we've done." Duvoisin later told the *L.A. Downtown News* that "allegations that I did anything but edit the [USC] story to a high standard have no substance. The story speaks for itself, and speaks loudly." It strangely echoed a statement Maharaj gave *L.A. Magazine* for its eviscerating article on his leadership: "We and I should be judged by the quality of our work, and by that standard the *Los Angeles Times* has done very well in the past five years. Our journalism speaks for itself, and it speaks loudly."

A few hours after the firings, I bumped into Ballard near the city desk. I thanked her for the effort she threw into the investigation and, most of all, for her integrity. I told her she was a "hero" to the staff. She returned my thanks with a smile and said, "We need more stories like the USC story."

The next morning, Harriet sent a mass email to the newsroom with the subject line, "Drink if you love the LA Times." It was an invitation to an after-work get-together at the Far Bar in Little Tokyo. "First round on the USC crew," Harriet wrote. The Far Bar was a fifteen-minute walk from the paper. Branded with a vintage neon sign that blared CHOP SUEY, the bar occupied an 1896 brick building. Its entrance off a shoulders-squeezing alleyway was, as the *L.A. Downtown News* described it, "near-secret." That was fitting considering all that had happened at the *Times* and all that was still underway, such as our efforts to form a union. On this Tuesday evening, dozens of us filled the second-floor landing of the bar to raise a glass to what we hoped would be a renewal for the paper—even knowing that much more needed to be done to right the *Times*.

Unknown to the reporting team was that our work on USC was also just beginning.

19

BILLIONAIRE BACKERS

Stories that come from tips tend to produce more tips, and we were busy with the ones that started rolling in on the day the first Puliafito piece ran. They yielded stories that showed USC administrators had received complaints about Puliafito's drinking and erratic behavior for years and, for the most part, ignored them. It was all kept very quiet, and that allowed Puliafito to continue seeing patients in whatever condition he might be in. (Medical board testimony later revealed that a vice dean reported to Michael Quick, Nikias's provost, his suspicions that Puliafito was doing drugs.)

One tip that came in an email was about Rohit Varma, Puliafito's successor as dean. The tipster wrote of hearing "many stories about alleged inappropriate behavior by Dr. Varma with trainees and staff." He did not provide details but stated that "it could demonstrate a pattern of disregard for the safety of both students and staff by the USC leadership."

Sarah Parvini took the lead in the reporting, with the rest of the team joining in as our inquiries expanded. We spent weeks calling and door-knocking potential sources and teasing confidential documents out of them. It was slow going, but we were able to prove that Varma had been the subject of a sexual harassment complaint years earlier. He was accused of trying to coerce a young woman, an international student who held a fellowship at Keck, to share a hotel bed with him during an out-of-town conference. When she refused, Varma allegedly threatened to have her visa revoked.

We learned that USC responded to the complaint with the university's trademarked secrecy: It paid a six-figure settlement to the woman and made certain no one blabbed. Varma had to pay a small portion of the settlement, and he saw his salary cut and was denied a promotion. But much of his punishment was later waived. USC liked him because he had secured millions in federal grants for the school—and now he led Keck.

After learning of our reporting, and just before we published our story, USC forced Varma out as dean (he remained a professor).

So now there were back-to-back medical school deans in back-to-back scandals. Shouldn't that toss the university president's job up in the air?

Not at USC.

Standing on the high corners of the clock tower of USC's Bovard Administration Building were statues of Abraham Lincoln, Theodore Roosevelt, Cicero, and Plato. They were stationed on hundred-foot pedestals like sentinels guarding over the Italianate structure. Hunkered down inside Bovard was Max Nikias, who was determined to cling to the presidency with no end in sight.

That seemed more than likely, because by all appearances Nikias still enjoyed the protection of the ultrarich industrialists, sports and entertainment moguls, bankers, construction barons, real estate investors, and financiers who controlled USC's bloated board of trustees. Throughout our reporting on Puliafito and then Varma, the trustees were as silent as the Bovard statuary, much as they were during previous controversies. They were no more forthcoming after Nikias and Quick abandoned the tactic of suggesting that our reporting might not be true and expressing concern for Puliafito. The apparent reason for the abrupt change in tone: According to the Warrens, the Geragos firm had shown USC's representatives some of the images of Puliafito smoking meth and otherwise partying with his young cohort. Quick seemed to be referring to photos and videos—which we did not yet have the Warrens' permission to publish—when he said this in a letter to the faculty:

"Today, we were provided access to information of egregious behavior on the part of the former dean concerning substance-abuse activities with people who aren't affiliated with USC. This was the first time we saw such information firsthand. It is extremely troubling and we need to take serious action."

Quick added that USC was firing Puliafito. Nikias endorsed the move in a letter to the campus community, in which he declared, "We are outraged and disgusted by this individual's behavior."

But the trustees uttered barely a word. And there were *fifty-seven of them*—a number much larger than what experts in academia governance said was optimal for a university board. Too many members, the experts warned, can render a board unruly and unfocused. Tommy Trojan and other USC insiders told me that Nikias and his predecessors went big in recruiting for their board because they wanted points of contact and influence across as many economic sectors as possible. About a dozen of the trustees were billionaires—most of the fifty states have fewer—which possibly made the board the most well-capitalized favor bank in higher education. Also serving as trustees were luminaries such as Hollywood icon Steven Spielberg and Los Angeles Lakers owner Jeanie Buss. Bringing more wealth and star power onto the board could help build wealth and star power for the university. Trustees of means, famous or not, were expected to donate to the institutions they oversee, and at least some of the Trojan board members did so in amounts that reflected the size of their fortunes.

Besides, as crowded as the USC board was, its power was centered in a much smaller subgroup of members who comprised its executive committee. That seemed like a good place to start when we sought reaction from the trustees to our Puliafito reporting for a follow-up story. Except that we encountered a problem: USC kept the membership of the executive committee a secret. There were two exceptions: The school bylaws stated that the committee must include the chair of the full board—at the time, John Mork, a Denver oil billionaire—and the university president. So we had Mork and Nikias, and that was it. USC refused to reveal who else was on the committee or even how many members it had.

In a written statement, Mork said: "I have utmost confidence and trust in President Nikias' and Provost Quick's ability to lead USC through this challenging time and to move the university forward."

Rick Caruso, a trustee who made his billions in upscale mall construction, and who was a candidate for L.A. mayor as of this writing, broke with the pack by speaking to *Times* columnist Steve Lopez. Caruso was skilled in media relations as a former president of the Los Angeles Police Commission and a member of the board that oversees the L.A. Department of Water and Power, the agency whose history of siphoning off Northern California H_2O for the city informed the plot of the movie *Chinatown*. "If the allegations are true . . . I'm very disturbed and condemn the illegal use of drugs, especially by someone who holds the highest level of trust and care," Caruso told Lopez.

But those words apparently were it. Caruso had the political leverage inside and outside USC to do more publicly, to demand openness by the board, but he chose not to.

Nikias maintained his silence except for the occasional letters he sent to the Trojan family. In one of them, he announced that the university had hired the former U.S. attorney for the Los Angeles region, Debra Wong Yang, to lead an investigation of the scandal, an inquiry that Yang promised would be separate from the administration.

That was hard to swallow. Yang was a partner in Gibson, Dunn & Crutcher, a mega-firm with an international presence whose connections to USC were circuit board–like. The firm's managing partner, Kenneth Doran, was a graduate of the university's Gould School of Law and served on its board of councilors. Doran and his colleagues at Gibson Dunn were donors to the school. And Yang taught at Gould in the 1990s and later represented USC in several lawsuits. Yang told the *Times* her investigation would be "independent," adding, "My job is to take it wherever the facts go."

The USC reporting team, the Trojan family, and L.A. at large never learned where those facts took Yang. Whatever she found remained secret, despite expectations that her report would be made public — and that *the whole point* of the investigation had seemed to be transparency and disclosure.

Yang wasn't the only lawyer with USC ties who played a role in the Puliafito affair; another was Jackie Lacey, the L.A. County district attorney.

Lacey was the first African American and first woman to hold the office. Her rise to the top of the nation's largest local prosecutorial agency was an inspirational tale of grit and toil and shouldering through closed doors. Lacey was born in L.A. to a father who cleaned parking lots and a mother who sewed clothes in the Garment District. She grew up in the Crenshaw area on the city's south side, at a time when predatory street gangs made her walk to school a fearsome adventure. The experience instilled in her a devotion to the law and an appreciation of the police. Those allegiances were reinforced years later when her father was wounded in the leg in a drive-by shooting. In the daughter's telling, he was shot while mowing the lawn, but it was shortly after he had painted over gang graffiti on a telephone box at their home.

Braving those walks to Dorsey High School paid off. Lacey got into the University of California, Irvine, where she studied psychology. She then earned her law degree at Gould, and four years later, she joined the DA's office. Lacey was quiet and hardworking and warm toward her colleagues. She willed herself to climb through the ranks of white and male prosecutors in the downtown Criminal Courts Building, which was renamed for Clara Shortridge Foltz, who was the first woman lawyer on the West Coast. Lacey eventually became the number two to District Attorney Steve Cooley, a blustery, heavy-faced man who was another USC alum. Cooley anointed Lacey his preferred successor when he decided to leave the office after three four-year terms and a losing run for California attorney general. Voters elected Lacey DA in 2012. She held her swearing-in ceremony at the Galen Center, USC's basketball arena. Nikias was among the speakers. "One dedicated Trojan, Mr. Steve Cooley, is passing on the baton to another dedicated Trojan," he told the audience, "and I am very proud and honored to be here today."

Lacey gave it back in her inaugural speech. "It is a privilege to be sworn into office on the University of Southern California campus," she said. "I thank President Nikias and the leaders of this distinguished university. . . . USC represents so much to me personally. It has been like the iconic center of some of the most important events of my life."

Nikias later awarded Lacey an honorary degree on behalf of USC. She keynoted a fundraising gala for the law school and participated in other university events. Now, medical board investigators were asking Lacey's office to consider bringing criminal charges against Puliafito, including a felony count for providing drugs to Charles Warren when he was underage. Finally, in covering the medical board's allegations against Puliafito, we were able to report that he gave meth, heroin, and other drugs to his coterie of desperate young people. It was the information that we had gathered seven months earlier and that Maharaj and Duvoisin cut from our story three and a half months after that.

After they were fired, I tried to get a separate story published that detailed Puliafito's actions as a drug purveyor. Grad wouldn't go for it. He wanted the team to focus on what USC administrators knew about Puliafito's conduct. I disagreed, and I believed we could pursue both those stories at once. But the piece on Puliafito gifting drugs did not run. As it languished, Sarah and Charles Warren gave sworn statements to the medical board investigators identifying Puliafito as their drug supplier, telling them everything they had told me. (Stokes gave conflicting statements on whether Puliafito was his source of drugs. He told me later he didn't want to suggest to the investigators that he knew Puliafito had bought the drugs, only that the ex-dean "shared" them with him.)

The evidence presented to Lacey's office was compelling, but the investigators struck out.

During Lacey's first term, three USC football players were accused of violent crimes, but none was prosecuted. Among the players who walked free was Osa Masina, who later pleaded guilty in a Utah sexual assault case, in which the victim was the same woman he had been accused of attacking in L.A.

Another case Lacey's prosecutors took a pass on involved a Trojan with much more clout than a football player. Jack Leonard and I published an investigative story that showed thousands of dollars in taxpayer-financed improvements were made to the home of L.A. County supervisor Mark Ridley-Thomas. We reported that county crews performed the work—all without permits—on the orders of administrators who ultimately reported to Ridley-Thomas, one of the most powerful politicians in L.A. In response to our story, Lacey's office opened an investigation into whether the work amounted to a misappropriation of public funds. It brought no charges after stating in writing that the spending was legal "if the witnesses are to be believed." Jack and I scratched our heads. Wasn't it the DA's *job* to determine whether the witnesses were credible?

Seven years later, a federal grand jury indicted Ridley-Thomas on charges of accepting bribes from a USC social sciences dean in exchange for directing county funds to the school. The bribes were in the form of a USC job and scholarship for Ridley-Thomas's son. The supervisor denied the charges.

At least Lacey's office conducted something of a probe, even if half-blinkered, into Ridley-Thomas's home improvement project. It extended no such effort to Puliafito. A month after the medical board investigators referred their findings to the office, prosecutors decided not to charge him, stating that the "current state of the case does not establish sufficient evidence to prove the charges beyond a reasonable doubt."

The DA's office arrived at that conclusion without even speaking to the Warrens, the family told me. Lacey said in an interview that she and her office never cut USC a break and that she had only a "very formal" relationship Nikias. "We're not close," she said. "We're not buddies."

With Lacey's team passing on the case, USC did not have to worry about a more thorough criminal investigation of Puliafito than the medical board could do. Nor would it face the daily headlines of a Puliafito trial. But there were still all those photos and videos of the drug parties Puliafito paid for. The Warrens had shared many of the images with the medical board investigators but kept copies on their phones and computers and a hard drive. The photos and videos in the family's possession would be available if they were subpoenaed in any future civil or criminal case. And they would remain a potential source of embarrassment to USC.

Unless they vanished.

Geragos had told the Warrens that their civil claim against USC and Puliafito could be worth $10 million or more. He persuaded them to go into mediation for a quicker payout than would be possible through a lawsuit. The mediator Geragos agreed to was Dickran Tevrizian, a retired federal judge who was a Trojan through and through. Tevrizian held degrees in finance and law from USC, a USC scholarship fund was named for him, and the university honored him with its prestigious Alumni Merit Award. His wife and three siblings were also Trojans. The Warrens told me they had been unaware of any of Tevrizian's USC connections until after his selection as the mediator—and then they were told only that he was an alumnus. Even that didn't sit well with Paul Warren, who asked Geragos how Tevrizian could be an impartial arbiter of the family's claim against his alma mater. Geragos assured him that Tevrizian was a good choice. (Tevrizian later insisted to me that he had disclosed his Trojan ties to all the parties in the mediation. When I asked him if he had anything in writing to support that, he replied that he would no longer engage with me.)

Everything about the mediation was secret—the participants, the nature of the claim, and the outcome—so my reporting on it had been limited, including with respect to Tevrizian's role. But I did learn that USC's lawyers played hardball with the Warrens, with threats to shame them publicly over their own conduct, which the family saw as a smear in the making. One of Geragos's associates handled most of the case, and the hoped-for $10 million became a $1.5 million offer from USC. The associate persuaded the Warrens to accept it to avoid an interminable and vicious court battle. Of the $1.5 million, $600,000 went to the Geragos firm, a handsome payday for the lawyers.

In return for their end of the money, the Warrens had to agree in writing to never speak publicly about the issues in the mediation—meaning all their encounters with Puliafito—and to help USC quash any subpoenas that might be issued for testimony or records about the ex-dean. It was the sort of nondisclosure agreement that the #MeToo movement, ignited months earlier by the sexual assault allegations against Hollywood mogul Harvey Weinstein, wanted scraped from the legal landscape.

There were two more conditions for the Warrens: The family had to surrender to USC all those photos and videos of Puliafito doing drugs, along with any emails, text messages, or anything on paper about him or the university. And the Warrens had to destroy their copies of the images. If they didn't, there would be no money. Who were they to reject the advice of a famous lawyer? So the deed was accomplished when the lawyers marshaled Paul, Mary Ann, Sarah, and Charles to a tech shop in downtown L.A., where the photos and videos were deleted from their phones and computers—a wipe so thorough that they had to create new Apple IDs when it was completed.

Puliafito was part of the mediation agreement. He and his lawyer signed it, as did attorneys for USC—including Yang. She apparently saw the muzzling of the Warrens and the destruction of their evidence of Puliafito's drug crimes as part of her charge to conduct an "independent" investigation of the scandal. After I learned of the wiping of the devices, I contacted Yang. She would not speak to me or answer written questions I sent her. Geragos also refused to be interviewed. Through his attorney, Nikias said he knew nothing about the mediation agreement, even though one of the attorneys who signed it for USC, the university's general counsel, reported to him.

Lacey said she was unaware that the photos and videos and other material were destroyed.

"That should be looked into," she said. As far as I could determine, it was not.

The Warrens' devices were wiped in November 2017. That was a month after the death of Dora Yoder's infant boy, a twenty-five-day-old who had meth in his body. The tragedy brought Los Angeles County sheriff's homicide detectives into Puliafito's life.

20

A BABY

For an Amish girl, teenage Dora Yoder was out of control. She was cruising the internet all hours—meeting guys out there on the Web. And then she was meeting them in person and staying out late and doing God knows what. Her big sister, Miriam, said it was "just normal teenage stuff." But it wasn't to their parents. The Yoders were from small-town Missouri by way of small-town Pennsylvania, where they were part of the Old Order Amish community in Smicksburg.

They made their living in Smicksburg on a two-hundred-acre farm of cattle, pigs, horses, and wheat, and they stayed true to their faith by shunning electricity, indoor plumbing, motor vehicles, modern tools, and even buttons on their clothes, which they made themselves. In time, an inheritance dispute over the farm caused Dora's parents to question their devotion to the order. In 1996 they plotted an "escape"—the commitment to the order is supposed to be lifelong—with the help of a Jehovah's Witnesses family. Dora and Miriam's dad, Menno Yoder, bought a car to spirit them out of Smicksburg. He kept it hidden in the barn under bales of hay and still used their horse-drawn buggy in public while one of the

Jehovah's Witnesses helped him learn to drive. The getaway came in the middle of the night. Dad and Mom woke up fifteen-year-old Miriam, Dora, who was just five, and their four brothers and sisters and bundled them into the car. They had never ridden in one before and had to make frequent stops so one of the kids could throw up. After they settled in Wright City, Missouri, Menno found work as a truck driver. The new life for the Yoders brought temptations. Menno got addicted to meth. It got so bad that Miriam had to go to court to have him involuntarily committed to rehab.

Miriam bolted when she was twenty-three. She moved to L.A.'s Silverlake, a hilly district favored by hipsters that was a time machine away from Smicksburg and Wright City. Four years later, her parents sent the misbehaving Dora, who was just seventeen, to live with her.

"Their solution was to send her to Los Angeles," Miriam recalled with weary sarcasm. "My parents were not equipped to live in the real world after leaving the Amish."

Dora had her own troubles adjusting. She became a party girl, hanging out in clubs and ignoring her sister's advice about the underbelly of the city. One night, she didn't come home. And then it was two nights and then three. "I freaked out," Miriam said. "I couldn't find her." She feared the worst until the police brought Dora home— and then it was almost the worst: Dora had been savagely assaulted. Her back was matted black with bruises. She wouldn't talk about it with Miriam. And she was never the same after that.

Blond and willowy, Dora photographed like a porcelain figurine. She began making good money modeling nude for fashion and art shoots, and she found herself invited into the more rarefied circles of L.A. She dated Todd Phillips, the writer-director of the *Hangover* novies and *Joker,* but the relationship ended as Dora started to drift away from people who were close to her. That's when Miriam suspected drugs were changing her sister into someone she didn't know.

The suspicions were confirmed when Ariel Franko, a guy in his early twenties from the nicer neighborhoods of the San Fernando

Valley, became Dora's latest companion. He was on his way to com-
piling an impressive record of arrests for drug possession for sale and
being accessory to burglary. Franko sold heroin and used it, too. He
didn't traffic in the volume of drugs that could financially support two
people in L.A., especially when they were consuming so much of the
merchandise. And Dora's modeling fees only went so far. But after a
while, money became no problem. Because Dora met Carmen Puliafito.

Miriam first encountered Puliafito at the house Dora moved into
in Altadena, the one on Ventura Street with all the trash in the front
yard. Dora was still modeling; the drugs had not yet left their visible marks. Miriam stopped by to check on her, and the old man was
standing in the entry to her kitchen. He looked and sounded like he
had been sleeping in the street—or was coming down from a high.
Dora introduced him as Tony. He avoided eye contact with Miriam
and mumbled when he spoke. He was wearing flip-flops and shorts
and a dirty white shirt whose buttons were misaligned. Tony wanted
no conversation with Miriam and left soon after she walked in.

"He's just a friend," Dora told her sister.

I'll bet, Miriam thought.

"I know what's going on," she said to Dora. And she pleaded with
her to be careful.

Miriam saw Puliafito only two or three times after that, the last as
he was driving away from a red-sided duplex he had leased for her
on Alameda Street in Altadena, an improvement from the Ventura
Street house. Dora's life now revolved around Franko and Puliafito.
The people they hung out with were users as well—Kyle Voigt, Sarah
Warren, and the others who blew in and out of their party scene.
The meth cut lines into Dora's fragile beauty and booby-trapped her
moods. She had recurring bouts of paranoia. The most innocuous
question or remark set her off. When Miriam asked about her new
kitchen table—just making conversation—Dora flared up, her eyes
darting everywhere: "Why? Why do you want to know?"

"She's not my sister when she's on drugs," Miriam said.

Months went by with no contact. And then Dora got pregnant. Franko was the father. Miriam didn't know her sister was expecting a child until a month and a half before baby Boaz was born. She never got to see her nephew or coo at him or hold him.

Boaz died on October 5, 2017. It was Puliafito who called 911.

"Baby not breathing," he told the dispatcher. Puliafito identified the mother as his "girlfriend."

"She called me crying," he said.

In January 2018, Matt and Harriet published a story on the death of baby Boaz and quoted Sarah Warren as saying Puliafito was the source of Dora's drugs. (Sarah had told me she witnessed Puliafito give Dora heroin or meth forty to fifty times.) Matt and Harriet interviewed Miriam, who remembered her sister saying she "never paid for her drugs and that he would supply them." The story noted that the Yoders' father, Menno, had called the L.A. County Sheriff's Department in August 2016 to report Dora missing. Menno is heard on a recording of the call telling a sheriff's deputy about Puliafito's involvement with his daughter.

"My daughter's been known to do drugs, and she's involved with a doctor that's also been known to do drugs," he said. "He gives my daughter money, and he pays for her rent, and he pays for all that stuff."

Dora turned up at the Westin Hotel in Pasadena, and there was no indication the sheriff's department, like the Pasadena police that same year, looked much further into Puliafito.

But now an infant was dead, and Puliafito wasn't talking. And two months later, a coroner's toxicology screening was completed, and it found meth in the baby's body. Sheriff's homicide detectives Mike Davis and Gene Morse opened an investigation into Puliafito with Lacey's office. A memo from the office laid out the reason for the inquiry:

Puliafito was at Yoder's home with the victim. It is suspected that Puliafito provided Yoder methamphetamine, which they both allegedly used. Later on, Yoder breastfed the victim and then put him to sleep in his crib. Yoder placed heavy blankets over the victim because it was cold. In the morning of October 5, 2017, both suspects discovered that the victim had died. Puliafito left Yoder's home before he called 911 to report the baby was not breathing.

For once, Puliafito was feeling real heat. Not that he shrank from it. He put his money to work, including to hire a law firm to assert that he never gave drugs to Yoder and to threaten the *Times* with a libel lawsuit over the Boaz reporting. He used lawyers to fend off the detectives. Puliafito sent his own private investigator to confront potential witnesses—including Dora's relatives—and ask them to sign pre-written affidavits stating that he did not use drugs.

Dora, like Sarah, could have been my own daughter. Her Pennsylvania pedigree hit close to home as well. I was also from small-town Pennsylvania—only the northeast coal region, not Amish country—and most of my extended family remained there. I understood the lure of L.A. for someone like Dora. If my parents hadn't moved us west when I was in grade school, I'd like to think I would have made my own way to L.A. And I could see my daughters doing the same if they had been in Dora's circumstances. Would they have been strong enough to resist the temptations someone like Puliafito could bankroll? I was certain they would have been. But then the parents of Sarah and Dora probably had been just as certain.

And Puliafito kept getting away with it. Dora's baby died nearly three months after we exposed Puliafito's degenerate preying on young people. We had published follow-up story after follow-up story on the scandal, and he was still on the street. It was maddening. I wondered then, and always will wonder, whether Boaz would be alive if any of the law enforcement agencies that were alerted to Puliafito and his world of drugs had just brought him in for questioning. Or at least *tried* to question him before he cowered behind his lawyers. Or tailed him. Or interviewed people close to him. Would that have spooked him? Scared him away from Dora? And would that have allowed her to get whatever help she needed to keep her baby drug-free?

Davis and Morse stayed on Puliafito for more than two years, trying to build a case of involuntary manslaughter based on the suspicion that he was the source of the meth in Boaz's bloodstream. They got little help from Dora. She admitted she used meth the night before Boaz died, but she otherwise maintained her transactional loyalty to Puliafito. He continued to pay her rent and her other expenses, as far as Yoder's family knew. Critical to Puliafito and Dora avoiding legal landmines was the coroner concluding that Boaz died of accidental asphyxiation—not drug poisoning—because of the weight of the blankets on his chest.

Matt and Harriet monitored the inching progress of the investigation as best they could, given the secrecy enveloping it. In an exhaustive recap of the inquiry, they wrote that the autopsy on Boaz found "nothing definitive as to why he died. The toxicological report was similarly inconclusive."

It all came down to whether the trace amount of meth in the infant's blood was enough to kill him. If that was the case, and if the detectives could prove Puliafito was the source of the drug, he could be charged in the death.

Matt and Harriet reported that the deputy medical examiner who conducted the autopsy changed her initial conclusions after learning the *Times* was asking questions about the death. The examiner no longer said it was not possible to determine how Boaz died but instead reported the cause of death as asphyxiation from the blankets, with "methamphetamine exposure" from breast milk as a contributing condition "not related to the immediate cause of death."

That was no doubt the result Puliafito had been hoping for.

Matt and Harriet quoted experts who questioned some of the methods and conclusions in the coroner's inquiry. But what frustrated the detectives in the end was the relatively small amount of meth the toxicology lab found—just fifty nanograms per milliliter, which was a little less than what had been detected in other cases when the drug was determined to be the cause of death. That fact and the finding about the blankets doomed the criminal investigation. The district attorney's memo on a possible involuntary manslaughter prosecution ended with language that echoed the Pasadena drug case. It said there was "insufficient evidence to prove beyond a reasonable doubt" that Puliafito committed a crime.

Miriam was angry and distraught. She was one of the family members visited by Puliafito's private investigators. A man and a woman knocked on her door. "I told them he killed my nephew, he's holding my sister hostage, and he's a piece of shit," Miriam said. They left.

The last time Miriam saw Dora, her sister's teeth were either missing or blackened. What little fat remained in her body seemed to have clumped around her calves. She was still in the duplex, which Puliafito had equipped with security cameras. He also monitored Dora's emails and even placed a tracking device on her car, Miriam said.

Twice I visited the duplex house, under the watchful lenses of the cameras eyeing me from under the yellow eaves; when I pressed the bell, no one came to the door. And Dora did not return my phone calls or text messages.

The system handed one more break to Puliafito. Even as the baby investigation unfolded, he was fighting to keep his physician's license in the medical board hearing, which Adam and I covered. The hearing was held in an undersize room at a state building on Fourth Street downtown. Khan had been subpoenaed to testify, so he told his story for the first time publicly. He was an important witness, recounting what he had found in room 304 and Puliafito's resistance to a 911 call. Puliafito's testimony went on for hours. He blamed his drug-fueled relationship with Sarah on bipolar disorder and a "hy-pomanic" state. But he denied ever giving drugs to anyone, including Sarah and Charles and Don Stokes and Dora. He denied having a sexual relationship with Dora—never mind his "girlfriend" statement on the 911 recording—and said he was her "healthcare consultant." Puliafito also denied having any ongoing contact with Kyle Voigt or Ariel Franko.

Adam and I knew from our reporting that he was lying about the drugs. And after Puliafito made his denials about Voigt and Franko, the deputy state attorney general presenting the case against him produced recordings of jailhouse phone calls made by the two dealers. Puliafito was on more than a dozen of those calls, talking with Voigt and Franko about drugs and overdoses and addicts. The calls were proof that Puliafito stayed in touch with the two men—proof that he lied under oath.

"He perjured himself on the stand here today," deputy attorney general Rebecca Smith told the administrative law judge presiding over the hearing.

Perjury is a felony punishable by up to four years in prison in California.

Puliafito lost his medical license, but he was never charged with perjury. No one in the offices of the attorney general or district attorney would tell me why.

21

ANOTHER BAD DOCTOR

On a Friday morning in February, Harriet was at her desk when she received a call from a blocked number. It was two weeks after publication of the story on Boaz's death and two days after we ran a piece showing how the Puliafito scandal had pummeled USC fundraising. Matt and I had been exchanging emails with Harriet about possible follow-up stories when the call came in. After she got off the phone, Harriet emailed us: "Just got a potentially good tip. Involves a creepy gynecologist in the student health services."

Matt and I waited for more. Less than an hour later, Harriet emailed us again: "Source is very squirrely. Doesn't have documents. But gave me a few leads."

The gynecologist was George Tyndall, a name that had never come up in our nineteen months of reporting on Puliafito—not in all those face-to-face meetings with sources, interviews over the phone, email and text exchanges, and record searches.

Could it be that Puliafito hadn't been the only bad doctor on campus?

· · ·

Nearly six years earlier, Lucy Chi walked into Tyndall's office at the student health center for what she thought would be a routine visit. She was immediately struck by the map of China on the wall.

What is that about? she thought.

Then the doctor asked her if she ever modeled.

Is he serious?

Chi wasn't tall, and she wasn't thin. She didn't have the unblemished complexion the camera loved.

"No," Chi said after a moment. *It was such an odd question.* "I don't think I look like a model."

For that matter, Tyndall didn't look like much of a doctor. The tall, baggy-face man was wearing an oversize Hawaiian shirt—or maybe it was a barong—and his white lab coat was wrinkled and splotched with food stains. The mess of hair on his head could have come out of a blender. If Chi saw him on the street, she might expect him to ask her for spare change. And his disheveled, unclean appearance was reflected in the office itself. Boxes overflowing with patient files were scattered around the room. One of two desks was buried under heaps of paper and old take-out cartons. A trash basket brimmed with used examination gloves. The office was humid and had a mulch-like odor.

Chi gave Tyndall the benefit of the doubt: *Doctors are so busy. They don't have time to take care of themselves. They have more important things on their minds than a tidy office. And this doctor worked for USC—a leading university.*

After she had entered the room, Tyndall locked the door behind her. *Was that weird?* Maybe not. Maybe it was for her privacy. He volunteered that the clutter of boxes in the office was in preparation of the clinic's upcoming move to a new building. Then he asked her what she was studying. When she said health policy, he eyed her warily: Was she a nurse? he asked. Was she studying medicine? No, she said, but she did attend medical school for a couple of years. Really? Did she learn to examine patients? How about gynecology exams? Chi said she didn't get that far in the program. And next he asked what she knew about the exam. Chi replied that she had a general understanding of the exam, the basic purpose of it.

And did her previous doctors wear gloves when they examined her? Did they put their hand inside her?

Chi asked herself if these were normal questions. She decided she hadn't any reason to believe they weren't.

But the doctor's manner? Well, that was something else.

Tyndall was in his midsixties and had been practicing at the school for twenty-three years. A native of upstate New York, he crisscrossed the country and the Pacific before finding his way to USC. Tyndall had enlisted in the navy and was stationed in the Philippines after studying at the Defense Language Institute in Monterey. At the end of his navy hitch, he returned to New York to earn his bachelor's degree at SUNY but traveled back to the Philippines to begin medical school. Tyndall finished his M.D. at the Medical College of Pennsylvania, which later became Drexel University College of Medicine. He headed west again and completed an obstetrics and gynecology residency at Kaiser Permanente's colossal medical center in Hollywood, a rampart of coldly institutional buildings along Sunset Boulevard. His next and last stop was the much smaller and more intimate student health clinic on USC's main campus.

Chi had known none of that. She hadn't been to the clinic before. It was an October afternoon in 2012, and Chi had just started at the university, where she was enrolled in a master's degree program in public policy. Her journey to USC was also circuitous, beginning as it did in Taiwan, where her parents ran a small publishing company. Her father and mother split up, but both immigrated to the L.A. area. Chi was six years old when she made the move with her mother. They had very little money and stayed first with her mother's brother, sleeping on a mattress in the living room of his apartment in Alhambra, a suburb where Asian immigrants made up a large and growing share of the population. Chi's mother had a degree in business and accounting from one of the best universities in Taiwan; in L.A., however, she had to settle for jobs in the underground economy because she lacked a green card. She never made much more than minimum wage, first as a bakery assistant and later as an off-the-books accountant for companies owned by Chinese immigrants.

The family had only one path to the American dream—education. And so when Chi was in first grade and came home in tears, crying day after day because she didn't know the language and couldn't keep up with the other kids, her mother only pushed her harder. The fierceness of her mother's insistence was often hurtful, but it worked. Chi became an honor student by the end of elementary school and continued to excel all through middle school and into high school, with college on the horizon. But good grades didn't pay the bills, and the financial stresses at home had not let up. In her senior year at Wilson High, Chi dropped out to help her mother, who was now caring for her own mother. The three of them were living in a small, two-bedroom apartment. Chi worked odd jobs and took the bus to save money. Eventually, she was able to fit community college classes into her work schedule. She did well enough to transfer to the University of California, Berkeley. The dream seemed to be coming true, and Chi's ambitions grew. She decided she wanted to become a doctor, and her performance at Berkeley earned her a spot at the University of Minnesota Medical School.

Leaving her mother and California for the Midwest wasn't easy. Her mother was struggling again, although her troubles this time were more emotional than financial. She had the irrational notion that Chi had abandoned her. In more desperate moments, her mom imagined having terminal cancer. The pressures of medical school were intense enough; her mother's distress made them unbearable. Chi felt she had no choice but to give up on a medical degree and returned home. She was twenty-eight when she landed back in L.A., and she had no long-term goals to pursue, no thought-out plans for the future. It made her despondent.

After all her achievements, all her hard work, would she still be consigned to the circumscribed life of an immigrant? To have her opportunities narrowed? Would she relive her mother's disappointments? Those thoughts haunted her as she regressed into a doldrums of jobs from the help-wanted listings, clerical work that paid the rent but hardly required a degree from Berkeley.

A year of that dead-end existence became an incentive for Chi to resume her studies. She had developed an interest in public policy, with an emphasis on health care—expanding health care to underserved communities like hers. Chi applied to several master's programs, including those at USC and UCLA. USC was not her first choice. It was much more expensive than UCLA; Chi's savings wouldn't come close to covering the tuition. She would have to keep working and hope for some financial aid.

Both schools accepted her—and the Trojans upped the ante for their more affordable rival: The USC School of Public Policy offered Chi a scholarship. It was a *full ride*!

All at once, the road ahead brightened with prospects. She would not be saddled by student loan debt. An advanced degree from USC promised a career that she would find rewarding. She might even be given a choice of jobs through L.A.'s vaunted "Trojan network"— the multitudes of alums with connections to share.

The news that arrived in the big envelope from USC sent a jolt through her. She jumped up and down in the living room of the apartment. And she hugged her mom for a long time.

And now, to make conversation with the strange doctor, Chi said, "My mother could've been a model."

"Was she beautiful?" Tyndall said.

"Yes."

He asked if her parents were from China. Chi said they were

from Taiwan, but her grandparents were from the mainland. Tyndall turned to the map on the wall and asked her to point to her grandparents' home province.

"I don't know where it is," she said.

And a feeling began to come over her. *Something isn't right here. Does this guy have an interest in women of Asian descent? Does that explain the modeling question?*

Other things started to make sense: When she had called the clinic to make an appointment, the woman who answered said it would take a month to see a female gynecologist. A *month*? Then the woman said in an obligatory way that the male doctor at the clinic had an opening the next day. Chi said that would be fine—and it was like she had given the wrong answer. "Are you sure?" the woman asked. There was a note of caution in her voice. "Are you sure?" she said again. Chi didn't know what to make of it or if she should make anything of it, but she was eager to get the exam behind her. It was just a routine visit. So she booked the appointment with the male doctor.

The following day was clear and calm—warm for fall but not too warm. The clinic was in a two-story brick building next door to the University Religious Center. Chi arrived late at the clinic; she might have ambled as if the balmy weather demanded a slower pace. The waiting area was dated, some of the chairs banged up a bit, but it was also neat and clean and had a cheerful air. And it was busy. Most of the students waiting for prescriptions or sports physicals or someone to check their sore throats were younger than Chi. She apologized to the receptionist for her tardiness. The receptionist smiled and said not to worry, and she checked the appointment calendar.

"You're here to see Dr. Tyndall?" she asked flatly. Her smile was gone.

Chi nodded.

The receptionist suddenly seemed concerned about her being five or ten minutes late.

"Do you want to reschedule?"

"Reschedule?"

"The doctor has time, but maybe you should reschedule."

A funny thing to say, Chi thought. If he has time, why reschedule? She said she preferred to keep the appointment. The receptionist gave her a look of resignation and directed her to a chair right at the door to Tyndall's office, some distance from the waiting area for the other doctors. It wasn't long before Tyndall opened the door and greeted her.

"Are you Lucy?"

"Yes."

Tyndall said, "I could see you now, without a nurse. Is that okay?"

Chi said it would be—why would she need a nurse?—and he led her into the office.

And he locked the door.

Yes, she was getting a bad feeling about this Dr. Tyndall, even as he sat there grinning at her. She was starting to wonder if both the receptionist and the woman who'd booked the appointment over the phone had been trying to steer her away from him—to warn her without actually saying anything about him. But warn her about what? His street-person appearance? The dumpy office? *Maybe his thing for Asian women?*

Or was she letting her imagination get the better of her? Was she overreacting to something she couldn't really describe?

Tyndall motioned to the exam area across the room. He asked her to remove her clothes and put on a hospital gown. She found that the privacy curtain around the exam table was not closed. Why wouldn't he close it? He turned to the side as she undressed, but she could sense his eyes on her body before she could cover herself in the gown. Creepy. *Let's just get this over with.*

She got on the table, and he began probing her. He told her she was "too tight," and he would need to massage her vaginal muscles so that the speculum would fit. She felt him using his hand on her. Could this be right? No doctor had ever done anything like this to her. But she remembered reading that training for gynecologists differed in certain regions of the country. Was that it? He was trained in methods she was unfamiliar with?

He was bent down as he kept his fingers inside her. She could hear him breathing—or was he panting?

Chi told him she had never had a problem with the speculum before and what he was doing was unnecessary. "Please stop," she said.

But he didn't stop. "I'm almost finished here," Tyndall said.

And then he asked, "Are you sexually active?"

She said yes, and that prompted him to ask if she enjoyed having sex with her boyfriend and what her usual positions were.

No gynecologist had ever asked her questions like that before. Was this also part of some alternative training?

Let's get through this. Let's get this done and get out that door.

He finally inserted the speculum and performed the exam.

Then someone was knocking on the door.

"What's going on in there?" a woman said. "Are you in there with a patient?"

Chi was startled. Tyndall did not respond to the woman.

"Unlock this door!" the woman yelled.

"I'm in here," Chi said. "We're almost done."

When Tyndall finished the exam, she waited for him to leave so she could get dressed. But he stood there and said he needed to examine her breasts. He said he had to feel them for lumps and to examine both at the same time to check for symmetry. She hadn't heard of a breast exam for symmetry, but the word *lumps* was always scary, so she let him continue.

Tyndall squeezed both of her breasts hard as he mumbled about checking for this and checking for that. She was frozen—shocked—and couldn't take in what he was saying. He squeezed and squeezed.

He wasn't examining her. He was *groping* her.

I need to leave! Chi told herself. *Now!*

She pulled her clothes on and hurried out the door. The woman on the other side of the door was a nurse, a middle-aged African American woman whose face was creased with concern.

"Are you okay?" she said to Chi. "Are you okay?"

Chi nodded. She wanted only to leave. *Escape.*

She all but ran toward the exit. The receptionist and other women staffers joined the nurse in calling out to her:

"Are you all right?"

Another receptionist, a younger woman, followed her out the door.

"Do you want to talk?" the receptionist asked gently.

"No," Chi said, "I have to get to class." And she walked away, unsteady—trembling.

Years later, Chi had a chilling realization: *They all knew.* The nurses, the receptionists, everyone working there, all of them. That's why they had tried to nudge her toward another doctor, and that's why they wanted to talk to her. They knew Tyndall was a danger to young women like her. And the way the nurse had pounded on the door and shouted at Tyndall to unlock it—that told Chi they had some protocol in place for him, special rules they hoped would limit his opportunities to hurt the women who came to him for help.

So why was he still allowed to treat patients?

Who else knew about him?

And for how long?

A view of the white-capped evening surf greeted Matt and me at the end of our drive from downtown L.A. to Long Beach. That was the best of the welcomes awaiting us. We made the trip to knock uninvited on the door of a USC administrator who lived in an ocean-view apartment on the coast highway. We hoped to speak to her about George Tyndall. The administrator's arms were filled with grocery bags when we approached her at the elevator. As soon as we identified ourselves, she shooed us away.

"I have nothing to say to you," she said.

We'd parked on a darkened side street; on the way back to our car, Matt stepped in a fresh pile of dog shit. He had to tear pages from his notebook to excavate it from his shoe tread. It was that kind of outing. Matt and I had thought the administrator might be one of the more helpful people on our door-knock list, which had taken us to points in the San Fernando Valley and in the opposite direction to the far edges of the San Gabriel Valley. All those road miles didn't get us much.

But we kept going because we badly wanted the story about Tyndall.

After Harriet got the tip from the blocked number, she and Matt searched for any criminal cases, civil lawsuits, or medical board actions involving Tyndall. He came up clean in the document scrubs, but then so had Puliafito. I asked Tommy Trojan and two sources at Keck I had cultivated during the Puliafito reporting what they knew about Tyndall. All three told me they hadn't heard anything troubling about the gynecologist, although they didn't work with him.

Harriet and Matt next compiled a roster of current and former employees of the health clinic, collecting names from a source inside USC as well as from LinkedIn and archived staff directories online. That launched weeks of home visits, navigating the freeways, boulevards, and suburban streets of L.A., mostly after hours and on weekends. Harriet and Matt focused primarily on doctors, nurses, and medical assistants; all but a few were too scared to speak on the record, if at all. We couldn't blame them. Nikias was still in power, and neither he nor the trustees showed any indication they were newly tolerant of whistleblowers—or anyone they might see as disloyal to the Trojan family.

As we dropped in on the frightened people, nearly all of them not expecting us, we kept in touch with each other by phone, car to car. Harriet would tell me how heartrending it was that lower-level clinic employees who earned such miserly salaries were willing to risk their scrap of financial security to tell the truth about Tyndall. Matt would remark on the fear in their faces.

We often returned to the same home more than once. I spent a combined four hours in repeated sittings in one living room. On their visits, Harriet and Matt asked the people who answered the door if they would be comfortable sending their loved ones to Tyndall—their daughters. The responses were a universally visceral *no,* and some of those who worked with Tyndall opened up about what they witnessed. A break came when one source told Harriet and Matt of Tyndall's sexually abusive pelvic exams of his young patients, his gawking at their exposed bodies, and his prurient commentaries.

And then interview by interview, conducted in secret with these employees, the outlines of a horror story emerged.

The current and former staffers of the clinic told us that complaints about Tyndall's behavior dated to the 1990s—*the nineties*! The earliest included a report that Tyndall was photographing his young patients' genitals for no apparent medical purpose. To nail down the details of that complaint, Matt and I drove out to Glendora to door-knock a retired nurse, Bernadette Kosterlitzky, one of the few people who spoke on the record. Kosterlitzky, who was in her eighties, gave us a brief interview at her front door, and she confirmed that the clinic director back then, Dr. Larry Neinstein, had Tyndall's camera confiscated after learning of the photographs. No other action was taken against Tyndall, however.

As the weeks went by, other people whom Harriet and Matt interviewed said the complaints about Tyndall's conduct only grew worse through the years, and many described acts of sexual abuse similar to what he inflicted on Lucy Chi. The sources said Tyndall was reported time after time to Neinstein and his management staff, with no noticeable result. Neinstein had been dead for two years, so others would have to speak for him. Two people who had been close to Neinstein told me he would have taken to his superiors any serious complaints about Tyndall. Those administrators would have included Michael Jackson, who had overseen the clinic as USC's vice president for student affairs. Jackson had retired from USC, but I caught up with him by phone in Northern California.

"I know why you're calling," he said. "I have nothing to say to you. I no longer work at USC, so I have nothing to say." And he hung up.

Most of the people I visited at home, like the woman in Long Beach, would not speak. Those who did insisted on anonymity, and they described Tyndall in terms that echoed what Harriet and Matt heard in their interviews: creepy, weird, unclean. He smelled, one source told me. Another recalled that Tyndall had to be ordered twice to remove a graphic image of a vagina from his wall. Between runs at USC administrators, I tried to learn more about Tyndall through the woman he identified as his wife, Daisy Patricio, and her family. She had left him and returned to her native Philippines, although we were not sure they had divorced. Patricio's relatives here would not speak to me; I briefly made contact with her new partner in the Philippines, but then he went silent. I arranged to have a *Times* stringer in the Philippines try to engage Patricio; the stringer fared no better.

But Harriet and Matt continued to make inroads with their interviews of the medical staffers and patients. They learned that USC only began to move against Tyndall when a longtime nurse supervisor at the clinic decided to put everything on the line in a last effort to take him down.

Her name was Cindy Gilbert.

22

TYNDALL'S HUSH-HUSH DEAL

Nesting on the windowsill inside George Tyndall's office were cans of Raid insect killer and Febreze air freshener. Neither helped. The room where the gynecologist saw his patients had become infested with fruit flies. It reeked of body odor.

Cindy Gilbert spotted the Raid and Febreze when she inspected the office with Dr. Mildred Wenger, a colleague at the student health clinic. This was in June 2016. Four days earlier, Gilbert had calculated the risks of trying to stop Tyndall once and for all. They were considerable. The executives who ran USC did not like people in the trenches stirring up trouble. Staffers who broke ranks and spoke out were not exactly rewarded for acting on principle. But it no longer mattered to Gilbert, a slender woman with a soft smile and a hard-nosed devotion to protecting her patients. It no longer mattered to her if what she was about to do got her fired. Her husband was a USC physician, and his job could also be put in jeopardy, but that didn't matter, either. All that mattered anymore was preventing Tyndall from ever again abusing another young woman.

Gilbert had taken the steps she was supposed to take within the clinic's internal procedures. She had done so year after year, repeatedly—

complaining about Tyndall to the clinic's executive director and to the head of nursing. All she heard in response was that Tyndall had been counseled about his behavior.

Counseled, but not stopped.

And this wasn't "behavior." It was abuse. It was *sexual assault.* So Gilbert resolved to report it for what it truly was. If it was her last act as a USC employee, that was the way it had to be. At the suggestion of the clinic's quality control manager, Gilbert reported Tyndall to USC's Relationship and Sexual Violence Prevention and Services—the rape crisis center. Gilbert reported him to the center's executive director, just as she would a rapist. And it appeared to work. At long last, the university seemed to pay attention.

Tyndall was on vacation, so Gilbert and Wenger could get a good look at his office. Everyone on staff who had peeked inside Tyndall's office knew he was a hoarder—all those cartons and files, the extra broken chairs, the old slides and pamphlets, books, lunch boxes, fast-food wrappers, half-empty water bottles, a dirty container of hypodermic needles, the lot of it pack-ratted in there. But what Gilbert and Wenger found was nauseating. The fruit flies fluttered everywhere and covered the entire surface of Tyndall's desk. The source of the flies was a plastic bag of fruit lying on top of a cloth suitcase; the fruit had decayed into a liquid, which leached through the bag and into the fabric of the suitcase. The stench had a tangible quality to it. There was the usual trash everywhere. Gilbert took photos to document the clutter and filth that Tyndall's patients had to sit in.

How could this have gone on so long? For twenty-five years, complaints about Tyndall were passed up the chain of command at the clinic. Some came from patients whose accounts of how Tyndall examined them were punctuated by the word "creepy." *Shouldn't that be enough to remove him from campus? Who would want to see a creepy gynecologist?* The female medical assistants and nurses had complaints of their own. Clinic policy required them to serve as chaperones for Tyndall's patients during exams, and they told of witnessing him cross just about every line of appropriate conduct for a doctor, up to what looked very much like sexual abuse.

Three years before Gilbert turned to the rape crisis center as a last resort, she and a group of chaperones took another batch of complaints about Tyndall to Neinstein. What he heard could not have surprised him. Neinstein had been running the clinic for eighteen years and had spent most of his professional life at USC, where his two sons and daughter all received degrees. He was now sixty-three, a cherubic-looking man with a dusting of white beard. Neinstein had his critics, but he seemed well liked overall and was widely admired beyond USC as an expert in adolescent health. Under Neinstein, the clinic had tripled in size and moved into its new, five-story head-quarters, named the Engemann Student Health Center after a donor. Neinstein called it "a dream come true." The doctor was also a two-time survivor of aggressive cancers, having beat melanoma in medical school and multiple myeloma in middle age.

At the clinic, Neinstein's affliction was George Tyndall.

He had been fielding complaints about Tyndall since the time he had to take the gynecologist's camera away because he was photographing his patients' genitals, supposedly to document the absence of cancer or the presence of conditions like warts. Back in 1997, a patient who completed a clinic comment card seemed to know just what a malignancy Tyndall would become. She wrote that Tyndall, "a doctor I have seen in the past—but will never see again—is the worst doctor I have ever seen in my life. He has mis-diagnosed myself + 20 other people I could name off-hand, including telling a girl I know she had cancer when she didn't." The patient's next comment warned of something ruinous: "If you don't want a huge future lawsuit on your hands, I highly suggest the termination of this man."

As the months and the years and then more than a decade went by, the complaints about Tyndall persisted and became increasingly disturbing. Most of them came to Neinstein. He learned that Tyndall was not allowing chaperones behind the privacy curtain to monitor him when he performed pelvic exams. A patient told Neinstein that Tyndall did not wear gloves when he used his fingers to examine her. Others said Tyndall liked to ask his young patients about their sex lives, for no apparent medical reason. Tyndall complimented a patient on the appearance of her pubic hair. With another patient, he shared an anecdote about a rock musician having sex in a Chicago street with a woman who had to remove her tampon. The patient complained in writing, saying it was "degrading and humiliating" to have to listen to Tyndall's "disgusting" story.

Neinstein confronted Tyndall and admonished him to not engage in such behavior again. But the message never seemed to sink in, and Neinstein had to rebuke him once more. Tyndall could be menacing in his response to criticism. A well of potential violence seemed to hide behind his dull gaze. He made Neinstein afraid for his physical well-being. In 2004, Neinstein took his fears to Jackson.

"I am concerned that we have an employee who is very disgruntled," Neinstein told Jackson in an email.

Apparently, nothing was done. (Jackson later denied receiving reports of Tyndall's abusing patients.)

The patient who complained about Tyndall not wearing gloves said he insisted on teaching her exercises to strengthen her pelvic walls—with no chaperone present. She wrote that Tyndall had her lie down and then penetrated her with his bare finger while telling her to "squeeze." Tyndall disputed the woman's account. Neinstein's contemporaneous notes on the matter showed that he informed a lawyer in USC's Office of the General Counsel of the complaint; the office reported to the president of the university. Neinstein also notified the school's Title IX coordinator in the USC Office of Equity and Diversity, known as OED. Title IX is the federal law that bans sexual discrimination and sexual harassment at universities that receive federal funding.

As Neinstein's notes documented, however, the general counsel and the OED responded with a yawn: *The conduct the woman alleged happened a long time ago—so forget about it, the complaint wouldn't "go anywhere."* And it didn't. No one came close to following the prescient young woman's advice to terminate him.

In his notes, Neinstein commented on the lack of any discipline of Tyndall. "Not good idea," he wrote.

That was in 2010. Neinstein did not have to accept the administrators' refusal to act. As a physician and as the director of a clinic that served vulnerable young people, he could have done more—and he *should* have done more. He could have reported Tyndall to the medical board, but there was no indication that he did. And he could have reported him to the police. There was no indication he did that, either.

Three years later, a patient had complained that Tyndall had wanted to do a second Pap smear on her, even though she told him she'd had one recently. She said Tyndall also suggested that she not leave his office and then remarked on his "beautiful wife" who was a "Filipina" and how he found "women so attractive." It gave her the "sceevies," the student said. The complaint led Neinstein to meet with Gilbert and the chaperones to hear the latest about Tyndall, and he took notes: Tyndall was locking his door during exams to keep chaperones out. Several patients said they would never see him again because of his "strangeness" and "creepiness." Tyndall asked patients "personal questions." He used a "different technique" in exams, and some patients suffered pain. Neinstein again decided to keep matters in-house. He reported Tyndall to the OED, citing those complaints and the earlier ones. This time, Neinstein wasn't merely forwarding complaints—he was the named complainant. The document alleged that Tyndall engaged in sexual harassment—a broad category under Title IX that could include sexual assault—and that he subjected patients to "national origin discrimination" through his remarks about his Filipina wife and comments such as "Mexicans are taking over."

The report prompted a senior investigator for the office to open an inquiry—the strongest word for what followed, because it wasn't much of an investigation. Despite the number and variety and extended time frame of the complaints, and despite the seriousness of the alleged misconduct, the investigator interviewed just eight people. Among those she didn't question: Tyndall himself. And she didn't go very deep into the records. The investigator did not even ask to review Neinstein's file on Tyndall. The inquiry carried from June into July of 2013 with no action taken. In the interim, Neinstein and the clinic's lead physician met with Tyndall to discuss the complaints and, one more time, ordered him to refrain from making sexist, racist, and harassing comments. Tyndall responded by going on the offensive: In a written rebuttal to Neinstein, Tyndall portrayed himself as the victim—that he had to endure a "hostile work environment" because he was a male gynecologist.

Neinstein kept the OED investigator in the loop. He called her to say that it "may be that he just doesn't get it," meaning Tyndall. Neinstein told her that Tyndall's personnel file—the one she didn't ask for—was four to five inches thick.

It was all for naught. On July 26, 2013, the investigator closed the inquiry. In a confidential memo, she wrote that she found "no actionable evidence of any policy violation," and there was "insufficient evidence of any university policy violation to justify continuing an investigation."

Neinstein did not give up. He turned to an administrator in human resources to express his frustration with the OED investigation. Neinstein filled the administrator in on the complaints about Tyndall to determine if it was enough to fire him. The administrator sympathized and took the matter up with the executive director of HR, only to be told that Tyndall could not be fired without first receiving three warnings. It was as if he had three free passes to sexually harass and even sexually assault his patients. As long as he didn't do it a fourth time, his job was safe. That may not have been a written policy, but it was the actual result.

Tyndall's position remained secure for another three years—until Gilbert did what Neinstein had failed to do—she forced the university to act, regardless of the cost to her. Neinstein would not live to see this. The cancer had returned, and he went on leave. He died less than two months before the Tyndall inquiry got underway.

Twenty-some years after Neinstein confiscated Tyndall's camera, Gilbert and Wenger made a shocking discovery: On the same day they encountered the swarm of fruit flies, they found more than two hundred photographs and slides from the early 1990s that were locked in a cabinet in the gynecologist's office. The images were of female genitalia; some were labeled with the names of the women who were photographed. The images escalated the administration's concerns about Tyndall. OED and the university's Office of Compliance opened investigations. The OED probe also included the 2013 accusations that Tyndall had made racially discriminatory statements.

Tyndall was placed on leave and banned from campus during the inquiry. A second OED investigator interviewed several chaperones, and their accounts had not changed. The investigator interviewed a patient who complained that Tyndall had asked her if she was sexually inactive because of her family's religious views; he shared with the patient that he had waited to have sex with his wife until they were married because she was Asian. And then he offered the patient some advice: If she wasn't a virgin when she got married, she could fool her husband by surreptitiously popping a small bag of blood on the bed during sex on their wedding night. The patient told the investigator she was "shocked."

The inquiry stretched into the beginning of 2017. USC retained a medical consulting firm, MDReview of Colorado, and a gynecologist from Kansas to bolster the case against Tyndall. Examiners from MDReview interviewed Tyndall and sixteen clinic staff members and reviewed more than two dozen medical records. Tyndall made no admissions of wrongdoing. Unsurprisingly, though, MDReview concluded in its report that Tyndall's conduct would raise "serious questions about patient physical and psychological safety" if he were to return to practice. The report stated that Tyndall used "physical exam techniques that vary from standard accepted practices and could be, and likely were (based on patient feedback), considered to represent inappropriate physical contact with patients that would likely be considered serious boundary violations by a professional conduct, licensing, or credentialing committee."

Tyndall's methods "could be considered a violation of [a patient's] body," the report said. And it stated that "some of Dr. Tyndall's behaviors are potentially indicative of underlying psychopathy."

MDReview noted that the "bulk of the patients" Tyndall saw were "unusually vulnerable" because of their age and lack of knowledge of what is "normal" for a gynecological exam and, in many cases, "language and cultural barriers." The latter seemed to refer to the large number of students from China and other Asian countries whom Tyndall saw.

USC now had more than enough to fire Tyndall and report him to the medical board and the police. Instead, it allowed him to file an appeal of the investigation's findings. That process and the university's general slow-footedness kept Tyndall on the payroll until the middle of 2017. The campus remained off-limits to Tyndall during that time, but nothing prevented him from engaging in private practice with unsuspecting patients (he later claimed he did not).

Finally, USC agreed to pay Tyndall off in exchange for his resignation. And the Nikias administration kept everything under wraps—everything secret—and not just from the authorities and the public but from the staffers who complained and Tyndall's patients as well.

Tyndall left the university with his medical license unblemished and money in his pocket. And he was free to do as he pleased.

That remained unchanged until Nikias and his team got wind

that we were interviewing people about Tyndall. Suddenly, the administration decided it *should* report Tyndall to the medical board, which it did—some eight months after USC decided to cut him loose for the same behavior it now deemed worthy of a report. And USC waited three more months to notify the police. And that was only after learning that our reporting was delving into allegations of sexual assault. The Nikias administration was quicker to alert clinic staffers to our queries. Many took that to mean they were to keep their mouths shut.

Not long after our aborted interview of the USC administrator in Long Beach, Matt and I zeroed in on another potential source we believed could confirm crucial parts of the story. The problem was that the person happened to be out of town at that time. But we couldn't let that stop us, not on a story this important. So we headed to LAX and boarded a plane for an *extreme* door-knock—extreme because we were traveling a vastly greater distance than our jaunts around greater L.A. And because we were doing so at considerable expense to the *Times* with an exceptionally slim chance that the person we intended to surprise would talk. The person had much to lose and nothing to gain by speaking to us—nothing, that is, except the satisfaction that comes from doing the right thing. In my experience, that was the most common motivation of people who spoke to me at risk to themselves. They simply wanted to do the right thing. And after Matt and I cajoled our way through the door, broke the ice with some small talk, and then made our pitch, that's what our long-distance source did. The right thing. The source had to remain anonymous; the alternative would have meant career death. We interviewed the source for two hours. What we learned confirmed much of the foundation of our reporting. The source told us from an authoritative perspective that we were right.

We flew back to L.A. the following day and returned to a *Times* newsroom that was very different from the one ruled by Maharaj and

Duvoisin. Under interim executive editor Jim Kirk, the leadership supported our pursuit of the Tyndall story and was prepared to throw all the resources of the paper at getting it published, as the trip Matt and I took to knock on a single door demonstrated.

And Soon-Shiong was in the process of buying the *Times* and tronc's other West Coast paper, *The San Diego Union-Tribune*.

Like Neinstein, Cindy Gilbert had given essentially the whole of her career to USC, and the institution played an even larger part than that in her life. She did her nursing training at County/USC Medical Center, where she met her future husband, Paul, who was doing his residency there as an orthopedic surgeon. Paul Gilbert was a Keck graduate and later a professor at the school. Cindy Gilbert didn't stray far in marrying a physician; her father was a cardiologist. She was drawn to nursing because it offered so much variety in the field of health care, allowing her to move between specialties. She started out in pediatrics; decades later, she was just as passionate about her work with the older teens and young adults at the clinic.

But the minute she reported Tyndall to the rape crisis center, Gilbert's commitment to her patients and colleagues seemed to become academic to her superiors. She was now a troublemaker, a loudmouth, a problem employee. And that's how she was treated by the administrators who should have taken action against Tyndall but did not. By going around them and over them, Gilbert had embarrassed them. She'd made them look bad, and there was a price to pay for that.

We're watching you. That was the bosses' message for her. From then on, in their estimation, she couldn't do anything right. They rescinded a promotion she had been promised. They began taking away her supervisorial duties and undermined her with her colleagues, telling them they did not have to take direction from her. Then they called her into a closed-door meeting with two of her managers and representatives from HR. *An ambush,* she thought. She was accused—falsely, Gilbert insisted—of making an inappropriate remark to a coworker. But that wasn't the real point of the session; they told her she had been "communicating poorly" with her supervisors, a catchall accusation that was more like a verdict—and an unspoken invitation to resign.

"Their goal was to push me out," Gilbert told me, her eyes moist with the memory.

Gilbert couldn't fight them any longer. The administrators hadn't even told her what happened with Tyndall. *Did he get fired? Was it possible he could return to the clinic?* There were rumors he was gone for good, but no one would confirm that for Gilbert. The administrators kept her in the dark, the woman who had the courage to report him at the cost of what she was losing now.

"I wasn't trying to hurt SC," Gilbert said in our interview. "I was trying to protect the students and the staff."

Her husband made the case that it wasn't worth her emotional health to stay. Gilbert resigned in July 2017.

"It was hard. There was so much I loved about the job. It should have been a good experience—and there were lots of positives."

She widened her eyes and caught the first of the tears with her finger. Then she shared her biggest regret about her time at the clinic—that she had failed for so long to stop Tyndall.

"I told the staff I would get him out, and it didn't happen," Gilbert said.

And she cried.

23

THE FALL OF MAX NIKIAS

At the Shrine Auditorium, the Moorish landmark that has hosted the Grammys, Emmys, and Oscars, Oprah Winfrey was delivering a spirited commencement address to graduates of USC's Annenberg School for Communication and Journalism. She roused the class of 2018 with lines such as "The truth has always been and will always be our shield against corruption." Just around the corner on Figueroa Street, a product of USC's journalism school, Matt Hamilton, sat in a university conference room with Harriet. They were there to give three of Nikias's administrators an opportunity to address our findings about Tyndall. It was not a fruitful meeting. The Nikias delegates dodged the tougher questions about the years of ignored complaints. They said the school did everything right with Tyndall, based on the information that had been available to them. Nothing the administrators said challenged our reporting.

USC was trying desperately to get ahead of the story before it was published. In addition to belatedly reporting Tyndall to the authorities, the university said that it had emailed a survey in 2016 to hundreds of patients of the clinic, vaguely soliciting feedback about any of the physicians on staff during the spring of that year. USC

244 · BAD CITY

would not give the *Times* a copy of the survey. The university said fewer than two dozen patients responded to the survey, including two who complained about Tyndall but not in relation to his exams. Four days after the meeting with Harriet and Matt, the Nikias administration issued a lawyerly statement to the paper saying it did not believe it violated a California statute requiring hospitals and clinics to report problem doctors to the medical board *because USC was a school and not a hospital or clinic.* The statement did add that "in hindsight, while not legally obligated, USC now believes it should have filed a consumer complaint with the Medical Board earlier in 2017 when Tyndall resigned."

Nikias emailed another of his letters to the USC community, this one saying, "On behalf of the university, I sincerely apologize to any student who may have visited the student health center and did not receive the respectful care each individual deserves."

Hours after the statement and letter were sent, our story went up on the *Times* website. The story was as hard-hitting and detailed and loaded with legal hazards as the Puliafito piece, if not more so, but with Jim Kirk now leading the newsroom, the editing barely took three weeks, not three or four months. The published version began:

For nearly 30 years, the University of Southern California's student health clinic had one full-time gynecologist: Dr. George Tyndall. Tall and garrulous, he treated tens of thousands of female students, many of them teenagers seeing a gynecologist for the first time.

Few who lay down on Tyndall's exam table at the Engemann Student Health Center knew that he had been accused repeatedly of misconduct toward young patients.

The complaints began in the 1990s, when co-workers alleged he was improperly photographing students' genitals. In the years that followed, patients and nursing staff accused him again and again of "creepy" behavior, including touching women inappropriately during pelvic exams and making sexually suggestive remarks about their bodies.

In recent years, some colleagues feared that he was targeting the university's growing population of Chinese students, who often had a limited understanding of the English language and American medical norms.

Still, Tyndall was allowed to continue practicing. It was not until 2016, when a frustrated nurse went to the campus rape crisis center, that he was suspended.

An internal USC investigation determined that Tyndall's behavior during pelvic exams was outside the scope of current medical practice and amounted to sexual harassment of students. But in a secret deal last summer, top administrators allowed Tyndall to resign quietly with a financial payout.

The university did not inform Tyndall's patients. Nor did USC report him at the time to the Medical Board of California, the agency responsible for protecting the public from problem doctors.

The story detailed Gilbert's long struggle to get anyone to move on the complaints. "It became clear he wasn't going to stop," Gilbert said. "Some things you can ignore. Some things you can't."

Gilbert described what she believed were acts of retaliation that followed her report to the rape crisis center. In its prepublication statement, USC denied she was retaliated against.

The university also tried to make Neinstein, two years in the grave, the fall guy. In an online letter to the USC community, Nikias wrote that Neinstein "chose to manage" the complaints about Tyndall "independently." He mentioned Neinstein's report to OED, but said it only involved "alleged racist comments" by Tyndall. Nikias's statement included a link to a "statement of facts" from Todd Dickey, who was USC's senior vice president for administration; Gretchen Dahlinger Means, the OED executive director who served as the Title IX coordinator; and Laura LaCorte, the school's associate senior vice president for compliance. A key line in the statement unloaded further on Neinstein; it said: "Rather than elevate these complaints for proper investigation, the former director's notes indicated that in each case he took steps to address Tyndall's behavior independently, including in some instances discussing the complaints with the patients, conducting chart reviews of Tyndall's clinical practice, and bringing in outside experts to review his clinical practices."

There was nothing in Nikias's letter or the statement of "facts" about Neinstein's complaints to OED of locked doors, blocked chaperones, ungloved fingers, sexist commentary, or prurient anecdotes. Nothing about Neinstein's earlier reports to the general counsel and the Title IX coordinator. Nothing about his appeal to HR to fire Tyndall.

Instead, Nikias and his administration tried to pin the worst of it on a dead man.

Tyndall's denials—his insistence that he did nothing improper— were noted in our story. They came from his combined ten hours of interviews with Harriet and Matt in a park near his home. The story included his stated desire to practice medicine into his eighties, as well as this comment by him: "When I am on my deathbed, I want to think there are thousands and thousands of Trojan women out there whose health I made a difference in."

Like the Puliafito story, the Tyndall piece became a sensation online. Media outlets across the nation and around the world chased it. And unlike the Puliafito story, it landed in the heat of #MeToo. Nikias now had to find a way to survive not just his second massive scandal in ten months but also a legal and moral reckoning sweeping through America's institutions. He gave it his best shot— largely by returning to the Puliafito playbook. First, he sought to deflect blame from himself, saying he had known nothing about

Tyndall until months after the physician left USC. Next, he issued an apology without quite taking personal responsibility for the inaction of his administrators, other than to say, "We let you down." And then he pledged to undertake a series of internal inquiries and reforms. USC also fired two clinic supervisors whom the university said should have done more about Tyndall, but Nikias offered no criticism of the role of the general counsel's office, the Title IX coordinator, and others in the administration.

The trustees remained in Nikias's corner. "The executive committee of the board has full confidence in President Nikias's leadership, ethics, and values and is certain that he will successfully guide our community forward," board chairman John Mork said in a statement.

But the drumbeat of our follow-up stories grew louder by the day. There were the accounts of more and more women who came forward to allege that Tyndall had abused them on the exam table. About three hundred former patients called a hotline USC set up for his alleged victims. The fact that Tyndall abused Asian students disproportionately became increasingly apparent. The Chinese consulate of Los Angeles gave me a statement demanding that USC "deal with the case in a serious manner, conduct an immediate investigation and take concrete measures to protect the Chinese students and scholars on campus from being harmed." That was the last thing the trustees—several of whom were from China and other Asian nations—and USC's fundraisers wanted to hear. The university had one of the largest enrollments of students from China in the United States—more than 5,400. The tuition those students paid and the money their parents donated were a significant piece of USC's business model.

The LAPD opened what would become one of the city's biggest sexual abuse investigations ever. Before arresting Tyndall and charging him with twenty-nine felonies (he pleaded not guilty), detectives would spend a year interviewing witnesses and alleged victims all over the United States. But there was one person they didn't even ask to

speak to: Max Nikias. As far as I could determine, the LAPD and the district attorney's office kept the investigation confined to Tyndall. They showed no interest in learning whether USC administrators had violated any laws in how they responded to the complaints about Tyndall's abuse of patients. That was in glaring contrast to the broader investigations of the sexual assault cases involving former Penn State football coach Jerry Sandusky and former Michigan State University physician Larry Nassar. In those probes, authorities examined the actions of university administrators, which resulted in criminal charges against the presidents of both schools. Former Penn State president Graham Spanier served two months in jail for not reporting an allegation that Sandusky molested a child. A judge dismissed the charges against former Michigan State president Lou Anna Simon, who was accused of lying to investigators in the Nassar case.

Audry Nafziger said Tyndall abused her when she was a USC law student in 1990. She went on to work for many years as a sex crimes prosecutor for the DA's office in neighboring Ventura County. "If you're not looking, you're never going to find anything," Nafziger said of the failure of L.A. investigators to conduct an inquiry into USC administrators. "Why is USC different from Penn State? Why is it different from Michigan State?"

She could think of no good answer.

By the week following publication of the Tyndall story, Nikias was taking fire from all directions. An online petition calling for his removal quickly garnered two thousand signatures from alumni, students, and others. More remarkable was a letter that two hundred faculty members sent to the trustees saying that Nikias "lost the moral authority to lead" and must resign. A constant in the previous scandals was the docility of the faculty, a reflection of Nikias's iron grip on the university. The letter set the stage for a bigger blow to Nikias's tenure: a vote by the Academic Senate, the body that rep-

resents the faculty, urging him to go. The vote followed a meeting in which faculty members lashed out at Nikias and the board. Said one: "The main problem is this institution does not have a Board of Trustees. Max has a Board of Trustees."

Rick Caruso, the mall builder with mayoral ambitions, saw the revolt only growing and was trying to persuade his fellow trustees behind the scenes to tell Nikias the time had come. Caruso turned for help to people like William Tierney, who belonged to a small and elite group of faculty members who held the title of University Professor, an honor reserved for the most accomplished of USC's researcher-educators. If Nikias had lost the support of the university professors, the likelihood that the board would ask for his resignation would increase dramatically. Tierney quickly determined that the group felt it was in the best interests of USC for Nikias to relinquish the presidency. So about a dozen of the professors met privately with Nikias to convey that conviction. The meeting in Nikias's office (some professors attended by phone) was polite but sad, Tierney said.

"Everyone said cordially, in their own way, 'Max, you have to go,'" Tierney recalled. "He said, 'I've got some thinking to do.'"

Soon after, on May 25, 2018, the word came down that Nikias was resigning. The top of our story:

USC President C.L. Max Nikias, whose tenure was marked by a significant boost in the university's prestige and fundraising prowess but tarnished by a series of damaging scandals, is stepping down from his post, the university's Board of Trustees announced Friday.

The move comes after more than a week of uproar over the university's handling of a longtime campus gynecologist accused of misconduct toward female students. More than 300 people, most of them former female patients of Dr. George Tyndall, have since come forward to USC, many with allegations of mistreatment and sexual abuse that date back to the early 1990s.

The revelations published by The Times heightened long-festering concerns about university leaders' ethics and management style and sparked calls for Nikias to resign.

"President Nikias and the Executive Committee of the Board of Trustees have agreed to begin an orderly transition and commence the process of selecting a new president," Rick J. Caruso, a USC trustee, said in a letter to the campus Friday. "We recognize the need for change and are committed to a stable transition."

But Nikias and the board did not fix a date for his departure. The transition turned out to be a protracted and mysterious one, with no signposts of a search for Nikias's successor. Faculty members and student leaders began to worry that Nikias might renege on his promise to leave. They knew that he maintained support among many trustees, some of whom believed the fallout from the scandal would wane over the summer and Nikias could remain as president indefinitely. By late July, the fears of that happening reached a boiling point. More than 670 faculty members signed a petition to the trustees seeking assurances that Nikias would be gone by the start of the fall semester. "We find ourselves in a state of turmoil and uncertainty," the petition said. "President Nikias cannot be the one who stands up to greet new students at the convocation." It was followed by a letter to the faculty from the Academic Senate president that stated "it would be inappropriate for Nikias to continue in office during the search for a new permanent President."

A week later, the trustees announced that Nikias was indeed relinquishing the presidency and would be replaced on an interim basis by Wanda Austin, a retired aerospace executive who held a seat on the USC board. She became the first woman and first African American to lead the university.

So the Nikias era finally came to a close. It was a steep and graceless fall—"an American tragedy," said Tierney—but Caruso and the other trustees feathered in a soft landing. They granted Nikias an exit package worth more than $7.6 million, kept him on the faculty in the School of Engineering, awarded him the title of president emeritus, and named him a "life trustee," a nonvoting but prestigious position on the board.

What the trustees likely didn't know when they cushioned Nikias's farewell was that another scandal was coming—one that also took root on his watch and would further tarnish USC on the national stage.

24

VARSITY BLUES

A knifing pain deep in his chest left Eric Rosen gasping for breath. *Was he having a heart attack?* He was in the back seat of an Uber on the West Side Highway in New York City, the traffic brought to a crawl by the motorcade of a visiting President Trump somewhere up ahead. Rosen was an assistant United States attorney from Boston, an expert in financial crimes. He had come to New York for a meeting with other federal prosecutors on a securities fraud case. It was an important case, but not the one that had him working sixteen-hour days month after month—a slog that likely led to whatever caused him to clutch his chest in agony. *He was only forty years old! Too young—too healthy—for this to be happening!*

Rosen phoned his wife, a physician; she ordered him to call an ambulance. He did, and somehow the EMS crew managed to punch through the gridlock to ease him out of the Uber and ferry him off to the hospital. The diagnosis there was a pulmonary embolism. A blood clot in his leg had traveled to his lung. Rosen remembered he'd felt what he thought was a muscle cramp in his calf when he was jogging. He took a foam roller to it, which might have only dislodged the clot and sped its journey north. His wife had been warning him about his schedule and the toll it could be taking on his health: *You're running yourself into the ground.*

She was right, but Rosen couldn't stop. He was out of the hospital and back to work in less than a week. He'd been eager to return to *the* case. The Big One. The case that had him flying around and across the country (all those hours on airplanes did not promote vascular health). There were several flights to L.A.

The yawning dimensions of the case had come into focus for Rosen during a trip to New York the year before. He'd been on an afternoon train from Boston, for a meeting with the Securities and Exchange Commission, when his phone rang with a call from the FBI. The agents he had partnered with wanted him to hear recordings an informant had secretly made of phone conversations with a man named Rick Singer. The train was too crowded for any privacy, so Rosen walked to the gangway connection between coaches. He stood there and listened to the recordings, pressing the phone close because of the din of clanging wheels.

Singer was a silver-haired and silver-tongued college admissions consultant based in Newport Beach, and he was recorded on the phone with a man named Rudy Meredith, who was the women's soccer coach at Yale University. He was making a sales pitch to Meredith, crowing about the hundreds of parents who turned to him for help in getting their children into the best universities—whether they were qualified or not. To Rosen's amazement, Singer was laying out the breadth and scope of what would become the largest college admissions scandal in U.S. history. He was the mastermind of a scheme in which parents bribed college coaches or administrators to admit their children as athletic recruits, even if they didn't play the sport they supposedly excelled at. Some parents also paid Singer to rig their children's SAT and ACT tests, ensuring they would receive world-beating scores for admission into the college of their choice.

Far more than any other school Singer targeted, USC was that choice.

Blithely, matter-of-factly, with the air of an accomplished con man who couldn't imagine anyone would dare turn on him, Singer told Meredith that he was doing so much corrupt business that he needed to bribe more coaches to admit students as phony athletes. "We've done it everywhere," Singer said. He needed more opportunities for well-heeled parents willing to hand over hundreds of thousands of dollars each to circumvent the normal admission process for their children. He needed more spots for those kids at schools like Yale. Singer felt safe sharing this with Meredith because Meredith was among the coaches who had accepted his bribes—at least $860,000 in total.

One parent who greased Meredith did not go through Singer: Morrie Tobin, an L.A. financier, was paying the coach in monthly installments to get his daughter into Yale as a soccer player. The payments started before the fifty-five-year-old Tobin got pinched in a stock-swindling case that had nothing to do with buying a spot in the freshman class. In March 2018, the stock investigation sent FBI agents to Tobin's French château–style mansion in L.A.'s Hancock Park neighborhood. They served him with a search warrant and nook-and-crannied their way through the 8,400-square-foot home, seizing documents and electronic devices. The evidence against Tobin was overwhelming. He had been a principal in an elaborate "pump-and-dump" scam that falsely inflated the value of stock to cheat unsuspecting investors out of millions. Rosen and his office asserted jurisdiction in the case because at least one of the victims lived in Massachusetts. At the time of the raid on Tobin's home, neither Rosen nor the FBI had any inkling that Tobin or anyone else was paying off coaches to get their children into college. Whoever heard of such a thing? As they finished their search, the FBI agents told Tobin that they had him cold—that he was going down—and that he should get in touch with Rosen if he wanted to help himself. Tobin was looking at years in federal prison; if he cooperated with the government, he might be able to cop a plea for a lighter sentence.

Tobin soon saw the wisdom in the FBI's advice and flew to the

Bay State to cut a deal. For two days, he met with Rosen, the FBI, and the SEC at the John Joseph Moakley U.S. Courthouse, in a ninth-floor conference room with a view of snowy Boston Harbor. Tobin gave up his coconspirators in the pump-and-dump case, name by name, detail by detail. And then he offered something of a cherry on top—information on a Yale coach who took money to admit applicants to the university who posed as recruited athletes.

Rosen was intrigued, and not just because he was a Harvard grad and Yale happened to be his alma mater's perennial rival. "It was the first time I had heard of bribing someone to get a spot," he recalled. He was impressed with the underhanded method of admission through a non-marquee sport like soccer: "It struck me as a very creative and crafty way of getting the ultimate prize of admission. At an Ivy League, no one really follows up on whether you play or not."

Initially, Rosen figured Tobin's bribery of Meredith was probably an isolated transaction between two dishonest men. Tobin selected Yale because he had attended the school, where he played hockey before transferring to the University of Vermont. "We obviously thought it was very interesting," Rosen said. "We thought it would be a good one-off case."

To get started, he had Tobin meet with Meredith in a hotel room to discuss the upcoming payments for his daughter's admission. The FBI had outfitted the room with hidden video cameras, which caught the dad and the coach settling on a $450,000 bribe.

"At the very end of the meeting, he tells Morrie there's this guy in L.A. and it's his job to do this," Rosen recounted. "He said, 'His name is Rick Singer.'"

That was the first time Rosen heard the name, and he began to wonder if this was a one-off after all.

Unknotting riddles was among the things Rosen loved about his job. He happened to be good at it, too. He was bulldog-ish and brought to the art of investigations a blend of technical skills he inherited from his engineer father and data analyst mother. Give him the slightest lead, and he would chase it relentlessly. And when the lead directed him to a problem—the kind that involved breaking the law and victimizing people—he solved it or exhausted himself trying.

Meredith's on-camera performance provided grounds to subpoena his bank records, which showed the $860,000 Singer had paid the coach over the past three years. That gave Rosen enough to have the FBI confront Meredith. Like Tobin, Meredith agreed to flip, and the agents had him call Singer on a recorded line. The result was the listening material for Rosen's train ride.

"He spoke of hundreds of kids all over the country," Rosen said of Singer. "He was bragging. It was like an empire of college admissions fraud."

The emperor's boasts enabled Rosen to subpoena his bank statements and emails and persuade the court to authorize wiretaps on his phones. Over the next three months, a river of evidence flowed from the documents and messages and calls. Once Rosen and the agents gave Singer a look at their findings, the fraudster went through a period of denial but then joined Tobin and Meredith in the cooperators camp. He then spent the fall and much of the winter surreptitiously recording his clients on the phone and in person. And, in March 2019, he appeared as Cooperating Witness 1 in an indictment that charged fifty people with crimes involving eight universities. Twenty-one were accused in connection with Singer's bribes and crooked tests for admission into USC, including three Trojan coaches and the senior associate athletics director, Donna Heinel. Lori Loughlin and Mossimo Giannulli—the Hollywood-and-fashion couple— were among the nineteen USC parents charged. None of the other schools came close to matching the number of defendants USC produced.

"USC is very unique," Rosen said.

The university was different from the other schools because it had a special committee that considered applications from athletes separately from other students. That made it easier for Singer to subvert the process. Heinel was the liaison to the committee—"the gatekeeper," Rosen called her. In the indictment, she was accused of conspiring to admit more than two dozen applicants who would never have passed muster as legitimate recruits. They included the daughters of Loughlin and Giannulli, who masqueraded as coxswains; a purported basketball player who stood five foot five; and a fake football player from a high school with no football team. All told, Heinel was charged with receiving $1.3 million in payments from Singer, which landed in USC accounts she largely controlled. She also was accused of collecting $20,000 a month in personal fees from Singer for what the government labeled sham consulting services. None of this was known to me or my colleagues before the indictment was handed up, and there was no suggestion by authorities that USC administrators above Heinel's level knew of the cheating. But the case did amplify questions of whether something in the university's leadership culture had allowed Singer's enterprise to thrive there.

Most of the Varsity Blues defendants were rich, abundantly lawyered, and influential in their fields. But they got the same treatment from the feds as street-crime suspects. FBI agents showed up at their homes without warning, usually around daybreak, and took them into custody. I had to wonder if the L.A. district attorney's office would have done the same if Varsity Blues had landed in its lap. And I could only guess what local investigators might have found if they'd shown up at Puliafito's door, unannounced, with a search warrant. Or what might have turned up if they had subpoenaed every email or text message sent or received by USC administrators about Tyndall.

Rosen said rank and privilege meant nothing to him when it came to following the evidence to wherever and whomever it led. And he didn't foresee what a huge splash Varsity Blues would make by crystallizing for people how easily money could further tilt a field that already favored the wealthy—and how an obsession with prestige could seed corruption in institutions of higher learning. Rosen began to realize how profoundly the case resonated with the public minutes after he stood before the cameras at the U.S. courthouse for the announcement of the indictment. The news conference was still underway when the phone in his breast pocket started vibrating with calls and texts from journalists from one end of the country to the other.

"I had no idea it was going to be this big," he said. "I had no idea it would be a national conversation starter."

25

SAVING THE *TIMES*, AND . . .

Lewis D'Vorkin was giving us a dose of what I and many of my colleagues had seen coming—the end of the *Times* as a reputable news organization. *Times* CEO and publisher Ross Levinsohn had hired D'Vorkin from *Forbes,* where he was chief product officer, to become our editor in chief. Just two weeks after he arrived at the *Times,* D'Vorkin had convened a staff meeting to complain about a *New York Times* story on his efforts to cozy up to the Disney Company. Disney had barred *L.A. Times* reporters from its film previews because it was unhappy with our coverage of financial incentives Disneyland received from its home city of Anaheim. D'Vorkin had earlier defended his private talks with Disney honchos and his directive that we not highlight on social media the company's boycott of our reviewers. Now he was steaming because someone leaked a recording of those remarks to *The New York Times.* D'Vorkin said whoever made and leaked the recording violated a state law barring surreptitious recordings. Moreover, he intoned, the leaker was "morally bankrupt." It was insane. We were *journalists;* leaks were our currency, including those about the waywardness of our own editors and publishers.

Well, I captured D'Vorkin's moralizing remarks on my phone

and leaked *that* recording to National Public Radio media reporter David Folkenflik. He used it to scathing effect in a piece that unclothed the fool in D'Vorkin.

By then, several of us had already set out to do whatever we could to unshackle the *Times* from tronc. We had become certain that D'Vorkin and Levinsohn were enemies of the type of journalism that elevated the paper. They spoke glibly about transforming legacy print publications like ours into digital properties that would prosper on the Web and mobile devices. But their strategy was naked in its aim to slash the staff and replace much of our reporting with lowbrow clickbait produced by underpaid freelancers, which was what D'Vorkin had done at *Forbes*. Our only hope for the long-term survival of the *Times* was a sale to a benevolent buyer like Soon-Shiong. But that did not seem in the cards; the signals we were getting from people close to Soon-Shiong were discouraging. So the best we could do was resist the downward direction that Levinsohn and D'Vorkin and their boss Michael Ferro were intent on taking the *Times*. We had to again operate in secrecy because our actions could get us fired on the spot. In an ethically sound newsroom, reporters cover their own paper's internal failings and file stories on them, just as they would with any other institution important to their readers. The *Times* had been lauded in the past, including with a Pulitzer Prize, for engaging in such self-examination. But that no longer seemed possible under tronc. So we were left to help our competitors bring out the truth.

I began looking into Levinsohn with an assist from my colleague Ron Lin. We plowed through public records going back to the late 1990s, when Levinsohn became an executive at ill-fated search engine AltaVista. He later worked at Fox Sports and, after his stint at Yahoo!, led the parent company of *The Hollywood Reporter, Billboard,* and *Adweek*. We found a long-buried sexual harassment lawsuit against him, and I fed that and other material we dug up to Folkenflik, who was going deep and wide on Levinsohn for an upcoming profile. We also were providing tips, internal *Times* emails and memos, names of potential sources, and any other information that might be valuable to all manner of local and national media outlets covering the ferment at the *Times*. The number of staffers who became sources for outside reporters grew and grew. The newsroom soon was a fountain of leaks. And NewsGuild organizers were posting on the union's campaign website our findings about tronc's excessive pay for executives and Ferro's pirate-like perks, among them the private jet.

Folkenflik's story on Levinsohn was a devastating exposé that went well beyond what Ron and I had slipped to him. Folkenflik reported that Levinsohn had been named in two sexual harassment lawsuits, behaved like a "frat boy" in previous places of employment, and had used a derogatory term for gay people. Levinsohn said it was all lies, but the story finished him at the *Times*.

The next day, the National Labor Relations Board announced the results of the NewsGuild election: We won with *85 percent* of the vote. For the first time in its 135-year history, the *Times* had a unionized newsroom, joining at last the ranks of *The New York Times, The Washington Post, The Wall Street Journal,* and scores of other publications.

And we were just warming up. I had been in touch with reporters from the *Columbia Journalism Review, Fortune* magazine, and other news organizations, so I had a good idea of what was coming next. Less than a week after the NPR scorching of Levinsohn, *CJR*'s Lyz Lenz weighed in with a lengthy takedown of D'Vorkin and his huckster's approach to covering the news. Headlined LA JOURNALISM'S "PRINCE OF DARKNESS," the story opened with a reference to his "morally bankrupt" statement. One line in Lenz's report said it all: "Even those who speak positively about him acknowledge he can be difficult, threatening, and, in the words of one writer who worked with D'Vorkin for more than four years and actually likes him, 'without journalistic ethic.'"

The article poleaxed D'Vorkin, and he completed his fall by

suspending the *Times*'s business editor because he wrongly suspected her of being a source of the leaks. Shortly thereafter tronc removed him as editor in chief.

As the chaos intensified, so did Soon-Shiong's interest in a purchase, including through a possible hostile bid. I had a Wall Street–savvy contact who knew Soon-Shiong and thought that, given the upheaval at the *Times,* a judge might be persuaded to extend the elapsed deadline for staging a proxy battle for control of the tronc board. That could allow Soon-Shiong to buy the company out from under Ferro. My contact made some inquiries, but the tactic was a no-go. Something else was in the works, however: *Fortune* writers Kristen Bellstrom and Beth Kowitt were closing in on a story detailing sexual harassment allegations against Ferro by two women. I learned that Ferro had gotten wind of their reporting and thus was suddenly eager to sell (he later would retire as tronc chair, just hours before Bellstrom and Kowitt posted their story). In the first week of February 2018, he presented Soon-Shiong with a take-it-or-leave-it proposition.

It was a critical moment, because we had information tronc had been preparing to cut the staff by at least 20 percent and eliminate our Washington, D.C., bureau. Soon-Shiong later told an interviewer that Ferro and the board called him with an even worse ultimatum: tronc intended to shut down the *Times* and shift all operations to the corporate base in Chicago. To prevent that, Soon-Shiong was given seventy-two hours to agree to a crazily inflated price of $500 million for the *Times* and our much-smaller sister paper, *The San Diego Union-Tribune.* Soon-Shiong knew he would be overpaying, and any financial adviser would have told him to walk away. But he didn't hesitate. Soon-Shiong accepted Ferro's terms and pulled the *Times* back from the abyss.

Three years after Devon Khan delivered his tip about the Hotel Constance, a senior editor at the *Times* got a tip of his own: A news media insider told him our Tyndall coverage was in the running for the

Pulitzer Prize for Investigative Reporting. It was a few days before the Pulitzers were to be announced at Columbia University, and the winners were always a closely kept secret. On occasion, though, the names of some awardees leaked from the Pulitzer board, although it would be bad form to go public with them. We were tantalized by the tip but tried not to get excited. Even tips from journalists to other journalists about journalists could be wrong. I called the editor with the Pulitzer source and pressed him in a humorous way about how solid the tip seemed. "Very solid," he said, because his source was in a position to know. But that was still not confirmation.

The next day, confirmation came from another insider. And the day after that, the staff gathered on the seventh floor of the paper's new headquarters, a 1960s office building next door to Los Angeles International Airport. Soon-Shiong had spent millions more to renovate the structure, including with a modern newsroom that was the clean and orderly opposite of our bruised and cluttered space in the old (but still cherished) Times Building. Before Tribune became tronc, it had sold that building to a commercial developer, which wanted it as an anchor for high-rise condos and shops. Now, in our new digs, Harriet, Matt, and I stood side by side in the newsroom, surrounded by scores of our colleagues, all of us with eyes on overhead monitors where the announcement of the Pulitzer winners was being livestreamed from New York. Some of us joked—half joked?—about the possibility of a mix-up, a miscommunication, and that maybe we *hadn't* won. But then the investigative prize was awarded, our names appeared on the screen, and the newsroom erupted in cheers and applause.

For me, the moment transcended the joy that comes from winning journalism's highest honor; it shouted *vindication*. The prize was further proof that fighting for journalism principles and ethics, even at the risk of tanking your career, pays off in the end. And in that light, I believed the Pulitzer also belonged to Adam Elmahrek and Sarah Parvini. Their courageous work on the Puliafito investigation was crucial in laying the foundation for the Tyndall reporting.

After the last prize was announced, Harriet, her eyes brimming with emotion, addressed our colleagues and thanked and saluted the women of USC who bravely came forward to make the Tyndall story possible. Then she spoke to the paper's near-death experience and recognized our narrow rescue by Soon-Shiong and his wife, Michele B. Chan.

"I don't know if any award will ever be as sweet as this one when there are so many people in this building who know we almost died," she said. "When there are so many people, so many of my colleagues in the newsroom who fought to save the paper. When so many people still remember the hope that we felt when Michele and Pat walked into the newsroom for the first time."

Right on point. The Pulitzer recognized our work from the previous year, but it said something more about the future of the *Times*, the one made possible by the resilience and resolve of the staff, the newsroom that refused to allow the journalism standards of the paper to tumble into the past. Harriet, Matt, Adam, and Sarah represented that future. Unlike me, they had long careers ahead of them.

Long after the Pulitzer win, there were still some loose ends in the newsroom. That was loudly evident in the way Norman Pearlstine, the *Times*'s executive editor, began screaming at me one day in early 2020. He demanded that I stop investigating him. "You're looking up *my* ass?" he bellowed.

I was sitting in Pearlstine's office with Jack Leonard, who was now my editor. The windows looked out on the runways of LAX and then beyond to the mountain-silhouetted skyline of downtown. The view was much more inviting than the one Pearlstine accused me of taking in. He was red-faced as he stood in front of me, his arms folded tightly against his chest.

"Please, could we lower the temperature?" Jack said to him.

"Let's *not* lower the temperature!" Pearlstine howled. "My asshole is clean!"

When he bought the *Times*, Soon-Shiong hired Pearlstine, the former top editor at *The Wall Street Journal* and Time Inc., to run our newsroom. He'd been in the job for eighteen months when Jack and I walked into his office to discuss a possible conflict of interest involving two largely softball pieces Pearlstine had written about Huawei, the Chinese communications giant U.S. officials suspected was an arm of Beijing. Another *Times* reporter and I had learned that Pearlstine, before joining the paper, served as a consultant to a Toronto-based company whose subsidiary claimed to do business with Huawei. And a Chinese national whom Pearlstine had hired for a tech position at the *Times*, Max Wu, was actually an officer in the Toronto company; he had a byline with Pearlstine on one of the Huawei stories and a credit line on the other. Jack and I believed that, at minimum, the stories should have included an editor's note informing the reader of the ties between the Toronto firm and Pearlstine and Wu. But Pearlstine started shouting almost as soon as we asked him about it. He said there was no conflict. And an editor's note never appeared.

Jack and I expected there would be a penalty for challenging Pearlstine, and we believe it came a few months later. Pearlstine spiked three follow-up stories to a major investigation that I produced with colleagues Alene Tchekmedyian and David Pierson. The investigation explored accusations that Marc Ching, a Hollywood-backed animal rights advocate, had paid butchers in Asia to torture and kill dogs while he filmed it. Pearlstine said he just wasn't interested in more stories on Ching and later claimed the initial piece did not attract a large online audience. In fact, it did exceptionally well on the Web. I suggested to Jack that we resign in protest of Pearlstine's refusal to publish the follow-ups. We considered that move for a good part of the day, but then we concluded that would only please him, and the stories would remain dead. So we fought back. I filed a grievance under our new union contract, while Jack quietly lobbied managing editor Scott Kraft to get the stories in the paper. One of the pieces dove into allegations that Ching was practicing veterinary medicine without a license and hurting the pets he "treated."

Thankfully, Pearlstine had been losing more and more support in the newsroom, including for making only anemic moves to diversify our mostly white staff. He rebuffed calls for his resignation. A fresh sexual harassment scandal shook the paper, forcing the resignation of the man Pearlstine had hired to run the *Times*'s Food section. With the walls drawing close, Pearlstine's resolve to block the Ching stories seemed to falter. The piece on Ching's dabbling in veterinary medicine finally ran, and it triggered an investigation by the L.A. city attorney and then criminal charges. Ching eventually was convicted after pleading no contest. Pearlstine had almost spared him that fate.

Over the ensuing months, allegations of other ethical transgressions at the *Times* surfaced, including those involving conflicts of interest. There were embarrassing stories about the paper in other publications, and then in our own pages, and that was it for Pearlstine. In December 2020, he announced his retirement and returned, with no fanfare, to New York.

The search for a successor settled on Kevin Merida, the highly regarded former managing editor of *The Washington Post* who headed ESPN's The Undefeated. I and several other staffers called and emailed Merida to encourage him to come west. After a long courtship, Merida accepted Soon-Shiong's offer to become executive editor. We had reason to hope that the salvation of the *Times*, at least as a force for fearless and ethical journalism, was now complete.

Matt had been expecting the calls he got from two sources on a March evening in 2021. He was at his desk in the West Hollywood apartment he shared with his partner, the lights of Sunset Boulevard visible through his second-floor window. The calls were a heads-up about the Tyndall civil case, in which more than seven hundred women who claimed they were abused by the doctor had sued him and USC. Matt had been following the pitched wrangling over a proposed pretrial settlement; throughout the coronavirus pandemic, he was often the only journalist in the courtroom when the two sides appeared before the judge overseeing the case. USC was represented by three law firms—at a fierce burn rate in fees. And discovery had been going poorly for the school. There were just too many incriminating facts USC's administrators and trustees would not want to see presented to a jury. So a settlement was imminent, it would be big, and Matt was working late to make certain he didn't get beat on the story.

The two sources told him the settlement had been reached and would be read in open court the next morning. Matt asked how much it was . . . and then his jaw dropped:

Eight hundred fifty-two million dollars!

And that was on top of more than $215 million USC already had agreed to pay to two other groups of Tyndall's accusers.

Nothing will ever undo the harm that George Tyndall inflicted on his patients, much of it life-altering for the women. But more than $1.1 billion in settlements brought them a measure of justice (Lucy Chi was among the recipients). The sum was the largest on record for a sexual abuse case in academia and one of the biggest in any field. In journalism, this is what we call *impact*. It is the real-life results our work can produce for people—often for people on the margins. Impact usually goes unrecognized by journalism award committees (there are only so many prizes out there), but it is far more meaningful. It is the umbrella term for why we do what we do.

And a payout north of $1 billion was a hell of a lot of impact. Not just in terms of restitution for the women but also for the message it sent to corrupt institutions and their leaders: Be warned that the price for tolerating abusive behavior could extend far beyond the moral and ethical condemnations.

The settlements renewed calls by faculty members and students for Nikias to be stripped of his teaching and board positions and removed from campus. In their story on that settlement, Harriet and Matt quoted Caruso, who had become chair of the board, on Nikias.

"I think this is a time where Max really has to reflect on what's best for the university, what's best for the students, and make a decision himself," Caruso said. "I think there's clarity to the answer to that, but I think that's for him to answer."

The following month, Nikias answered that question in an email exchange with me through his attorney. He said, in short, that he wasn't going anywhere. "I have devoted the last three decades of my career to USC," Nikias wrote, "and in all the positions I have held from faculty member to President, I worked to advance the academic excellence of the University and looked after the very best interests of students and faculty."

In that and subsequent exchanges, always through the lawyer, he did not take personal responsibility for any of the scandals and rejected the suggestion that he or his administrators should have been the subject of a criminal investigation. And he revealed something that, if true, confirmed that I was right to fear that he enjoyed special access to the *Times* newsroom during our reporting on Puliafito. In response to my queries about why he didn't open the note I delivered to his house and why he instead complained about my visit, he wrote, "I was told at that time by an editor in the newsroom that you and your group of reporters followed me on Instagram, so you should have known that I was out of town."

I asked him to identify the editor. The attorney refused on his behalf. "Dr. Nikias was told in confidence by an editor in the newsroom that you and your group of reporters followed him on Instagram, and he does not want to betray that confidence," the attorney said in an email. First, there was no group of reporters at that time—just me. And as I informed Nikias earlier, I was not following him on Instagram.

To deeply understate it, editors are not supposed to have confidential communications about their reporters with a subject of their reporting.

I emailed Maharaj and Duvoisin about Nikias's claim that he had an editor source in the newsroom. Maharaj's lawyer responded by saying my query was another of those based on a false predicate; Duvoisin replied, "I have never met Max Nikias or communicated with him on any subject."

A year and a half after his firing, Maharaj's tenure at the *Times* made news again. NPR's Folkenflik, with some clandestine help from me, reported that Maharaj had received a secret payment of more than $2.5 million from pre-tronc Tribune after threatening to sue the company for wrongful termination. Folkenflik's story revealed that Maharaj made a surreptitious recording of Ferro saying that Southern California billionaire and philanthropist Eli Broad was part of a "Jewish cabal" that ran L.A. The decision by Tribune and Ferro to pay off Maharaj, as Folkenflik wrote, kept Ferro's anti-Semitic epithet hidden from the public. Maharaj should have immediately exposed it, but he instead concealed it ultimately for his financial benefit. Through a spokesman, Ferro denied to NPR that he uttered the slur. Maharaj's attorney told the outlet his client was not paid to keep anything secret and the settlement reflected his "almost 30 years of exceptional service" to the *Times*. Apart from a role in a small journalism nonprofit based in Jamaica, Maharaj faded from view in the media world.

Duvoisin fared better in the business. He landed an at-large editing job at the *Houston Chronicle* and later became editor in chief of the *Chronicle*'s sister paper, the *San Antonio Express-News*. Nobody at either publication had reached out to the USC reporting team for a reference on him.

Paul Warren lost his job in L.A. The Warrens retreated to Texas in a state of damage and despair. The money from the USC settlement helped the family relocate and buy a home in Houston. And it allowed Sarah to stay for a while in Huntington Beach. But it ran out while the family was still struggling to get back to normal. That was especially true for Charles, whose introduction to drugs and heavy drinking in the company of Puliafito had led to severe addiction. The last time I checked in with the family, he had been hospitalized more than a dozen times.

Sarah remained sober and rejoined the family in Texas. The record of drug arrests followed her, which turned the search for any job with a future into a series of frustrations. Sarah told me she blamed herself for that, but I disagreed. She'd barely reached adulthood when she met Puliafito—and she was troubled. He used his privilege to exploit her pain and loss of control. None of that could be gleaned from the arrest records. And while Puliafito suffered once he was exposed, he dodged the hammer end of justice—as did his boss, Nikias. Puliafito was still living the free life in Pasadena, although with a bit of downsizing. He sold his mansion for $5.7 million and moved into a condo valued at less than half that.

Waiting tables was the best gig Sarah could find in Texas. But she assured me she didn't plan to be a server forever. Her goal was to get back on the path to a college education, find her calling, and put behind her everything that had happened in L.A.

My bet was on Sarah. This was the young woman who'd tornadoed through the baddest latitudes of the city, setting in motion a cascade of events that toppled some of L.A.'s most powerful men, upended two of its most important institutions, and brought redress to hundreds of women abused by Tyndall. I'd always kept a clinical distance from Sarah because she was both a subject and a source of my reporting. But I couldn't stop seeing my daughters in her, and I was taken by how much stronger she was than others close to me. She beat Puliafito and his high position and his money. And she was tough enough to tell the hard truth about herself and live with it.

I had no doubt that truth tellers like Sarah and journalists like my colleagues at the *Times* would continue to team up and do more damage—*righteous* damage—for years to come.

ACKNOWLEDGMENTS

I hope it's clear in these pages how much I and many others owe Devon Khan and Sarah Warren, her brother, Charles, and their parents, Paul and Mary Ann. Without their courage, the Puliafito and Tyndall scandals might have never come to light.

I owe a similar debt to my *Los Angeles Times* colleagues, present and past, who chased the USC stories with no quit in them. They are Matt Lait, Matt Hamilton, Harriet Ryan, Adam Elmahrek, and Sarah Parvini. Special thanks to Adam for his help in bringing the book home.

Colleagues Jack Leonard, Hector Becerra, Carlos Lozano, Nathan Fenno, and Steve Clow bucked me up as cheerleaders for the Puliafito investigation, and Jack later showcased his considerable skills in editing the Tyndall story.

This book exists because of the brilliant and relentless Will Lippincott of Aevitas Creative Management. It was his idea. Will deserves more applause for bringing into the mix his Aevitas colleague Jen Marshall, whose razor-sharp contributions and infectious enthusiasm elevated the whole enterprise. I had great luck in Will and Jen—and in Allison Warren, Shenel Ekici-Moling, and Kaleigh Choi, also of Aevitas.

I could not have done better in my editor at Celadon, Ryan Doherty. All working relationships should be so inspiring and, in every other sense, delightful. The same goes for the rest of the Celadon team: Jamie Raab, Deb Futter, Cecily van Buren-Freedman, Christine Mykityshyn, Heather Orlando-Jerabek, Audine Crosse, Diana Frost, Elisa Rivlin, Clay Smith, Anne Twomey, Erin Cahill, Sara Lynn, Chris Ensey, Rachel Chou, Jennifer Jackson, Sandra Moore, Jaime Noven, Rebecca Ritchey, Frances Sayers, Emily Walters, and Karen Lumley.

Heaps of thanks go to my former editor at the *Times*, Linda Rogers, who read every word of the book even before Will, Jen, and Ryan did. Linda provided invaluable advice and critiques. I'd known for a long time that nothing escapes Linda, which is why I imposed on her.

I thank and admire Lucy Chi, Audry Nafziger, Riley Ransom, Allison Rowland, and Ja'Mesha Morgan for their bravery in sharing their experiences of the abuse they suffered at the hands of George Tyndall. Cindy Gilbert is a hero for blowing the whistle on Tyndall and his protectors; I am deeply grateful for her help. I salute five other women who understandably asked to remain anonymous in relating to me their encounters with Tyndall or their attempts to hold him accountable.

There are more sources for the USC stories I wish I could thank by name, including "Tommy Trojan," but they also requested anonymity—for sound reasons. A source who helped me behind the scenes and now allows me to identify him is Jim Haw.

Miriam Yoder was strong and selfless in sharing the trials of her family. Eric Rosen graciously told me the "Operation Varsity Blues" story in a different and very interesting way.

John Mack Faragher, Tom Sitton, Raphael Sonenshein, and Sue Mossman were generous with their time and insights.

I can only guess whether the *Times* would have survived the

Tribune/tronc years if it weren't for Jon Schleuss, Anthony Pesce, and Natalie Kitroeff. They were the original organizers of the NewsGuild at the paper. Because of the gutsy efforts of those "troublemakers," and those of the NewsGuild organizing and bargaining committees (and their offshoots), as well as Nastaran Mohit and Ben Dictor, the *Times* has remained a place where excellent journalism could be produced.

I'm proud of my colleague Rong-Gong Lin II for the risks he took in our stealth campaign to run tronc out of town. I thank the many colleagues who also took risks in coming forward in the HR investigation that grew out of the USC reporting.

The book's dedication is to my wife and daughters, but they deserve more recognition here as indispensable readers of the rough drafts. Their feedback made everything better. So did my brother Pete's. He vetted the drafts and offered spot-on perspectives I did not get elsewhere.

They're gone now, but I thank my mother for the love of language and inquiry she instilled in me, and my father for his harder-nosed lessons in life. And I thank my Aunt Mary and Uncle George for being there.

For decades, I've found grounding in my friendships with Bob and Sherry Pool and Dennis Harvey; they've tolerated my faults, provided wonderful company, and kept me on my toes as a journalist. More grounding came from my extended family in California and points east—particularly nieces Corrine, Melissa, Amy, and Hanna, and nephew Mike; the Pringle/Brown clan of Pennsylvania, starting with Dee Dee, Linda, George, and Donny; and many other cousins, among them Annie, Kathleen, Toni, Danny, and Judy.

I'm fortunate in my family-by-marriage in England, anchored by Caroline and Ursula.

And I've been blessed with the friendship of Shante Morgan and the honor of being godfather to her marvelous daughter Christina.

The tireless charity of Ronald Harper is something I wish I had the capacity to repay.

Which brings me to the Adler family. Jeremy Adler was a source of light in our lives who left us decades too soon. His memory was an inspiration through all of this, as were his brother, Pierre, and their mother, Charlene. We miss you terribly, Jeremy. And Pierre, we have more work to do, buddy.

AUTHOR'S NOTE

This book is based primarily on interviews with people who provided firsthand accounts of the events, experiences, and observations presented on the page. The interviews were conducted from April 2017 through March 2022. Several of the people featured prominently in the book were interviewed a great many times over a period of months or even years. For simplicity's sake, the specific dates of each of those interviews are not included in the endnotes.

The author's personal experiences and observations account for much of the material in the book. Otherwise, in addition to interviews, the reporting comes from emails and text messages; municipal, state, and federal records; University of Southern California statements and publications; news media accounts; and a variety of other published sources, as the endnotes detail.

Quoted remarks and conversations that the author did not hear were drawn from the accounts of at least one firsthand source. Descriptions of the thoughts or motivations of people who did not share them with the author came from the accounts of sources with whom the thoughts and motivations were shared; in some cases, they reflect the viewpoint of the sources based on their observations of the actions of the people whose thoughts and motivations are presented.

Some sources for the book were granted anonymity for journalistically sound reasons, such as credible claims that they would face reprisals if identified by name. As noted in the relevant passages, pseudonyms were used for three people for the same reasons or in consideration of their personal circumstances. The accounts of the unnamed and pseudonymous sources were corroborated through on-the-record sources or documentation.

The author contacted the major figures in this story to give them an opportunity to respond to criticism or complaints directed at them. This occurred during the author's reporting for the *Los Angeles Times* and afterward as he expanded on that work for the book. The responses are included as appropriate.

NOTES

1. THE OVERDOSE

3   **A fog scented by canyon pines:** Devon Khan, interviews by the author, April and May 2016; March and April 2017; April 2018; October, November, and December 2020.

5   **the seven-story Constance was a 1926 showpiece:** Cuyler Gibbons, "The Historic Hotel Constance Completes a Long-Awaited Renovation," *Pasadena Magazine,* https://pasadenamag.com/people-places/community/the-historic-hotel-constance -completes-a-long-awaited-renovation/.

5   **Khan was the highest-ranking employee:** Devon Khan, interviews by the author.

9   **With that, Khan walked out of the room:** Pasadena Police Department records and 911 recordings; Langham Hotel & Resorts, https://www.langhamhotels.com/en/the -langham/pasadena/; Valli Herman, "Pasadena Ritz-Carlton to Be Rebranded," *Los Angeles Times,* November 28, 2007, https://www.latimes.com/archives/la-xpm-2007 -nov-28-fi-ritz28-story.html; Michelle Higgins, "Pasadena, Calif.: Ritz-Carlton Huntington Hotel and Spa," *New York Times,* September 24, 2006, https://www .nytimes.com/2006/09/24/travel/24check.html.

2. SARAH AND TONY

14   **Two months earlier, on a January night:** Sarah Warren, interviews by the author.

15   **Puliafito had plenty of money:** Jon Weiner, "Puliafito Named Keck School Dean," USC News, August 20, 2007, https://news.usc.edu/18094/Puliafito-Named-Keck -School-Dean/.

15   **he had spent lavishly on her:** Sarah Warren, interviews by the author; Carmen A. Puliafito's testimony at hearings of the Medical Board of California.

15   **Sarah had become the singular focus:** Transcripts of Puliafito's testimony at hearings of the Medical Board of California and the board's decision against Puliafito, July 20, 2018, https://www2.mbc.ca.gov/BreezePDL/document.aspx?path=%5CDIDOC S%5C20180820%5CDMRAAAGL3%5C&did=AAAGL180820181338333.DID.

15   **Sarah had checked in to Creative Care:** Sarah Warren, Charles Warren, Mary Ann Warren, and Paul Warren, interviews by the author.

16   **Staffers at the center knew Puliafito:** Creative Care source, interview by the author.

16   **Puliafito graduated magna cum laude:** Paul Pringle, Harriet Ryan, Adam Elmahrek, Matt Hamilton, and Sarah Parvini, "An Overdose, a Young Companion, Drug-Fueled Parties: The Secret Life of a USC Med School Dean," *Los Angeles Times,* July 17, 2017, https://www.latimes.com/local/california/la-me-usc-doctor-20170717-htmlstory .html.

17–18   **It did not mean much to campus presidents:** "Former Temple University Business Dean Convicted of Fraud in Rankings Scheme," NBC News, Nov. 30, 2021, https://www.nbcnews.com/news/us-news/former-temple-university-business-dean -convicted-fraud-rankings-scheme-rcna7089.

18   **The day USC hired Puliafito, the university issued a news release:** Weiner, "Puliafito Named Keck School Dean."

18   **They bought one of Pasadena's signature homes:** Ping Tsai, "An English Tudor Revival Home in Pasadena That Was Once Home to a Manufacturing Tycoon," *Pasadena Magazine,* https://pasadenamag.com/homesandrealestate/english-tudor -revival-home-pasadena-home-manufacturing-tycoon/.

19   **And when he wasn't talking jargon:** "Technology and Entertainment Moguls Headline Most Successful Fund-Raising Event for USC Center for Cancer Research," Keck Medicine of USC, https://www.keckmedicine.org/technology-and -entertainment-moguls-headline-most-successful-fund-raising-event-for-usc-center -for-cancer-research/.

19   **That extended to his pastime:** "The Dr. Carmen A. Puliafito Collection of U.S. Independent Mails—May 4, 2016," Stamp Auction Network, 2016, https:// stampauctionnetwork.com/y/y1124.cfm; "Outstanding United States Stamps Featuring the Dr. Carmen A. Puliafito Collection of 19th and 20th Century Issues," Siegel Auctions, 1999, https://siegelauctions.com/1999/818/818.pdf; the Chairman's Chatter of the U.S. Philatelic Classics Society, Inc., September 2009.

3. THE TIP

21   **Devon Khan couldn't let it go:** Devon Khan and Tanja Khan, interviews by the author.

22   **The department wasn't known:** Hayley Munguia, "A Black Man's Death in Pasadena Police Custody Is Latest in Recent History of Fraught Incidents," *Pasadena Star-News,* September 30, 2016, https://www.pasadenastarnews.com/2016/09/30 /a-black-mans-death-in-pasadena-police-custody-is-latest-in-recent-history-of -fraught-incidents/.

22   **There had been questionable police shootings:** Richard Winton and Adolfo Flores, "Pasadena Police Shooting of Kendrec McDade Was Justified, D.A. Says," *Los Angeles Times,* December 17, 2012, https://latimesblogs.latimes.com/lanow/2012/12 /kendrec-mcdade-pasadena-police-shooting-justified.html.

22   **And last summer, they arrested:** Marina Pena, "Hundreds Protest Sentencing of Black Lives Matter Activist in Pasadena," *Pasadena Star-News,* June 7, 2016, https:// www.pasadenastarnews.com/2016/06/07/hundreds-protest-sentencing-of-black -lives-matter-activist-in-pasadena/.

22   **The police claimed she tried:** Victoria M. Massie, "What Activist Jasmine Richards's 'Lynching' Conviction Means for the Black Lives Matter Movement," Vox, June 21, 2016, https://www.vox.com/2016/6/6/11839620/jasmine-richards-black-lives-matter -lynching; "Pasadena Black Lives Matter Organizer Sentenced to 90 Days in Jail,"

Pasadena Star-News, June 7, 2016, https://www.pasadenastarnews.com/2016/06/07/pasadena-black-lives-matter-organizer-sentenced-to-90-days-in-jail/.

23 **Khan began typing:** Devon Khan, anonymous email to city attorney, March 11, 2016.

24 **the bistro that occupied:** Bistro 45, http://bistro45.com/.

28 **Veteran *L.A. Times* photographer Ricardo DeAratanha:** Matt Hamilton, "L.A. Times Photographer Arrested After Covering Nancy Reagan Funeral Motorcade," *Los Angeles Times,* March 9, 2016, https://www.latimes.com/local/crime/la-me-times-photographer-arrest-20160310-story.html.

28 **prosecutors later decided to charge him:** Kate Mather, "L.A. Times Photographer Charged with Misdemeanor After Nancy Reagan Funeral Motorcade," *Los Angeles Times,* April 5, 2016, https://www.latimes.com/local/lanow/la-me-in-photographer-charged-20160405-story.html.

29 **Khan's "eyes became as big as moons":** Ricardo DeAratanha, comment relayed to the author.

29 **Pete Carroll, a revered figure on campus, violated:** Paul Pringle, "Carroll's Rules Violation Could Hurt USC," *Los Angeles Times,* July 14, 2010, https://www.latimes.com/archives/la-xpm-2010-jul-14-la-me-pete-carroll-20100714-story.html.

4. HITTING A WALL

34 **Pasadena was an early bastion:** "Heritage: A Short History of Pasadena," City of Pasadena, https://www.cityofpasadena.net/about-pasadena/history-of-pasadena/; "Pasadena at 125: Early History of the Crown City," KCET, https://www.kcet.org/shows/lost-la/pasadena-at-125-early-history-of-the-crown-city; interview of Eric Duyshart, City of Pasadena, January 14, 2021; Cuyler Gibbons, "The Evolution of Eva Fenyes," *Pasadena Magazine,* https://pasadenamag.com/artsandculture/the-evolution-of-eva-fenyes/.

34 **A Pasadena thoroughfare, Orange Grove Boulevard:** Paul Pringle, "Don't Even Think About Joining This Club," *Los Angeles Times,* September 18, 2004, https://www.latimes.com/archives/la-xpm-2004-sep-18-me-club18-story.html.

34 **USC graduates served on the Pasadena City Council:** "Councilmember John J. Kennedy Bio," City of Pasadena, https://www.cityofpasadena.net/district3/bio/; "Councilmember Steve Madison Bio," City of Pasadena, https://www.cityofpasadena.net/district6/bio/.

34 **The eight-bedroom, eleven-bathroom:** Jack Flemming, "USC's Presidential Mansion Lists for the First Time Ever at $24.5 million," *Los Angeles Times,* February 12, 2021, https://www.latimes.com/business/real-estate/story/2021-02-12/uscs-presidential-mansion-lists-for-the-first-time-ever-at-24-5-million.

35 **And city hall itself became a crime scene:** Alejandra Reyes-Velarde, "Former Pasadena City Employee Gets 14 Years in Prison for Embezzling $3.6 Million," *Los Angeles Times,* January 11, 2019, https://www.latimes.com/local/lanow/la-me-ln-pasadena-city-employee-sentenced-20190111-story.html.

35 **whose tall whitewashed arches:** "Pasadena Police Department," Los Angeles Conservancy, https://www.laconservancy.org/locations/pasadena-police-department.

36 **Ibarra was a longtime veteran:** "Pasadena Police Officer Retires After 35 Years of Living Her Purpose," Behind the Badge, February 19, 2019, https://behindthebadge.com/pasadena-police-officer-retires-after-35-years-of-living-her-purpose/.

36 **Or maybe it was because the *Times*:** Richard Winton, "Pasadena Police Union Loses Bid to Bar Release of Shooting Report," *Los Angeles Times,* September 10, 2015, https://www.latimes.com/local/crime/la-me-pasadena-police-shooting-20150911-story.html.

36   **The newspaper was winning that fight:** Nathan Solis, "LA Times Wins in Public Records Case," Courthouse News Service, April 12, 2018, https://www.courthousenews.com/la-times-wins-in-public-records-case/.

36   **I walked back to my car and sent her an email:** Author's email to Pasadena police media contact Lisa Derderian, April 12, 2016.

37   **Later that day, shortly before 6:30 P.M.:** Pasadena police supervisor Melissa Trujillo, email to author, April 12, 2016.

37   **The document was two pages of call times:** Pasadena police Call for Service log, March 4, 2016.

39   **Then, out of the blue:** Dr. Carmen A. Puliafito, email to author, April 20, 2016.

40   **All together, our stories led to six indictments:** Andrew Blankstein, Paul Pringle, and Rong-Gong Lin II, "Coliseum Case Widens; Six Are Charged," *Los Angeles Times,* March 24, 2012, https://www.latimes.com/local/la-me-0324-coliseum-20120324-story.html; Rong-Gong Lin II, "Panel OKs Coliseum Lease Deal," *Los Angeles Times,* May 15, 2012, https://www.latimes.com/local/la-me-coliseum-20120515-story.html.

41   **This was nine years after the *Times*:** Gary Cohn, Carla Hall, and Robert W. Welkos, "Women Say Schwarzenegger Groped, Humiliated Them," *Los Angeles Times,* October 2, 2003, https://www.latimes.com/local/la-me-archive-schwarzenegger-women-story.html; Ann Louise Bardach, "USC's Arnold Schwarzenegger Problem," *Los Angeles Magazine,* April 24, 2019, https://www.lamag.com/citythinkblog/usc-arnold-schwarzenegger.

45   **I complained in writing to my supervisor:** Author's email to then *L.A. Times* city editor Matt Lait, September 13, 2015.

45   **So I partnered on it with Fenno:** Paul Pringle and Nathan Fenno, "Outside of USC, Pat Haden Holds More Than a Dozen Roles That Pay at Least a Half-Million Dollars a Year," *Los Angeles Times,* October 23, 2015, https://www.latimes.com/local/california/la-me-usc-haden-20151024-story.html.

45   **Haden placed him on indefinite leave:** Gary Klein and Lindsey Thiry, "USC Coach Steve Sarkisian, Called 'Not Healthy,' Placed on Indefinite Leave," *Los Angeles Times,* October 11, 2015, https://www.latimes.com/sports/usc/la-sp-usc-sarkisian-20151012-story.html.

46   **Our investigation of the Haden charity:** Paul Pringle and Nathan Fenno, "L.A. Education Foundation Became a Lucrative Source of Income for USC's Pat Haden and His Relatives," *Los Angeles Times,* June 18, 2016, https://www.latimes.com/local/lanow/la-me-ln-mayr-foundation-20160617-snap-story.html.

5. SEARCHING FOR SARAH

50   **The newsroom was an aesthetic affront:** "Times Mirror Square," Los Angeles Conservancy, https://www.laconservancy.org/locations/times-mirror-square.

50   **My first CPRA request was to the Pasadena city attorney:** Author's email to Pasadena city attorney, May 26, 2016.

50   **My request for the Pasadena police:** Author's email to Pasadena police lieutenant Tracey Ibarra, May 26, 2016.

51   **Kaufmann's monument-evoking:** Lorena Iniguez Elebee, Ellis Simani, and Thomas Curwen, "Inside the Historic Buildings That Have Defined the *Los Angeles Times,*" *Los Angeles Times,* July 20, 2018, https://www.latimes.com/projects/latimes-building/; Cecilia Rasmussen, "'Wall Street of the West' Had Its Peaks, Crashes," *Los Angeles Times,* June 11, 2000, https://www.latimes.com/archives/la-xpm-2000-jun-11-me-39908-story.html.

51   **Spring Street was once known as "the Wall Street of the West":** Cecilia Rasmussen,

"'Wall Street of the West,'" *Los Angeles Times,* June 11, 2000, https://www.latimes.com/archives/la-xpm-2000-jun-11-me-39908-story.html.

51   **At the request of the school's athletic director:** Bill Plaschke, "The Original Man of Troy," *Los Angeles Times,* February 23, 2012, https://www.latimes.com/sports/usc/la-xpm-2012-feb-23-la-sp-0224-plaschke-usc-trojans-20120224-story.html.

51   **a young *Times* sports columnist, Owen Bird:** Bill Plaschke, "The Original Man of Troy," *Los Angeles Times,* February 23, 2012, https://www.latimes.com/sports/usc/la-xpm-2012-feb-23-la-sp-0224-plaschke-usc-trojans-20120224-story.html; "USC to Mark 100th Anniversary of Trojans Nickname," USC News, February 23, 2012, https://news.usc.edu/26134/usc-to-mark-100th-anniversary-of-trojans-nickname/.

51   **The road to the White House for Nixon:** David Halberstam, *The Powers That Be* (New York: Knopf, 1979); Dennis McDougal, "The Perils of Picking Presidents," *Los Angeles Times,* January 20, 2008, https://www.latimes.com/archives/la-xpm-2008-jan-20-op-mcdougal20-story.html.

52   **The $8 billion merger:** Felicity Barringer and Laura M. Holson, "Tribune Co. Agrees to Buy Times Mirror," *New York Times,* March 14, 2000, https://archive.nytimes.com/www.nytimes.com/library/financial/031400tribune-mirror.html.

52   **Carroll resigned in 2005 rather than:** Elaine Woo, "John Carroll Dies at 73; Editor Led L.A. Times to 13 Pulitzers in 5 Years," *Los Angeles Times,* June 14, 2015, https://www.latimes.com/local/obituaries/la-me-john-carroll-20150614-story.html.

52   **real estate wheeler-dealer Sam Zell:** "Sam Zell Settles Lawsuit over Tribune Leveraged-Buyout 'Deal from Hell,'" *Los Angeles Times,* June 14, 2019, https://www.latimes.com/business/la-fi-sam-zell-tribune-20190614-story.html.

52–53   **A *New York Times* story on Michaels's boorish:** David Carr, "At Flagging Tribune, Tales of a Bankrupt Culture," *New York Times,* October 5, 2010, https://www.nytimes.com/2010/10/06/business/media/06tribune.html; David Carr and Tim Arango, "Tribune Chief Accepts Advice and Backs Out," *New York Times,* October 22, 2010, https://www.nytimes.com/2010/10/23/business/media/23tribune.html.

53   **Maharaj became the editor *and* publisher of the *Times*:** Christopher Goffard, "Davan Maharaj Is Named Editor-Publisher of the L.A. Times in Tribune Publishing Shake-Up," *Los Angeles Times,* March 2, 2016, https://www.latimes.com/business/la-fi-maharaj-los-angeles-times-20160302-story.html.

6. THE WARRENS

58   **Sarah Warren was spending a December day:** Sarah Warren, interviews by the author.

58   **Civil War veterans were buried in the cemetery:** Brittany Hanson, "Magnolia Park's History and Mystery," *Orange County Register,* November 2, 2011, https://www.ocregister.com/2011/11/02/magnolia-parks-history-and-mystery/; "Magnolia Memorial Park & Gardens—Garden Grove, Orange County, California," Interment.net, http://www.interment.net/data/us/ca/orange/magnolia/index.htm.

59   **a twenty-five-minute drive from Ocean Recovery:** Ocean Recovery, https://www.oceanrecovery.com.

7. THE CELEBRATION

75   **Set in gold borders and topped by the USC shield:** Newsroom source; email with attached invite forwarded to the author, May 31, 2016.

80   **That's where Sanchez stumbled into a trap:** Letter to the author from Pasadena police chief Phillip Sanchez, June 20, 2016.

8. WE NEED THE PD

87   **His voice was easily recognizable:** Pasadena 911 recording, March 4, 2016.

88   **He noted in his message:** Steve Mermell, email to the author, September 23, 2016.

9. A PROTECTED PERSON

92   **Henry Huntington was a union-bashing:** Carolina A. Miranda, "The Huntington Library Has a History of Inequity. Can It Pivot Toward Inclusivity?" *Los Angeles Times,* April 1, 2021, https://www.latimes.com/entertainment-arts/story/2021-04-01/reckoning-with-history-and-equity-at-the-huntington-museum.

92   **His name lived on:** Lauren Gold, "Langham Celebrates Huntington Hotel's 100 Colorful Years," *Pasadena Star-News,* February 8, 2014, https://www.pasadenastarnews.com/2014/02/08/langham-celebrates-huntington-hotels-100-colorful-years/.

92   **the palatial Langham Huntington Hotel:** "Historical Property Tour of the Langham Huntington, Pasadena," Langham Hotels, https://www.langhamhotels.com/cdn-225ef196/globalassets/lhr/tl-pasadena/pdf/others/historical_property_tour_map.pdf.

93   **They were mostly a series of denials:** Pasadena public information officer William Boyer, email to the author, October 7, 2016.

96   **I emailed this to Puliafito:** Author's email to Dr. Carmen A. Puliafito, October 28, 2016.

97   **A few days later, I tried again:** Author's email to Dr. Carmen A. Puliafito, November 1, 2016.

99   **On Maharaj's watch, investigative stories sat for weeks:** Ed Leibowitz, "What's the Matter with the *L.A. Times?*," *Los Angeles Magazine,* December 7, 2016, https://www.lamag.com/culturefiles/whats-matter-los-angeles-times/.

101   **I was preparing written responses when I and much of the newsroom:** Tracey Lien, Paige St. John, Peter H. King, and Joe Mozingo, "A Night of Music and Dancing Turns into a Deadly Inferno at Oakland Warehouse," *Los Angeles Times,* December 4, 2016, https://www.latimes.com/local/lanow/la-me-ln-main-oakland-fire-story-20161203-story.html.

104   **And to create a paper trail for myself:** Emails between the author and Matt Lait, Marc Duvoisin, and Shelby Grad, January 7, 2017.

10. SPIKING THE STORY

106   **The property would later sell for *$25 million:*** Jack Flemming, "USC's Presidential Mansion Lists for the First Time Ever at $24.5 Million," *Los Angeles Times,* February 12, 2021, https://www.latimes.com/business/real-estate/story/2021-02-12/uscs-presidential-mansion-lists-for-the-first-time-ever-at-24-5-million.

110   **"Davan's going to think on it":** Emails between the author and Marc Duvoisin, February 15, 2017.

11. SECRET REPORTING TEAM

119   **Tribune had spun the *Times*:** Andrew Khouri, "L.A. Times Building Sold to Canadian Developer," *Los Angeles Times,* September 28, 2016, https://www.latimes.com/business/la-fi-times-building-sale-20160926-snap-story.html.

122   **a radical unionist bombed the newspaper:** Carolina A. Miranda, "The 1910 Bombing of the Los Angeles Times Has Been the Subject of Books and Film. Now It's a Bus Tour," *Los Angeles Times,* September 22, 2017, https://www.latimes.com /entertainment/arts/miranda/la-et-cam-esotouric-los-angeles-times-bombing -20170922-story.html.

122   **Chandler pampered his journalists:** Joe Mozingo, "Visionaries and Scoundrels Made the Los Angeles Times, Which Returns to Local Ownership After 18 Years," *Los Angeles Times,* June 17, 2018, https://www.latimes.com/local/california/la-me-latimes -owners-20180617-htmlstory.html.

125   **I sent Khan three Facebook photos:** Text messages between the author and Devon Khan, February 22, 2017.

12. SARAH'S ESCAPE

128   **Sarah Warren found herself sitting:** Sarah Warren and Don Stokes, interviews by the author.

128   **The get-together at the Balboa was a send-off for Sarah:** Ibid.

128   **Puliafito paid for the room and the drugs and a new bong with a bowl the size of a grapefruit:** Ibid.

129   **"I'm out of here," he told her:** Don Stokes, interviews by the author.

130   **He met Sarah there when she was staying:** Sarah Warren and Don Stokes, interviews by the author.

130   **He became a source of free meth for Stokes:** Ibid.

130   **Stokes visited Sarah at her apartment:** Ibid.

131   **So he warned Sarah:** Sarah Warren, interviews by the author.

131   **she and Kyle, her heroin-dealing boyfriend:** Ibid.

132   **The Newport Beach police booked Sarah:** Orange County Superior Court, criminal case records for Sarah Warren.

132   **Two days after they checked out of the Constance:** Los Angeles County Superior Court criminal case records for Sarah Warren, San Fernando Courthouse.

133   **The drug business didn't keep Kyle in much money:** Los Angeles County Superior Court criminal case records for Kyle Voigt, San Fernando Courthouse.

133   **"It's just you and me here":** Sarah Warren, interviews by the author.

133   **"Skittles surgery":** Ibid.

134   **Ryan opened the door:** Sarah Warren and Ryan Cea, interviews by the author and *Los Angeles Times* staffer Adam Elmahrek; Medical Board of California decision against Dr. Carmen A. Puliafito, July 20, 2018.

135   **Ryan was booked at the Huntington Beach jail:** Huntington Beach Police report in Medical Board of California documents.

136   **And then Sarah introduced him to Carmen:** Sarah Warren and Charles Warren, interviews by the author; Medical Board of California decision against Dr. Carmen A. Puliafito, July 20, 2018.

137   **Charles sprinted across the boulevard:** Sarah Warren and Charles Warren, interviews by the author.

140   **a total of $500,000 in bribes:** Matthew Ormseth, "Lori Loughlin Wants FBI Reports, Says They Would Show Her Belief Payments Were Legitimate," *Los Angeles Times,* December 16, 2019, https://www.latimes.com/california/story/2019–12–16 /lori-loughlin-wants-fbi-reports-says-they-would-show-her-belief-payments-were -legitimate.

13. NO SNITCHES

143 **In July 2015, the University of California sued USC:** Bradley J. Fikes, "UC San Diego Sues USC and Scientist, Alleging Conspiracy to Take Funding, Data," *Los Angeles Times,* July 5, 2015, https://www.latimes.com/local/education/la-me-ucsd -lawsuit-20150706-story.html.

145 **the "cottage industry" of expensive rehab:** Paul Pringle, "The Trouble with Rehab, Malibu-Style," *Los Angeles Times,* October 9, 2007, https://www.latimes.com /archives/la-xpm-2007-oct-09-me-rehab9-story.html.

145 **The industry had since outgrown the cottage category:** "Rehab Riviera," series of investigative articles, *Orange County Register,* 2017, https://www.ocregister.com /rehab-riviera/.

153 **Grad emailed the team:** Shelby Grad, email to author and USC reporting team, March 6, 2017.

14. ECSTASY BEFORE THE BALL

161 **"The problem is you and you," the cop said:** Mary Ann Warren and Paul Warren, interviews by the author.

15. HAZEL AND WILLY

166 **She had been arrested for possession:** Criminal case records, Los Angeles, Orange County and Riverside County Superior Courts.

166 **Willy also had an arrest sheet:** Criminal case records, Riverside County Superior Court.

16. DISAPPEARING THE WHISTLEBLOWER

176 **But the relationship between the two men soured:** Sydney Ember, "Billionaire Investor Raises Stake in Tronc, and Feud with Its Chairman," *New York Times,* March 23, 2017, https://www.nytimes.com/2017/03/23/business/media/tronc-investor-chairman-feud-patrick-soon-shiong-michael-ferro.html.

180 **The *Times* had a written policy:** Deirdre Edgar, "Ethics Guidelines," *Los Angeles Times,* June 18, 2014, https://www.latimes.com/local/readers-rep/la-rr-la-times-updates -newsroom-ethics-guidelines-20140618-story.html.

17. PULIAFITO STORY EXPLODES

184 **July was just ahead when I sent the complaint:** Author's email to Tim Ryan and Julie Xanders, June 26, 2017.

188 **He let me know after the fact:** Marc Duvoisin, email to the author, July 14, 2017.

190 **The story appeared in print and online:** Paul Pringle, Harriet Ryan, Adam Elmahrek, Matt Hamilton, and Sarah Parvini, "An Overdose, a Young Companion, Drug-Fueled Parties: The Secret Life of a USC Med School Dean," *Los Angeles Times,* July 17, 2017, https://www.latimes.com/local/california/la-me-usc-doctor-20170717-htmlstory .html.

18. PURGING THE MASTHEAD

192   **USC's media office issued a statement:** Adam Elmahrek, Sarah Parvini, Paul Pringle, Matt Hamilton, "Former USC Medical School Dean No Longer Seeing Patients; Pasadena Police Discipline Officer," *Los Angeles Times,* July 17, 2017, https://www .latimes.com/local/lanow/la-me-ln-usc-dean-patients-20170717-story.html.

193   **The city did release an audio recording:** Adam Elmahrek, Paul Pringle, Sarah Parvini, and Matt Hamilton, "Pasadena Officer Who Investigated Overdose Was Skeptical of USC Med School Dean's Story, Recording Shows," *Los Angeles Times,* July 25, 2017, https://www.latimes.com/local/lanow/la-me-usc-dean-pasadena-overdose -20170725-htmlstory.html.

197   **Shelby, the bottom line:** Author's email to Shelby Grad, August 2, 2017.

198   **some of Maharaj's masthead editors joined in a letter:** Gene Maddaus and Ricardo Lopez, "L.A. Times Masthead Massacre Capped a Month of Newsroom Turmoil," *Variety,* August 22, 2017, https://variety.com/2017/biz/news/los-angeles-times -firings-davan-maharaj-tronc-ross-levinsohn-1202535485/.

198   **Our story on the statement:** Paul Pringle, Harriet Ryan, Matt Hamilton, and Sarah Parvin, "USC Downplays Fundraising Efforts of Ex-Dean at Center of Drug Scandal," *Los Angeles Times,* August 18, 2017, https://www.latimes.com/local/lanow/la -me-ln-usc-fundraising-letter-20170818-story.html.

200   **The *Times*'s story referred to the firings:** "Ross Levinsohn Is Named the New Publisher and CEO of the L.A. Times as Top Editors Are Ousted," *Los Angeles Times,* August 21, 2017, https://www.latimes.com/business/hollywood/la-fi-ct-los-angeles -times-20170821-story.html.

201   **Duvoisin later told the *L.A. Downtown News:*** Jon Regardie, "Dragons, Firings and the L.A. Times," *L.A. Downtown News,* August 28, 2017, http://www .ladowntownnews.com/news/dragons-firings-and-the-l-a-times/article_ae7a9374 -89de-11e7-9f61-230190569853.html.

201   **"Drink if you love the LA Times":** Harriet Ryan, email to newsroom staffers, August 22, 2017.

19. BILLIONAIRE BACKERS

202   **Medical board testimony later revealed:** Adam Elmahrek and Paul Pringle, "Top USC Medical School Official Feared Dean Was 'Doing Drugs' and Alerted Administration, He Testifies," *Los Angeles Times,* June 5, 2018, https://www.latimes.com/local /lanow/la-me-usc-medical-school-dean-20180605-story.html.

203   **After learning of our reporting:** Sarah Parvini, Harriet Ryan, and Paul Pringle, "USC Medical School Dean Out Amid Revelations of Sexual Harassment Claim, $135,000 Settlement with Researcher," *Los Angeles Times,* October 6, 2017, https://www.latimes .com/local/lanow/la-me-usc-dean-harassment-20171005-story.html.

204   **Quick seemed to be referring to photos and videos:** Paul Pringle, Sarah Parvini, and Adam Elmahrek, "USC Moves to Fire, Ban from Campus Former Medical School Dean over 'Egregious Behavior,'" *Los Angeles Times,* July 21, 2017, https://www .latimes.com/local/lanow/la-me-usc-dean-drugs-investigation-20170721-story .html.

204   **most of the fifty states have fewer:** Sara Clarke, "States with the Most Billionaires," *U.S. News and World Report,* https://www.usnews.com/news/best-states/slideshows /states-with-the-most-billionaires.

205   **USC kept the membership of the executive committee a secret:** Sonali Kohli, Sarah Parvini, Matt Hamilton, and Adam Elmahrek, "Some of L.A.'s Richest People Oversee USC. They Will Decide What to Do After the Dean Drug Scandal. Only Three Have Commented," *Los Angeles Times,* August 6, 2017, https://www.latimes.com/projects/la-me-usc-trustees-respond/.

205   **Caruso told Lopez:** Steve Lopez, "USC Bosses Flunk the Leadership Test Amid Shocking Allegations About Former Medical School Dean," *Los Angeles Times,* July 20, 2017, https://www.latimes.com/local/california/la-me-lopez-puliafito-nikias-07202017-story.html.

206   **Yang was a partner:** Victoria Kim, "A Lawyer Who Has Been a Defender of USC Now Must Investigate the Dean Scandal. But Can She Be Impartial?," *Los Angeles Times,* August 12, 2017, https://www.latimes.com/local/lanow/la-me-usc-debra-yang-20170812-story.html.

206   **Her rise to the top:** James Queally, "Jackie Lacey Grew Up in South L.A. but in a Tough D.A.'s Race, Her Opponents Are Encroaching on Her Home Turf," *Los Angeles Times,* March 1, 2020, https://www.latimes.com/california/story/2020-03-01/jackie-lacey-grew-up-in-south-l-a-but-in-a-tough-d-a-s-race-her-opponents-are-encroaching-on-her-home-turf.

207   **Nikias was among the speakers:** Paul Pringle, "Former USC Campus Gynecologist's Accusers Call for Investigation of Top University Officials," *Los Angeles Times,* October 6, 2021, https://www.latimes.com/california/story/2021-10-06/usc-tyndall-gynecologist-sex-abuse-investigation.

208   **Jack Leonard and I published:** Jack Leonard and Paul Pringle, "Work at Ridley-Thomas' Residence Went Beyond Security System," *Los Angeles Times,* January 19, 2014, https://www.latimes.com/local/la-me-ridley-thomas-garage-20140120-story.html.

209   **a federal grand jury indicted Ridley-Thomas:** Michael Finnegan, Matt Hamilton, and Harriet Ryan, "L.A. Councilman Mark Ridley-Thomas and Ex-USC Dean Indicted on Bribery Charges," *Los Angeles Times,* October 13, 2021, https://www.latimes.com/california/story/2021-10-13/mark-ridley-thomas-usc-dean-bribery-indictment.

211   **There were two more conditions:** Paul Pringle, "A Secret USC Payout Had a Catch: Images of Ex-Dean Using Drugs Had to Be Given Up," *Los Angeles Times,* September 30, 2021, https://www.latimes.com/california/story/2021-09-30/secret-usc-payout-involved-images-ex-dean-using-drugs.

211   **Lacey said she was unaware:** Former Los Angeles County district attorney Jackie Lacey, interview by the author, June 15, 2021.

20. A BABY

212   **For an Amish girl:** Miriam Jones, interviews by the author, July 28 and August 10, 2021.

213   **The getaway came in the middle of the night:** Gale Holland, "Amish Journey from Homespun to Hipster," *Los Angeles Times,* January 9, 2012, https://www.latimes.com/local/la-xpm-2012-jan-09-la-me-holland-20120110-story.html.

215   **It was Puliafito who called 911:** 911 recorded call, October 5, 2017.

215   **quoted Sarah Warren as saying Puliafito was the source:** Matt Hamilton and Harriet Ryan, "After a Baby Suddenly Dies, a 911 Call from USC's Former Medical School Dean Sparks Detectives' Interest," *Los Angeles Times,* January 27, 2018.

215   **And two months later, a coroner's toxicology screening:** Matt Hamilton and Harriet Ryan, "An Infant Dies, a Millionaire Doctor Calls 911, and a Tale Emerges of Drugs, Love and Suspected Crime," *Los Angeles Times,* December 2, 2020,

https://www.latimes.com/california/story/2020-12-02/former-dean-usc-medical
-school-child-death-investigation.

21. ANOTHER BAD DOCTOR

221   **Lucy Chi walked into Tyndall's office:** Lucy Chi, interviews by the author, April 15,
2021.

222   **Tyndall was in his midsixties:** Matt Hamilton and Harriet Ryan, "How George Tyndall Went from USC Gynecologist to the Center of LAPD's Largest-Ever Sex Abuse
Investigation," *Los Angeles Times,* December 19, 2018, https://www.latimes.com
/local/lanow/la-me-george-tyndall-profile-usc-sexual-assault-allegations-20181219
-story.html.

22. TYNDALL'S HUSH-HUSH DEAL

233   **So Gilbert resolved to report it for what it truly was:** Cindy Gilbert, interview by
the author, July 27, 2021.

234   **Three years before Gilbert:** Report to USC President Carol Folt, U.S. Department
of Education Office for Civil Rights, Feb. 27, 2020.

234   **He had been fielding complaints:** Matt Hamilton and Harriet Ryan, "Secret USC
Records Reveal Dire Warnings About Gynecologist Accused of Abusing Students,"
Los Angeles Times, May 25, 2019, https://www.latimes.com/local/lanow/la-me-usc
-george-tyndall-secret-records-victims-sex-abuse-20190525-story.html.

235   **"I am concerned that we have an employee":** USC filing in U.S. District Court, Los
Angeles, May 23, 2019.

239   **And it stated that:** MDReview, "University of Southern California Engemann Student Health Center Consultation: Report of Consultation Performed by Kimberly
Schlichter, M.D. FACOG, and Sharon Beckwith, CEO, MDReview," report, n.d.,
https://change.usc.edu/files/2019/05/2019–05–23–143-Exhibits-14–16_FINAL.pdf.

23. THE FALL OF MAX NIKIAS

243   **Oprah Winfrey was delivering:** Jennifer Swann, "Oprah Winfrey Urges USC
Annenberg Graduates to Seek Truth," news release, USC Annenberg School for
Communication and Journalism, May 11, 2018, https://annenberg.usc.edu/news
/commencement/oprah-winfrey-urges-usc-annenberg-graduates-seek-truth.

244   **The published version began:** Harriet Ryan, Matt Hamilton, and Paul Pringle,
"A USC Doctor Was Accused of Bad Behavior with Young Women for Years.
The University Let Him Continue Treating Students," *Los Angeles Times,* May
16, 2018, https://www.latimes.com/local/california/la-me-usc-doctor-misconduct
-complaints-20180515-story.html.

247   **Next, he issued an apology:** Harriet Ryan, Matt Hamilton, Paul Pringle, and Sarah
Parvini, "Patients Flood USC with Reports About Doctor Accused of Misconduct;
LAPD Set to Review Cases," *Los Angeles Times,* May 18, 2018, https://www.latimes
.com/local/california/la-me-usc-doctor-firings-20180518-story.html.

247   **There were the accounts:** Harriet Ryan, Matt Hamilton, Sarah Parvini, and Paul Pringle, "Former Students Recount Decades of Disturbing Behavior by USC Gynecologist," *Los Angeles Times,* May 16, 2018, https://www.latimes.com/local/lanow/la-me
-usc-students-gynecologist-20180516-story.html.

247   **The Chinese consulate of Los Angeles:** Paul Pringle, Matt Hamilton, Harriet Ryan,
and Melissa Etehad, "Chinese Government Has 'Serious Concerns' About USC

Gynecologist and Allegations of Misconduct with Students," *Los Angeles Times*, May 17, 2018, https://www.latimes.com/local/lanow/la-me-ln-chinese-consulate -usc-doctor-20180517-story.html.

247   **The university had one of the largest enrollments:** Melissa Etehad, Paul Pringle, Rosanna Xia, and Matt Hamilton, "USC's Aggressive Recruiting of Chinese Students Faces Challenge Amid Gynecologist Scandal," *Los Angeles Times*, May 17, 2018, https://www.latimes.com/local/lanow/la-me-usc-chinese-20180517-story.html.

248   **In those probes, authorities examined the actions of university administrators:** Jaclyn Diaz, "Ex-Penn State President Will Serve Jail Time in the Jerry Sandusky Child Abuse Scandal," National Public Radio, May 27, 2021, https://www.npr.org/2021/05 /27/1000793762/former-penn-state-president-to-serve-jail-time-in-jerry-sandusky -child-abuse-sca.

248   **A judge dismissed the charges:** Sandra E. Garcia, "Charges Against Former Michigan State President Are Dismissed," *New York Times*, May 13, 2020, https://www .nytimes.com/2020/05/13/us/michigan-state-university-president-charges.html.

248   **More remarkable was a letter:** Harriet Ryan, Sarah Parvini, and Matt Hamilton, "200 USC Professors Demand Nikias Step Down; Trustees Express 'Full Confidence' in President," *Los Angeles Times*, May 22, 2018, https://www.latimes.com /local/lanow/la-me-ln-usc-faculty-petition-nikias-20180522-story.html.

248   **a vote by the Academic Senate:** Adam Elmahrek, Sarah Parvini, Alene Tchekmedyian, and Matt Hamilton, "USC's Academic Senate Calls on University President to Resign After a Series of Scandals," *Los Angeles Times*, May 23, 2018, https://www .latimes.com/local/lanow/la-me-ln-usc-academic-senate-vote-20180523-story.html.

249   **"Max has a Board of Trustees":** Sarah Parvini, Adam Elmahrek, and Paul Pringle, "Pressure Grows on Board of Trustees Amid USC Gynecologist Scandal," *Los Angeles Times*, May 24, 2018, https://www.latimes.com/local/lanow/la-me-usc-trustees -20180524-story.html.

249   **The top of our story:** Matt Hamilton, Paul Pringle, Harriet Ryan, and Steve Lopez, "USC President C.L. Max Nikias to Step Down," *Los Angeles Times*, May 25, 2018, https://www.latimes.com/local/lanow/la-me-max-nikias-usc-20180525-story.html.

24. VARSITY BLUES

253   **He stood there and listened to the recordings:** Eric Rosen, interviews by the author, July 10 and August 21, 2021.

254   **Tobin soon saw the wisdom:** Joel Rubin, Matthew Ormseth, Suhauna Hussain, and Richard Winton, "The Bizarre Story of the L.A. Dad Who Exposed the College Admissions Scandal," *Los Angeles Times*, March 31, 2019, https://www.latimes.com /local/lanow/la-me-morrie-tobin-college-admissions-scandal-20190331-story.html.

25. SAVING THE *TIMES*, AND . . .

259   **D'Vorkin had convened a staff meeting:** Sydney Ember, "Disney Ban Elevated Tension at Los Angeles Times Newsroom," *New York Times*, November 13, 2017, https://www.nytimes.com/2017/11/13/business/media/disney-ban-los-angeles -times.html.

261   **Folkenflik's story on Levinsohn:** David Folkenflik, "Accusations of 'Frat House' Behavior Trail 'LA Times' Publisher's Career," National Public Radio, January 18, 2018, https://www.npr.org/2018/01/18/578612534/accusations-of-frat-house -behavior-trail-la-times-publisher-s-career.

261   **We won with *85 percent* of the vote:** James Rufus Koren, "Los Angeles Times Jour-

nalils Vote 248–44 to Unionize," *Los Angeles Times,* January 19, 2018, https://www
.latimes.com/business/la-fi-times-guild-vote-20180119-story.html.

261 *CJR*'s Lyz Lenz weighed in: "L.A. Journalism's Prince of Darkness," *Columbia
Journalism Review,* January 24, 2018, https://www.cjr.org/business_of_news/la
-times-lewis-dvorkin.php.

262 *Fortune* writers Kristen Bellstrom and Beth Kowitt were closing in: Kristen
Bellstrom and Beth Kowitt, "Former Tronc Chairman and Investor Michael Ferro
Accused of Inappropriate Advances by Two Women," *Fortune,* March 19, 2018,
https://fortune.com/2018/03/19/tronc-chairman-michael-ferro-allegations/.

262 Soon-Shiong was given seventy-two hours: Kara Swisher, "Should We Worry as Billionaires Buy Up Newspapers?," *New York Times, Sway* (podcast), August 12, 2021,
https://www.nytimes.com/2021/08/12/opinion/sway-kara-swisher-patrick-soon
-shiong.html.

263 But then the investigative prize was awarded: Los Angeles Times Staff, "How the
Los Angeles Times Uncovered the George Tyndall Scandal," *Los Angeles Times,*
April 15, 2019, https://www.latimes.com/local/lanow/la-me-times-pulitzer-george
-tyndall-usc-20190414-story.html.

265 The investigation explored accusations that Marc Ching: Paul Pringle, Alene Tchekmedyian, and David Pierson, "Times Investigation: He Was a Hollywood Darling
for Fighting Dog Meat Trade. Butchers Say He Staged Killings; He Denies It," *Los
Angeles Times,* May 24, 2020, https://www.latimes.com/california/story/2020–05–24
/animal-cruelty-abuse-marc-ching-dog-meat.

267 But more than $1.1 billion in settlements: Matt Hamilton and Harriet Ryan, "USC's
$1.1-Billion Payout: Here Is Who Gets the Settlements and Other Details," *Los An-
geles Times,* March 25, 2021, https://www.latimes.com/california/story/2021–03–25
/uscs-1–1-billion-settlements-here-is-who-gets-the-payouts-and-other-details.

267 In their story on that settlement: Matt Hamilton and Harriet Ryan, "USC to Pay
$1.1 Billion to Settle Decades of Sex Abuse Claims Against Gynecologist," *Los An-
geles Times,* March 25, 2021, https://www.latimes.com/california/story/2021–03–25
/usc-payout-gynecologist-sex-abuse-claims-to-top-1-billion.

269 Maharaj had received a secret payment: David Folkenflik, "Tribune, Tronc and Beyond: A Slur, A Secret Payout and a Looming Sale," National Public Radio, December 12, 2018, https://www.npr.org/2018/12/12/675961765/tribune-tronc-and-beyond
-a-slur-a-secret-payout-and-a-looming-sale.

269 "almost 30 years of exceptional service": Ibid.

ABOUT THE AUTHOR

Paul Pringle is a *Los Angeles Times* reporter who specializes in investigating corruption. In 2019, he and two colleagues won the Pulitzer Prize in Investigative Reporting for their work uncovering the widespread sexual abuse by Dr. George Tyndall at the University of Southern California, an inquiry that grew out of their reporting the year before on Dr. Carmen Puliafito, dean of USC's medical school. Pringle was a Pulitzer Prize finalist in 2009 and a member of reporting teams that won Pulitzer Prizes in 2004 and 2011. Pringle won a George Polk Award in 2008, the same year the Society of Professional Journalists of Greater Los Angeles honored him as a distinguished journalist. Along with several colleagues, he shared in Harvard University's 2011 Worth Bingham Prize for Investigative Reporting. Pringle and a *Times* colleague won the California News Publishers Association's Freedom of Information Award in 2014 and the University of Florida's Joseph L. Brechner Freedom of Information Award in 2015. Pringle lives in Glendale, California.

CELADON
BOOKS

Founded in 2017, Celadon Books, a division of
Macmillan Publishers, publishes a highly curated list
of twenty to twenty-five new titles a year. The list of
both fiction and nonfiction is eclectic and focuses
on publishing commercial and literary books and
discovering and nurturing talent.